Grannie Mae's
CHRISTMAS
COOKY
BOOK

Cookie baking still takes work as it did years ago,
it still takes nuts, fruit and spice a dash of love and dough.
There's only one thing missing now and Grannie says, "My land"
where are all my grandchildren now with their little helping hands?

© Copyright 1995 G &R Publishing -Waverly, IA

Recipes and Poems Collected by: Maybelle McClure - Green Valley, AZ
Cover Design: Cullen & Floyd Design - Tucson, AZ

happiness is baking "cookies"
grannie Mae
green Valley, Az.

G&R Publishing Co.
507 Industrial Street
Waverly, IA 50677
1-800-383-1679

FOREWORD

This book was published with love for everyone to share. It is for those who bake occasionally as well as those having the time to bake quite often. I have given much thought and research to produce this "Christmas Cookie Book" to satisfy everyone's taste. I have searched and could never find enough cookie recipes in one book to satisfy my love for baking. I started baking at Mom's side when I was five years old and my love for it has never stopped. Mom always said "I must have been born with a 'Wooden Spoon' in my mouth". These recipes have been tested and tried by family and friends, including my husband and two boys, who loved sampling my creations. I've attended several cooking schools in Wisconsin with my Mother and guess what part of the course held my attention? Yes, the "Cookie Demonstration" part which included baking and decorating of the cookies.

I Feel Sorry For Children
Whoever They Are
That Live In A House
With No Cookie Jar.

Christmas Memories

Christmas is "Magic Time" - It seems bells ring louder, smiles are seen on more faces and how easy it is to go about humming "Jingle Bells" and say "I love you".

The sights, sounds, and fragrances of Christmas bring back many happy memories. Our Christmas holidays are laced with a web of memories way back in early childhood. Many of them start right in our kitchen. I can still see Dad cracking nuts with a hammer and me trying to take out the pieces so Mom could add them to the dough she was busily making. We were in such great spirits and our kitchen had such a spicy aroma that one could smell it way outside. The taste and smells of past Christmases are with us every year as we gather together. Parents and children working together produce memories that will last forever. This is how traditions start. They hold comfort as we grow older and it is the time to make and renew memories for our family.

Mom's everywhere begin to bake special "Holiday Treats". Things are different nowadays, but there isn't any change in the way a youngsters eyes light up at the sight of a gaily colored cookie. We try new recipes every year, however it seems Mom's old standbys are always included. I have happy memories sharing my baking experience with my sister-in-law, Marion. The Sunday before Christmas we would bake about 10 batches of cookies together, while our boys played outdoors and our husbands watched football. I recall some years we would take a break from baking and look outside and see these big white flakes coming down, it gave us such a warm feeling inside.

As our boys returned from outside the understanding was, No cookies were allowed to be eaten! or so we thought.

My son Michael loved "Mondchens". I put several baking sheets of them on the landing upstairs to his room. Sometime later he and a friend came downstairs and thanked me for the nice surprise! "Boy was I surprised when I saw they were all eaten". My younger son Mark liked to be near when I was baking. One day I gave him the task of removing the cookies to the cooling rack. His reward was to eat the broken ones. Strange how many broken cookies he found. There are so many memories I have and I'm sure you do, too. Cherish them and try to make new ones for your family to keep. Remember "Happiness is Baking Cookies" and should be shared with the underprivileged, family and friends. My husband's face would beam as he carried a large box of cookies to work to share with his fellow employees.

Many thanks to my Mom and Dad for helping me understand what memories are all about.

TABLE OF CONTENTS

Foreword

Christmas Memories

Rolled Cookies 1

Drop Cookies 47

Refrigerated Cookies 113

Molded Cookies 155

Bar Cookies 235

Press Cookies 315

Unbaked Cookies and Icings 329

Rolled Cookies

*Grannie said that we must pass
our blessings all around
and share them with all other folks
wherever they are found.*

Best Of All Sugar Cookies

Made tender by using confectioners' sugar.

1-1/2	cups sifted confectioners' sugar	1/2	teaspoon almond extract
1	cup butter	2-1/2	cups sifted flour
1	egg	1	teaspoon soda
1	teaspoon vanilla	1	teaspoon cream of tartar
		1/2	teaspoon nutmeg

Mix sugar and butter. Add egg and flavorings; mix thoroughly. Measure flour by sifting. Sift dry ingredients together and blend in. Refrigerate 2 to 3 hours. Heat oven to 375 degrees. Divide dough in half and roll 3/16 inch thick on lightly floured pastry cloth. Cut with cookie cutter; sprinkle with sugar. Place on lightly greased baking sheet. Bake for 7 to 8 minutes, or until delicately golden. Makes about 5 dozen large round cookies.

Chocolate Sugar Cookies

A good chocolatey different sugar cookie.

5	ounces unsweetened chocolate	2	large eggs
5	ounces semisweet chocolate	2	teaspoons vanilla
		1	cup flour
1/4	cup butter	1/2	teaspoon baking soda
1/2	cup sugar	1/2	teaspoon cinnamon
1/2	cup firmly packed dark brown sugar	1/2	teaspoon salt
		1	tablespoon milk
			sugar for sprinkling

Combine the chocolates and butter in a large heavy saucepan. Place over very low heat until melted. Remove from heat and gradually stir in sugars. Beat 1 egg lightly. Stir into chocolate mixture, then stir in vanilla. In a mixing bowl, sift together flour, baking soda, cinnamon and salt. Gradually stir this into the melted chocolate mixture, stirring until well blended. Form the dough into a ball, wrap with waxed paper, and chill for 30 minutes. Preheat oven to 375 degrees. Lightly grease baking sheets. Roll dough out between 2 sheets of waxed paper to a thickness of about 1/8-inch. Use a cookie cutter to cut out the cookies and place them on the baking sheets. Beat the remaining egg with the milk. Brush dough surface with beaten egg mixture and sprinkle liberally with sugar. Bake until the edges are browned, about 12 minutes. Cool cookies on pan for 5 minutes, then remove to wire racks to cool completely.

Dutch Sugar Cookies

You don't have to be Dutch to enjoy these.

3/4	cup butter	1-1/2	teaspoon cinnamon
1	cup plus 2 tablespoons brown sugar, packed	1/2	teaspoon baking powder
		1	egg white
1	egg yolk	1	tablespoon water
2	cups sifted flour	1/3	cup granulated sugar
1/4	teaspoon salt		

Cream butter. Add sugar gradually. Blend in egg yolk and sifted dry ingredients. Roll 1/8 inch thick on floured canvas. Cut with cookie cutter. Place on greased cookie sheets. Combine egg white and water. Brush over cookies. Sprinkle with granulated sugar. Bake at 375 degrees 8 to 10 minutes. Makes about 7 dozen 2-1/2 inch cookies.

German Anise Cookies

For a really different cookie, be sure to try these. Do not substitute lard for other shortening.

1/2	pound lard	1/2	pound cubed sugar
1/2	cup hot water	1/8	teaspoon salt
1	teaspoon hart shorn (may be purchased at a pharmacy)	1-1/4	teaspoon anise oil
		3	cups flour

Melt lard and cool. Add water to hart shorn. Pour over sugar. Add salt and anise oil. Stir in lard. Add flour to make a smooth dough. Roll on floured board to 1/8-inch thickness. Cut with floured cutter. Put onto greased baking sheet. Bake at 375 degrees for about 15 minutes, or until light brown. Makes about 72 cookies.

Austrian Butter Cookies

This recipe was given to me from a friend in Austria.

1	cup sifted flour	1/2	cup butter
1/3	cup sugar	1/2	cup currant jelly
2/3	cup pecans, ground		

Sift flour and sugar together. Add ground pecans. Cut in butter with dough blender until mixture resembles coarse meal. Work mixture with fingers until a ball of dough is formed. Roll 1/8-inch thick on floured surface. Cut with 1-1/2-inch cookie cutter. Place on ungreased cookie sheets. Bake at 375 degrees about 10 minutes. Spread bottom of half of cookies with jelly. Place another cookie on top sandwich fashion. Frost top of cookie with Chocolate Frosting.

Chocolate Frosting:

1	tablespoon butter	1	square unsweetened chocolate, melted
1/3	cup powdered sugar		
1	egg yolk	1/4	cup pecans, chopped

Cream butter and powdered sugar together. Add egg yolk and cooled chocolate. Beat well. Spread on cookie. Sprinkle with chopped pecans. Makes 3 dozen sandwich cookies.

Finska Kakor

Scandinavians delight - a rich different look to add to your pretty holiday basket for friends.

3/4	cup soft butter or margarine	1	teaspoon almond flavoring
		2	cups flour, sifted
1/4	cup sugar		

Mix thoroughly, butter, sugar, and almond flavoring, then stir in flour. Mix with hands thoroughly. Chill dough. Roll out 1/4-inch thick. Cut into strips 2-1/2- inches long and 3/4-inch wide. Brush tops lightly with 1 egg white, slightly beaten. Sprinkle with mixture of 1 tablespoon sugar and 1/3 cup finely chopped blanched almonds. Carefully transfer (several strips at a time) to ungreased baking sheet. Bake in a 350 degree oven for 17 to 20 minutes or until cookies begin to turn to a very delicate golden brown.

Paintbrush Cookies

Children will have special memories of these fine "Holiday Cookies".

1	cup sugar	1	teaspoon vanilla
3/4	cup shortening (part margarine or butter, softened)	2-1/2	cups flour
		1	teaspoon baking powder
		1	teaspoon salt
2	eggs		Egg Yolk Paint

Mix sugar, shortening, eggs and vanilla. Stir in flour, baking powder and salt. Cover and refrigerate at least 1 hour. Roll dough 1/8-inch thick on lightly floured cloth-covered board. Cut into desired shapes with cookie cutters. Place on ungreased cookie sheet. Prepare Egg Yolk Paint. Paint designs on cookies with small paintbrushes. Heat oven to 400 degrees. Bake until cookies are delicate golden brown, 6 to 8 minutes. Makes about 4 dozen 3-inch cookies.

Egg Yolk Paint:

Mix 1 egg yolk and 1/4 teaspoon water. Divide mixture among several small custard cups. Tint each with different food color to make bright colors. If paint thickens while standing, stir in a few drops of water.

Caramel Sugar Cookies

Cutting out these easy to roll cookies adapts itself to variations in shape.

1	cup butter	2	teaspoons vanilla
1	cup sugar	3-3/4	cups cake flour
1/2	cup brown sugar	1	teaspoon salt
3	eggs, beaten	1/2	teaspoon baking soda

Cream butter. Add sugar and sifted brown sugar a little at a time and cream well. Add beaten eggs and vanilla. Mix and sift the flour, salt and baking soda and combine with the cookie mixture. Chill. Roll about 1/4-inch thick. Cut in various shapes and bake in a 350 degree oven for 9 to 12 minutes. Makes about 5 dozen.

Viennese Specials

Spices and almonds make these every one's favorite.

2	cups sifted flour	2	egg yolks
3/4	teaspoon cinnamon	1	cup grated, unblanched, almond nutmeats
1/2	teaspoon cloves		
1	cup butter	1	teaspoon grated lemon rind
1	cup sugar		

Mix and sift flour and spices. Cream butter well, add sugar gradually and continue creaming until light and fluffy. Add unbeaten egg yolks, nutmeats and lemon rind and mix well. Add sifted dry ingredients gradually and mix. Roll 1/4-inch thick on lightly floured board and cut with a floured 2-inch scalloped cutter. Bake on baking sheets in a 350 degree oven for about 13 minutes. Store in covered container. Makes about 5-1/2 dozen.

Note:
Commercially grated almonds are best for these cookies.

Walnut Filled Treats

The filling shows on both sides of these pretty treats.

1/4	cup powdered sugar	1/2	cup sour cream
2	cups sifted flour	1-3/4	cups ground walnuts
1/2	teaspoon salt	3/4	cup pineapple preserves
1	cup cold butter		Powdered sugar for rolling
1	egg yolk, beaten		

Combine sugar, flour and salt; cut in butter with pastry blender until mixture resembles coarse crumbs. Stir in egg yolk and sour cream; form into a ball. Chill. Roll about 1/8-inch thick on surface sprinkled with powdered sugar; cut into 2-inch squares. Combine walnuts and preserves; place about 1/2 teaspoonful walnut mixture on each square. Start at 1 corner and roll towards opposite corner. Place point down on ungreased cookie sheets. Bake at 350 degrees about 15 minutes. Sprinkle lightly with powdered sugar. Makes about 6 dozen.

Candy Bar In-Betweens

A different look for your cookie display.

2	cups confectioners' sugar	1	teaspoon cream of tartar
1	cup butter, softened	1	teaspoon soda
2	eggs	1/4	teaspoon salt
1	teaspoon vanilla	12	(7/8-ounce) milk chocolate bars
1/2	teaspoon almond extract		
3	cups flour		

Cream sugar and butter in mixer bowl at high speed of mixer until light and fluffy. Add eggs and vanilla and almond extract, beating until well blended. At low speed of mixer, blend in dry ingredients. Cover; chill 1 hour. Roll out dough on well floured surface to an 18x11-inch rectangle. Cut into nine 11x12-inch strips. Place 2 chocolate bars, end to end, on long strip of dough, cover with second strip of dough, 2 more chocolate bars, then a third strip of dough. Round edges to enclose bars. Repeat with remaining strips of dough and chocolate bars. Cut into 1/2-inch slices. Place, cut-side up, on ungreased cookie sheets. Bake at 375 degrees for 10 to 12 minutes. Makes about 60 bars.

Make a Christmas tree for your children. Take an ice cream cone and cover with butter frosting. Put popcorn that has been tinted green all over and decorate with colored candies and tiny silver balls.

Nut Rolls

Extra tender cookies made with yeast.

1	package yeast	2	eggs, separated
3/4	cup plus 2 tablespoons sugar	1	teaspoon vanilla
		1/4	cup chopped nuts
1	cup butter, softened	1	teaspoon cinnamon
2	cups flour		

Dissolve yeast in 1/4 cup warm water and 2 tablespoons sugar. Add flour, softened butter and a little salt; mix as pie dough. Add egg yolks, vanilla and 1/4 cup sugar to the yeast mixture; mix well and divide into thirds. Roll each out into a long rectangle and cut each piece into 10 or 12 triangles. Make a filling with the egg whites, stiffly beaten, 1/2 cup sugar, chopped nuts and cinnamon. Spread a teaspoonful on each triangle and roll up, placing each on buttered tin, point down. Don't allow to rise. Bake at 350 degrees for 15 to 18 minutes and top with a thin icing.

Icing:

1	cup powdered sugar	1/4	teaspoon vanilla
1	teaspoon hot water	1/4	teaspoon almond extract

Put on rolls while they are still warm for a shiny glaze.

Ice Cream Cookies

So easy to do it's almost a sin to call it work.

1	cup soft butter	2	cups sifted flour
1	cup softened vanilla ice cream		apricot, raspberry or strawberry preserves

Combine butter and ice cream; add flour gradually and mix. Roll thin on floured board and cut with a floured 1-1/2-inch round cutter or with assorted cutters; decorate as desired. Bake on ungreased baking sheets in a 350 degree oven about 9 minutes. Indent centers of cookies immediately; fill with preserves. Makes about 8 dozen cookies.

Gateau Bonbons

Tiny frosted filled cookies from France.

2/3	cup soft butter or margarine	1	teaspoon finely grated lemon rind
1	cup sugar	2	cups sifted flour
1	egg	1/2	teaspoon baking powder
1	package (3-ounce) cream cheese, softened	1/2	teaspoon salt
		1/8	teaspoon soda
1/2	teaspoon lemon juice		orange marmalade

Mix first 6 ingredients until light and fluffy. Blend in dry ingredients; add to butter mixture, mix well. Chill. Using 1/4 of the dough at a time (keep rest refrigerated), roll 1/8-inch thick on lightly floured board. Cut 1-inch rounds. Place half the rounds on lightly greased baking sheet. Put 1/4 teaspoon marmalade in center of each. (For larger bonbons: cut 1-1/2-inch rounds; fill with 1/2 teaspoon marmalade.) Cover with remaining half of rounds; seal edges with floured finger. Bake in a 350 degree oven for 8 to 10 minutes, or until edges are slightly browned. When cool, frost with tinted frosting. Makes about 7 dozen 1-inch bonbons.

Store soft cookies in tins with a slice of apple added to keep them moist.

Zucker Hutchen

These delightful cookies are called little sugar hats.

1/3	cup butter or margarine	1	cup plus 6 tablespoons sifted flour
1/2	cup sugar		
1	egg yolk	1/4	cup finely cut-up citron
2	tablespoons milk	1/2	teaspoon baking powder
			Almond Meringue
			Decorator Icing

Cream butter and sugar until fluffy. Stir in egg yolk, then milk. Add citron which has been dredged in 4 tablespoons flour to butter mixture; stir in. Add 1 cup plus 2 tablespoons flour and baking powder; blend well. Chill. Heat oven to 350 degrees. Roll dough 1/8-inch thick on lightly floured board; cut out small rounds with cookie cutter (2-inch). Place 1-inch apart on a greased baking sheet. Put 1 teaspoon meringue in center of each round to make it look like the crown of a hat. Bake 10 to 12 minutes. When cookies are cool, pipe around crown of hat with icing to look like a hat band. Makes about 5 dozen cookies.

Almond Meringue:

Beat 1 egg white until frothy. Add 1-1/2 cups sifted confectioners' sugar; beat until meringue holds its shape. Fold in 1/2 cup almonds, finely chopped.

Decorator Icing:

Gradually add 1 egg white, slightly beaten, to 2 to 2-1/2 cups sifted confectioners' sugar, beating until icing is stiff. Add 1 to 2 drops blue food coloring.

Cinnamon Jelly Gems

Have a scalloped cutter? Use and cut in half for an unusual cookie.

1	cup sifted flour		currant jelly
1/4	cup sugar		candied cherries, citron,
1	teaspoon cinnamon		grated nuts for decoration
1/2	cup butter		

Combine flour, sugar and cinnamon in mixing bowl. Cut in butter with pastry blender and work mixture with a spoon until a ball of dough is formed; chill. Roll 1/8-inch thick on floured canvas and cut with 2-inch cutter. Place on ungreased cookie sheets and bake at 350 degrees for 12 to 15 minutes. Spread bottom half of the cookies with jelly; place another cookie on top sandwich fashion. Frost top with browned butter frosting; decorate as desired. Makes about 1-1/2 dozen.

Viennese Jam Rounds

These fancy cookies resemble stained-glass windows.

1	cup butter or margarine, softened	1/4	teaspoon salt
		3/4	teaspoon ground cinnamon
1	cup sugar	1/4	teaspoon ground cloves
2	egg yolks	1	cup ground almonds
1	teaspoon grated lemon peel		about 1/2 cup raspberry or apricot jam
2	cups flour		

In the large bowl of an electric mixer, beat butter and sugar until creamy. Beat in egg yolks and lemon peel. In another bowl, stir together flour, salt, cinnamon, and cloves; gradually add to butter mixture, blending thoroughly. Stir in almonds (dough will be very stiff). Gather dough into a ball, wrap tightly in plastic wrap, and refrigerate for 1 hour. Divide dough in half. Roll each half between 2 pieces of wax paper to thickness of 1/8-inch. Cut out with a 2-inch round cookie cutter and place about 2-inches apart on ungreased baking sheets. Top each cookie with about 1/2 teaspoon jam, spreading to within about 1/2-inch of edges. Cut dough scraps (re-roll, if necessary) into 1/4 by 2-inch strips; cross 2 strips over top of each cookie and press ends down lightly. Bake in a 375 degree oven for about 12 minutes or until edges are browned. Let cool for about a minute on baking sheets, then transfer to racks and let cool completely. Makes about 4 dozen.

Chocolate Filled Dreams

A great treat for your taste buds.

3/4	cup butter, softened	2	large egg yolks
1/2	cup confectioners' sugar	1	teaspoon vanilla
1/4	cup light brown sugar, firmly packed	1-1/2	cups flour

In a medium bowl cream butter at medium speed of an electric mixer. Add sugars and beat until smooth. Add yolks and vanilla, and mix at medium speed until light and fluffy. Add the flour and blend at low speed until thoroughly combined. Gather dough into a ball and flatten to a disk. Wrap dough tightly in plastic wrap. Refrigerate for 1 hour. Roll dough on floured board to 1/4-inch thickness. Cut circles with a 2-inch cookie cutter and place on ungreased cookie sheets, 1-inch apart. Drop 1 teaspoon of Chocolate Filling in center of each circle and top with another circle. Completely seal the edges using the tines of a fork. Bake in a 325 degree oven 15 to 16 minutes, or until cookies are golden brown. Transfer to a cool, flat surface. Sprinkle with white sugar, if desired. Makes 2-1/2 dozen.

Chocolate Filling:

- 1/2 cup heavy cream
- 1 cup semisweet chocolate chips

Scald the cream in a small saucepan over medium heat. Add the chocolate chips and stir until melted. Remove from the heat.

Chocolate Shortbread Hearts

For a sweet way to express your feelings, try this version of shortbread cookies in heart shapes. Other cutters may be used.

1	cup butter	2	cups flour
1/2	cup sugar	1/4	teaspoon salt
1/2	cup Dutch process unsweetened cocoa powder	1/3	cup crystal sugar for garnish

Cream butter and sugar until smooth. Add cocoa and blend in. Stir in dry ingredients just until blended. Do not overwork the dough. Gather dough into a ball and divide into halves. Roll out each half between 2 sheets of waxed paper to 1/4-inch thick. Cut out cookies and place on ungreased cookie sheet. Sprinkle the crystal sugar over cookies. Repeat with remaining dough. Bake in a 325 degree oven for 18 to 20 minutes. Transfer to rack to cool. Makes 40 to 50 cookies.

Swiss Chocolate Cookies

These yummy cookies have a crisp chewy texture and taste like chocolate macaroons.

1-1/4	cups blanched almonds	1/8	teaspoon cloves
1-1/2	cups powdered sugar	3	ounces bittersweet chocolate, chopped
3-1/2	tablespoons unsweetened cocoa powder	1/4	teaspoon almond extract
2-1/2	teaspoons cinnamon	2	large egg whites

Grind almonds and 1 cup powdered sugar in food processor to a powder. Add cocoa, cinnamon, cloves and chocolate and continue processing until chocolate is finely ground. Add remaining 1/2 cup powdered sugar, almond extract and egg whites, blend until mixture forms a mass. Dust a work surface with confectioners' sugar. Knead dough slightly. Roll dough out to 1/4-inch thick. Cut out cookies using a 2-1/2-inch trefoil shaped cutter. Put cookies on baking sheet that has been lined with foil. Space cookies 1-inch apart. Bake in a 325 degrees oven for 10 to 12 minutes. Cool on foil. When cool, pull off foil. Decorate cookies with White Chocolate.

White Chocolate Decoration:

Melt 1-1/2 ounces white chocolate. Remove from heat and let cool. Spoon chocolate into a pastry bag fitted with a very fine writing tip. Pipe lines diagonally across cookies at 1/4-inch intervals. Let stand until chocolate sets. Makes 3 dozen cookies.

Snowflakes

Cookies with sweet chocolate in center and top make these extra good.

1/2	cup sugar	1/2	teaspoons baking powder
1/3	cup butter or margarine	1/2	teaspoon salt
1	egg		sweet chocolate, melted
1/2	teaspoon vanilla		pistachio nuts, chopped
1-1/4	cups sifted flour		

Mix sugar, butter, egg, and flavoring well. Stir dry ingredients together and blend into shortening mixture. Chill 1 hour. Preheat oven to 400°. Roll dough 1/8-inch thick on floured board. Cut into small stars. Bake on ungreased baking sheet 6 to 8 minutes, until lightly browned. Cool. Put 2 cookies together with melted sweet chocolate; add dab of chocolate and sprinkling of chopped pistachio nuts on top. Makes about 32 cookies.

Merry Mints

Use different colored mint patties on these picture perfect cookies.

1	cup butter	1/2	teaspoon cream of tartar
1	cup powdered sugar	1/2	teaspoon salt
1	egg	1/4	cup finely chopped pecans for topping
1	teaspoon vanilla		
2-1/4	cups sifted cake flour	7-1/2	dozen thin candy mint patties
1	teaspoon soda		

Cream butter; add sugar gradually. Beat in egg and vanilla. Blend in sifted dry ingredients. Roll dough 1/4-inch thick on floured canvas. Cut with 1-1/4-inch cutter; place on greased cookie sheets. Sprinkle <u>half</u> the cookies with chopped pecans. Bake all cookies at 350 degrees about 8 minutes. Remove from oven; top cookies with mints; cover mints with nut topped cookies, sandwich fashion. Return cookies to oven for several minutes to soften mints. Makes about 7-1/2 dozen.

Parlies

A Scottish form of gingerbread. Cookies have a zippy flavor and an appealing crispness.

3/4	cup flour	3/4	cup plus 2 tablespoons butter
1	tablespoon plus 1 teaspoon ginger	1/2	cup dark molasses
3/4	teaspoon allspice	1	cup light brown sugar
3/4	teaspoon cinnamon	1	large egg
1/2	teaspoon baking soda		

Place butter, molasses and sugar in large mixing bowl and beat until light. Beat in egg; add dry ingredients. Divide dough in half, wrap each half in plastic wrap and refrigerate about 2 hours. Roll out 1/8-inch on light floured surface. Cut into rectangles about 2-1/2 by 3-inch. Bake on greased cookie sheets in a 375 degree oven for 7 to 9 minutes. Transfer cookies to wire racks immediately. Makes about 50 cookies.

Almond Cookies

Delicate tea cookie.

1/2	cup butter	2-3/4	cups flour
1	cup sugar	1/2	teaspoon salt
1	egg	1-1/2	teaspoon baking powder
1/2	cup milk	1	can almond filling
1	teaspoon grated lemon rind		

Cream together butter and sugar. Add egg and mix well. Blend in the milk and lemon rind. Sift flour with salt and baking powder, fold into mixture and mix carefully. Roll dough on a lightly floured canvas. Cut into various shapes. Be sure dough is rolled thin. Top each cookie with almond filling. Bake in a 400 degree oven about 10 to 12 minutes.

Note:
To top the cookies with almond filling, use pastry bag. Use small opening or tube and squeeze small amount on each cookie. Makes about 4 dozen cookies.

Ramunes (Daisies)

These are year around favorites - Taste like a rich sugar cookie.

1	cup butter	1	teaspoon vanilla
3/4	cup sugar	2	cups sifted flour
1	uncooked egg yolk	1/2	teaspoon salt
5	cooked egg yolks, mashed	1	egg, beaten, for topping
		1/2	cup chopped walnuts

Cream butter; add sugar gradually. Beat in uncooked and cooked egg yolks. Blend in vanilla, flour and salt. Roll 1/4-inch thick on well floured surface; cut with daisy or other fancy cutters. Place on lightly greased cookie sheets. Brush cookies with beaten egg; sprinkle centers with walnuts. Bake at 350 degrees 10 to 15 minutes or until golden. Makes about 4-1/4 dozen, depending on size.

Mississippi Cookies

Down Mississippi way, these cookies are rated #1.

1	cup sugar	1-1/2	cups seedless raisins
1	cup brown sugar	1/2	cup walnuts
3/4	cup shortening	1/2	teaspoon cloves
1	egg, beaten	1/2	teaspoon ginger
1-1/2	teaspoons baking soda dissolved in 1/4 cup hot water	1/2	teaspoon allspice
		1/2	teaspoon salt
		2-3/4	cups flour
1/2	cup buttermilk	1	beaten egg
2	cups ground oatmeal		sugar for garnish

Cream sugars, shortening, egg, soda mixture and buttermilk. Grind oatmeal, raisins and nuts together. Then add to sugar mixture. Sift dry ingredients together; stir into first mixture. If dough is not stiff enough, add more flour. Roll to about 1/8-inch thick, cut with a round cookie cutter, about 3-inches in diameter. Brush tops of cookies with egg. Sprinkle with sugar. Bake in 350 degree oven about 10 minutes or until cookies are crisp and chewy. Makes about 3 dozen cookies.

Molasses Wafers

A truly crisp and tasty cookie. Good for dunking!

1/2	cup dark molasses	1/2	teaspoon ginger
1/4	cup shortening	1	teaspoon grated orange rind
1-1/2	cups sifted flour		
3/4	teaspoon baking powder		

Combine molasses and shortening and bring to boiling point; cool. Mix and sift flour, soda, salt and ginger. Add molasses mixture and orange rind and mix well. Chill dough in refrigerator about 2 hours; roll thin as you can on floured pastry cover and cut with a floured 2-inch round cookie cutter or with assorted cutters. Bake on an ungreased cookie sheet about 8 minutes in a 350 degree oven, makes about 50 cookies.

Brown-Eyed Daisies

Orange flavored cookies made extra good with chocolate dabs.

1	cup butter	1-1/2	teaspoons orange extract
1	cup powdered sugar	2-1/2	cups sifted flour
1	egg	1	teaspoon salt

Cream butter, add sugar gradually; beat in egg and extract. Blend in sifted dry ingredients; chill. Roll 1/4-inch thick on floured surface. Cut with large and small daisy cutters. Place on ungreased cookie sheets. Bake at 375 degrees for about 10 minutes, depending on size. Make Glaze.

Glaze:

1	cup powdered sugar	yellow food coloring
2	tablespoons milk	cocoa
1/2	teaspoon orange extract	

Combine powdered sugar, milk and orange extract. Use several drops of yellow food coloring to tint mixture a pale yellow. Brush warm cookies with glaze. Add a small amount of cocoa and powdered sugar to remaining glaze to make a frosting. Place 1/4 teaspoonful chocolate frosting on center of large daisy cookie. Top with a small daisy cookie. Decorate with a bit of frosting. Makes about 2-1/2 dozen.

Merry Christmas Molasses Cookies

Here is a nostalgic sampling of an old Christmas favorite.

2/3	cup brown sugar, packed	4	teaspoons cinnamon
2/3	cup shortening	2	teaspoons ginger
1-1/3	cups molasses	2	teaspoons baking soda
2	eggs	1	teaspoon salt
5-1/2	cups flour		

Mix brown sugar, shortening and molasses. Stir in remaining ingredients. Cover and refrigerate at least several hours. Heat oven to 375 degrees. Roll dough 1/4-inch thick on lightly floured cloth-covered board. Cut into desired shapes with cookie cutters. Place about 1-inch apart on lightly greased cookie sheet. Bake until no indentation remains when touched, 7 to 8 minutes; cool. Frost and decorate as desired. Makes about 5 dozen 3-inch cookies.

Note:
Cookies can be decorated before baking with "Baked-on Decorators' Frosting" or afterwards with "Creamy Decorators' Frosting". To outline designs on baked cookies, place frosting in a decorators' tube.

Baked-on Decorators' Frosting:

1/3	cup flour	1-1/2	teaspoons hot water
1/3	cup margarine, softened	2	to 3 drops food color

Mix margarine and flour until smooth. Stir in hot water and, if desired, food color. Place in decorators' tube with number 3 writing tip. Outline, write or make designs on unbaked cookies. Bake as directed in recipe. Cool; store carefully, separating layers of cookies with waxed paper.

Creamy Decorators' Frosting:

1	cup powdered sugar	food color
1/2	teaspoon vanilla	
1	or 2 tablespoons half and half	

Beat powdered sugar, vanilla and about 1 or 2 tablespoons half and half until smooth and of spreading consistency. Tint with food color if desired.

Stone Jar Molasses Cookies

Sugar-free tasty molasses dunkers.

1 cup molasses	1-3/4 teaspoons baking powder
1/2 cup shortening	1 teaspoon salt
1 teaspoon baking soda	1-1/2 teaspoons ginger
2-1/4 cups sifted flour	

Heat molasses to boiling point; remove from heat, add shortening and soda, and stir until well blended. Sift together remaining ingredients and stir into molasses mixture. Blend thoroughly; chill. Roll dough out to 1/16-inch on a lightly floured board and cut with a 1-1/2-inch cookie cutter. Bake in a moderate oven, 350 degrees, for 5 to 7 minutes. Makes about 8 dozen cookies.

Crisp cookies are best kept in plastic containers or freeze them so they will stay oven fresh. They keep for at least six months.

Lecheri

Heart shaped moist cookies with honey and a touch of brandy glazed and decked with a cherry.

1/2	cup candied orange peel	3-3/4	cups unsifted flour
1/2	cup candied lemon peel		dash of salt
1-1/2	cups whole unblanched almonds	1	teaspoon baking soda
		1	teaspoon cinnamon
3/4	cup honey		dash of cloves
1-1/4	cups sugar		dash of nutmeg
2	tablespoons grated lemon peel		candied red or green cherries
1/4	cup lemon juice		citron
1-1/2	tablespoons kirsch or brandy	2	cups confectioners' sugar
		1/3	cup water

Chop fine the candied orange and lemon peel. Grind whole almonds in blender or food processor (makes 2 cups ground). In saucepan bring honey and sugar just to boiling, stirring constantly (do not boil). Add lemon peel and lemon juice; mix well. Cool 10 minutes. Add candied peel, ground almonds and kirsch; mix with wooden spoon until well blended. Into a large bowl, sift dry ingredients. With wooden spoon, make a well in center of flour mixture; pour in fruit-and-honey mixture; mix with spoon; with hands, knead in the bowl until blended. Dough will be quite stiff. Divide dough into 4 parts; place each part between 2 sheets of waxed paper. Roll each on slightly dampened surface into a 9x8-inch rectangle. Stack on cookie sheet; refrigerate 1 hour. Prepare cherries and citron for decorating. Preheat oven to 350 degrees. Combine confectioners' sugar with the water. Remove 1 sheet of cookies at a time. Peel off waxed paper. Using a 3-inch heart cookie cutter; cut 9 cookies. Flip dough over onto ungreased cookie sheet; peel off waxed paper. Remove trimmings. Bake about 8 to 10 minutes, or just until golden. Remove to wire rack. Brush icing over warm cookies. Decorate with candied fruit and citron. Re-roll trimmings; bake. Cool completely before storing in a covered plastic container in a cool, dry place. Store cookies with a piece of apple to make them moister; replace apple occasionally. Makes about 46 cookies.

Pepparkakor

Dad ate these unfrosted so he could "dunk" them in hot coffee.

1	cup shortening	2	to 3 teaspoons ginger
1	cup sugar	1-1/2	teaspoons baking soda
1	cup molasses	1	teaspoon cinnamon
1	egg	1	teaspoon cloves
2	tablespoons vinegar	1/2	teaspoon salt
5	cups flour		

Cream shortening and sugar. Beat in molasses, egg, and vinegar. Stir together flour, ginger, soda, cinnamon, cloves, and salt; blend into batter. Chill 3 hours. On lightly floured surface, roll dough to 1/8-inch thickness. Cut into desired shapes with assorted cookie cutters. Place 1-inch apart on greased cookie sheet. Bake at 375 degrees for 5 to 6 minutes. Cool slightly; remove cookies to wire rack to cool thoroughly.

Frosting:

1/2	cup shortening	3	to 4 cups sifted powdered sugar
1	teaspoon vanilla		
3	to 4 tablespoons milk		

Blend shortening and vanilla with an electric mixer. Gradually add powdered sugar; beat just until combined. Stir in milk. Insert small plain tip in pastry gag or cake decorator; fill with frosting. To decorate cookies, pipe frosting in straight or wavy lines.

Spicy Molasses Crisps

These crisp cookies are by far the most tempting and the hardest to stop eating that I ever encountered.

2	cups sifted flour	1/2	teaspoon nutmeg
2-1/4	teaspoons baking powder	1/2	cup shortening
3/4	teaspoon salt	3/4	cup sugar
1	teaspoon cinnamon	1	egg
1/2	teaspoon cloves	1/4	cup molasses

Sift together dry ingredients. Cream shortening. Gradually add sugar, creaming well; add egg and molasses; beat well. Blend in dry ingredients gradually; mix thoroughly. If desired, dough may be chilled. Roll out on floured pastry cloth or board to 1/16-inch thickness. Cut with pastry wheel or floured knife into various shapes. Or cut into rounds with 2-1/2-inch cutter. Place on greased cookie sheets. Bake at 400 degrees for about 5 to 7 minutes. Makes about 6 dozen cookies.

Spicy Crisps

Typically Danish, they are wafer-thin and rich with citron and almonds.

2-1/4	cups sifted flour	1/4	cup finely chopped almonds
1/4	teaspoon baking soda		
1	teaspoon cinnamon	2	tablespoons finely chopped candied citron
1/2	teaspoon ground cloves		
1/2	cup dark corn syrup	1/2	teaspoon grated lemon rind
1/4	cup sugar		
1/4	cup butter or margarine		

Combine syrup, sugar, and butter or margarine in a medium-size saucepan; heat, stirring constantly, just to boiling. Pour into a medium-sized bowl; stir in almonds, citron, and lemon rind. Stir in dry ingredients, half at a time, blending well to make a stiff dough. Cover bowl and let stand at room temperature for 2 days to ripen. When ready to roll dough, knead until smooth on a lightly floured pastry cloth or board. Roll out, half at a time, 1/16-inch thick; cut into rounds with a floured 2-inch plain or fluted cutter. Place, not touching, on greased cookie sheets. Brush very lightly with water; top each with a piece of candied cherry or fruit peel, if you wish. Repeat with remaining dough, then re-roll and cut out all trimmings. Bake at 375 degrees for 8 to 10 minutes, or until firm and brown. Remove from cookie sheet; cool completely on wire racks. Makes about 8 dozen.

German Spice Cakes

They have a hard texture and are good "dunking" cookies.

3/4	cup sugar	1	teaspoon cinnamon
3/4	cup honey	1/8	teaspoon allspice
2	eggs	1	cup chopped almonds
3-1/2	cups sifted flour	3/4	cup chopped candied orange peel
1	teaspoon baking powder		Egg White Icing

Heat oven to 400 degrees. Mix sugar, honey, and eggs thoroughly. Blend dry ingredients; stir into sugar mixture. Mix in almonds and orange peel. Roll 1/4-inch thick on lightly floured board; cut in fancy shapes. Place on lightly greased baking sheet, leaving 1/2-inch between cookies. Bake 10 to 12 minutes. While still hot, brush cookies with icing. Store cookies in covered container for 1 week to mellow. Makes about 4 dozen cookies.

Egg White Icing:

1	cup confectioners' sugar	1	teaspoon lemon juice
2	egg whites		

Blend sugar, egg whites and lemon juice. Beat for 5 minutes.

Mibs Molasses Cookies

Cookies warm from the oven - a glass of cold milk for dunking, what more would anyone want?

1	cup sugar	1	teaspoon ginger
1	cup shortening	1	teaspoon cinnamon
1	cup light molasses	1/4	teaspoon salt
1	tablespoon vinegar	2	teaspoons baking soda
5	cups flour	1/3	cup boiling water

In large bowl, cream the sugar and shortening. Add molasses and vinegar. Add baking soda to boiling water and add to creamed mixture with sifted dry ingredients. Mix well. On a lightly floured board, roll dough out to a little less than 1/4-inch thick. Cut with a 2-1/2-inch cookie cutter dipped in flour. Place on greased cookie sheets. Bake in a 375 degree oven about 8 minutes. Do not overbake. Makes 6 to 7 dozen cookies.

Gingerbread Cut-Outs

Decorated gingerbread cut-outs are fun to make and perennial favorites with the whole family.

1	cup butter	1/8	teaspoon salt
1/2	cup brown sugar, packed	1/8	teaspoon ginger
1/3	cup dark molasses	1/8	teaspoon nutmeg
2-2/3	cups sifted flour	1/8	teaspoon cinnamon
1/8	teaspoon soda		

Cream butter; add sugar gradually. Blend in molasses and sifted dry ingredients; chill. Roll 1/8 to 1/4-inch thick on floured canvas and cut into desired shapes. Place on greased cookie sheets; decorate before baking or frost and decorate when cool. Bake at 350 degrees for about 8 to 10 minutes depending on thickness of cookie. Cookies should be light in color. Makes about 7 dozen depending on size. Frost with decorator frosting.

Bread Crumb Cookies

These cookies are thin and dainty.

1-1/3	cups butter	1	teaspoon baking soda
2	cups brown sugar	1/2	teaspoon cloves
3	eggs, beaten	1	teaspoon cinnamon
1	cup molasses	2	teaspoons baking powder
5	cups fine dry bread crumbs		additional flour to make a stiff dough
1	cup cake flour		

Mix butter and sugar together, add molasses and beaten eggs. Add the bread crumbs and other dry ingredients which have been sifted together. Chill and roll thin. Cut and brush tops of cookies with beaten egg white or with milk before baking. Bake in a 350 degree oven for 6 to 7 minutes.

Speculass

A cookie made for the holiday's. Put into any Christmas mold or cut-out into special patterns.

4-1/4	cups flour	1/2	teaspoon salt
1	cup dark brown sugar, packed firmly	1	teaspoon cinnamon
		1/2	teaspoon cloves
1/2	cup butter	1/4	teaspoon nutmeg
3/4	cup grated almonds	1/4	teaspoon allspice
2	eggs	1/2	cup sliced almonds
4-1/2	teaspoons milk		

Beat together flour, brown sugar, butter, grated almonds, eggs, milk, salt and spices cover and refrigerate 1 hour. Preheat oven to 325 degrees. Grease baking sheets. Press dough firmly onto a floured speculass mold. Carefully turn out onto a greased cookie sheet. Repeat with remaining dough or roll out and cut into squares. Place on greased sheet. Sprinkle almonds over cookies. Bake 15 to 20 minutes. Remove and place cookies on coolers. Store in a tightly sealed container.

Make ginger cookies and trace your child's hand on the dough. Cut-out and after baking, have them write Grandma, Auntie or whoever they can think of.

Mickie's Date-Filled Oatmeal Cookies

Bring back childhood memories when cookies and milk were a must for an after school treat.

1	pound package pitted dates, finely cut	2	eggs
1	cup sugar	1	teaspoon vanilla
1	cup water	1-1/2	cups regular rolled oats
3/4	cup chopped walnuts	3-1/4	cups flour
1	cup margarine	1	teaspoon baking soda
1-1/2	cups firmly packed brown sugar	1	teaspoon cream of tartar
		1/2	teaspoon salt

In a medium-size saucepan, combine dates, sugar and water. Bring to a boil over medium heat. Boil 2 minutes, stirring constantly. Remove from heat and beat with a spoon until well blended. Stir in walnuts; cool. In a large bowl, cream margarine and brown sugar until well blended. Beat in eggs and vanilla until mixture is light and fluffy. Stir in oats. In a medium-sized bowl, combine flour, baking soda, cream of tartar and salt. Stir dry ingredients into creamed mixture; mix until well blended. Chill dough about 1 hour for easier handling. Preheat oven to 375 degrees. Remove 1/4 of dough at a time; refrigerate remainder of dough. On a lightly floured board or pastry cloth, roll dough 1/8-inch thick. Cut rounds with a 2-1/2-inch cookie cutter. Place rounds 1-inch apart on ungreased baking sheets. Spoon 1 teaspoon of date mixture near center of each cookie. Using back of a table knife, lift 1 side of cookie and fold it over other half. Edges will seal as cookies bake. Bake in preheated oven 8 to 10 minutes or until cookies are light golden brown. Remove cookies from baking sheet and cool on wire racks. Repeat with remaining dough and filling. Makes 48 cookies.

Chilled cookie dough often crumbles when you slice it. But if you first warm the blade of your knife in hot water and then wipe it dry, you can avoid the crumbling.

Trilby's

Use a small star cutter for these date filled goodies.

1	cup butter	1/4	teaspoon salt
1	cup light brown sugar, firmly packed	2	cups quick cooking oatmeal, ground
2	eggs		colored sugars for decorating
1-2/3	cups sifted flour		
1	teaspoon baking soda		

Cream butter. Add sugar gradually. Cream well. Add eggs one at a time. Beat well after each addition. Sift flour, soda and salt together. Add to creamed mixture. Add oatmeal. Blend. Roll 1/8 to 1/4-inch thick on floured canvas. Cut with small cookie cutters. Place on greased cookie sheets. Decorate half of the cookies with colored sugars. Bake at 350 degrees about 12 minutes. Cool. Spread bottom of plain cookies with date filling. Cover with decorated cookies. Makes about 10 dozen.

Date Filling:

1-1/2	cups finely cut, pitted dates	1	cup water
		1	cup sugar

Cook dates and water together until dates are soft. Add sugar. Cook until mixture is thick. Stir constantly. Cool.

Mondchens

It's not Christmas at our house without Mondchens; these crescent cookies are so different in taste, they automatically become every one's favorite.

2-1/2	cups commercially grated almonds	1	teaspoon grated lemon rind
1	cup butter	1-1/2	cups powdered sugar
1	cup sugar	1	teaspoon vanilla
1	cup sifted flour	2	tablespoons hot water
1/4	teaspoon salt		

Cream butter; add sugar gradually. Blend in almonds, flour, salt and lemon rind. Roll 1/4-inch thick on floured canvas; cut with crescent cutter; place on ungreased cookie sheets. Bake at 350 degrees about 10 minutes. Blend powdered sugar, vanilla, and water; spread on hot cookies. Makes about 7 dozen.

Pecan Praline Rounds

Pecans, cream, and sugar combine to make a praline topping for these irresistible buttery rounds.

1/2	cup unsalted butter, softened	2	teaspoons baking powder
1	cup plus 1 tablespoon sugar	1/4	teaspoon salt
		2/3	cup whipping cream
1	egg	1	cup finely chopped toasted pecans
1-1/2	teaspoons vanilla		sugar, for flattening cookies
1-3/4	cups flour		

Cream butter; gradually add 1 cup of the sugar and beat until light. Add egg and vanilla and beat thoroughly. Gradually add dry sifted ingredients beating until just blended. Gather dough into a ball and enclose in waxed paper or plastic wrap; refrigerate. Preheat oven to 325 degrees. In a small saucepan combine cream and remaining 1 tablespoon sugar. Simmer over moderate heat until reduced by half; do not let cream boil over. Stir in pecans and set aside. Divide dough in 42 pieces; roll each piece to form a ball. Place, 1-1/2-inches apart, on greased baking sheets. Flatten cookies with the bottom of a glass dipped in sugar. Place approximately a teaspoon of pecan mixture atop each cookie. Bake until lightly browned around edges, about 12 to 15 minutes. Transfer to wire racks to cool. Makes about forty-two 1-1/2-inch cookies.

Butter Horn Cookies

We all have eaten these yeast made cookies, now try baking some yourself.

2	cups sifted flour	1/2	cup sour cream
1	teaspoon baking powder	1/2	teaspoon vanilla
1/4	teaspoon salt	1/2	cup granulated sugar
1/2	cup butter	1/2	cup finely ground walnuts or pecans
1/2	package yeast		
2	tablespoons warm water	1/2	teaspoon almond extract
2	eggs, separated		confectioners' sugar

Stir flour, baking powder, and salt together in mixing bowl. Cut in butter. Dissolve yeast in water; stir in egg yolks, sour cream, and vanilla. Blend into flour mixture. Refrigerate 1 hour. Beat egg whites until foamy; gradually add sugar; beat until stiff. Fold in nuts and almond extract. Divide dough in 4 parts. Roll each part into 9-inch circle on board sprinkled with confectioners' sugar. Cut each circle in 12 wedges. Spread 1 heaping teaspoonful meringue on each. Roll, beginning at wide end. Bake on lightly greased baking sheet, or until golden brown in 350° oven for 10 to 12 minutes. Sprinkle with confectioners' sugar. Makes about 4 dozen cookies.

Bake your cookies weeks ahead, I start in early November. Most cookies freeze real good, but be sure to separate types or the flavor will transfer one to the other.

Date Crescents

Fond of dates? Then do try these extra delicious cookies.

1-1/4	cups sifted flour	1	cup uncooked oatmeal
1/2	teaspoon soda	1/2	cup cold butter
1/2	teaspoon salt	1/2	cup sour cream
1/2	cup sugar		

Sift flour, soda, salt and sugar into mixing bowl; mix in oatmeal. Cut in butter until mixture resembles coarse crumbs. Blend in sour cream; chill.

Date Filling:

3/4	cup cut dates	1/2	cup chopped pecans
1/4	cup sugar	1	tablespoon butter
1/2	cup orange juice		

Combine dates, sugar and orange juice in saucepan. Cook and stir until mixture boils and sugar is dissolved. Remove from heat; add pecans and butter; cool. Roll dough about 1/8-inch thick on floured surface. Cut into 2-inch squares. Spread 1/2 teaspoonful of filling on each square. Start at one corner and roll towards opposite corner; place point down on greased cookie sheets. Shape into crescents. Bake at 350 degrees about 15 minutes. Makes about 4-1/2 dozen.

Oatmeal Christmas Bells

Santa won't leave without finishing these delights.

2-1/2	cups flour	1	egg
1	teaspoon baking powder	1	teaspoon vanilla
1/2	teaspoon salt	1	cup oats
3/4	cup butter or margarine, room temperature		decorative red sugar, optional
2	tablespoons milk		

Sift together flour, baking powder and salt. Place in large mixing bowl along with butter, sugar, milk, egg and vanilla; beat until smooth. Stir in oats. On a floured board, roll the dough 1/8-inch thick. Cut into decorative bell shapes and sprinkle with red sugar if desired. Bake on an ungreased cookie sheet at 375 degrees for 15 to 18 minutes or until light golden brown. Remove from cookie sheet and cool on wire racks. Makes 2-1/2 dozen 3-inch cookies.

Sugar-Nut Sticks

A sugar cookie with raisins and nuts and glazed make this a pretty as well as tasty stick.

2	cups flour	1/4	cup butter or margarine, softened
1	tablespoon sugar		
3/4	cup butter or margarine, softened	1/4	cup raisins
		1/4	cup chopped nuts
1/4	cup milk	1	teaspoon almond extract
1	egg, beaten		glaze
1/2	cup sugar		

Mix flour and 1 tablespoon sugar. Cut in 3/4 cup butter until particles are the size of small peas. Stir in milk and egg until dough forms a ball and cleans side of bowl. Divide dough in half. Roll half of dough into rectangle, 12 by 4-inches, on lightly floured board. Place on ungreased baking sheet. Repeat with remaining dough. Preheat oven to 350 degrees. Mix 1/2 cup sugar, 1/4 cup butter, the raisins, nuts and extract. Spread half of the sugar mixture lengthwise down center of each rectangle. Bring long edges of dough together; seal securely. Bake 30 minutes. Cool slightly; drizzle with glaze. Cut crosswise into 1-inch sticks. Makes about 24 sticks.

Oatmeal Cookie Crackers

Excellent and healthy to serve with a big cold drink.

1/2	cup butter	1/4	teaspoon salt
1	cup sugar	2	cups quick-cooking oats
1	teaspoon baking soda	2	to 2-1/2 cups flour
1/2	cup hot water		*salt

Cream butter. Gradually add sugar; continue creaming until light and fluffy. Dissolve baking soda in hot water; add to creamed mixture. Blend in salt and oats. Add flour gradually to form a stiff dough; mix thoroughly. Divide into 4 parts. Shape into squares; flatten to 1/2-inch thickness. Roll out 1 part on floured surface to a 16x8-inch rectangle. Sprinkle with salt; roll in lightly. Cut into 2-inch squares, diamonds or triangles. Place on greased cookie sheets. Bake at 350 degrees for 7 to 10 minutes until delicately browned. Makes about 120 small cookies.

*Sugar, sesame seed, poppy seed, or caraway seed may be substituted for salt.

Honey Graham Crackers

A healthy after school snack for children.

1	cup sifted flour	1	teaspoon vanilla
1	teaspoon baking powder	1/2	cup dark brown sugar
1/2	teaspoon baking soda	1/4	cup honey
1/4	teaspoon salt	1/2	cup milk
1/2	teaspoon cinnamon	2	cups unsifted whole wheat flour
1/4	pound butter		

Sift together white flour, baking powder, baking soda, salt and cinnamon. In a large bowl, cream butter and sugar well. Add vanilla and honey, beat well. On low speed add dry ingredients and whole wheat flour alternately with milk. Scrape bowl often. Beat only until smooth. May be kneaded briefly on board if not smooth. Form dough into an even flattened oblong. Wrap and refrigerate several hours. Cut dough into quarters. Work with one at a time. Roll dough into an even 15 by 5-inch oblong. Trim edges, use a ruler and cut crosswise into six 5 by 2-1/2-inch oblongs. With back of dull knife score lightly across center of each, dividing it in two each 2-1/2-inch squares. Transfer to unbuttered cookie sheet 1/2-inch apart. With a fork prick in rows at 1/2-inch intervals. Bake 10 to 12 minutes until lightly colored at 350 degrees.

A cookie jar filled with an assortment of cookies is a welcome gift.

Swedish Wafer Cookies

A delicate tea cookie.

1	cup butter	2	cups sifted flour
1/3	cup half and half		sugar

Cream butter with half and half. Add flour; mix well. Chill thoroughly. Using 1/3 of dough at a time, roll out 1/8-inch thick on floured board. Keep remaining dough chilled. Cut with 1-1/2-inch round cutter. Coat each side with sugar. Place on ungreased baking sheets; prick with fork 3 or 4 times. Bake at 375 degrees for about 5 to 7 minutes. Watch carefully! Cool.

Filling:

1/4	cup butter	1	egg yolk
3/4	cup sifted confectioners' sugar	1	teaspoon vanilla food coloring

Blend together 1/4 cup butter, sugar, egg yolk and vanilla. For Christmas cookies, tint red or green; for tea cookies, pastel colors. Spread filling between 2 cookie halves. Press together gently. Makes about 5 dozen.

Swiss Almond Bites

Use tiny cutters for these unusual cookies.

1	pound almonds	1	teaspoon cinnamon
4	squares unsweetened chocolate	1/4	teaspoon cloves
2	cups plus 2 tablespoons sugar	1/4	teaspoon salt
		3	eggs

Chop almonds fine. Put almonds and chocolate in a blender and blend until fine. Mix thoroughly with remaining ingredients. Sprinkle a board with a mixture of half sugar and half flour. Pat out small amounts of dough to 1/4-inch thickness. Cut into any small shapes. Place on greased baking sheets and let stand in a cool place overnight. Bake in a 325 degree oven about 15 minutes. Cool slightly before removing from pan. Makes about 3 dozen cookies.

Viennese Almond Wafers

Simple rich cookies but elegant.

3/4	cup sliced blanched almonds, crushed	1/3	cup sugar
1/2	cup butter	3/4	cup plus 1 tablespoon sifted flour
	scant 1/8 teaspoon salt	1	egg white
1/4	teaspoon almond extract		

The almonds should be coarsely crushed. In a small bowl of an electric mixer, cream the butter with the salt and almond extract. Beat in the sugar and then the flour, beating only until mixed. If the dough is too soft to be rolled, chill it briefly. Transfer the dough to a well-floured pastry cloth. Turn it over to flour all sides, and form it into a square or an oblong. With a well-floured rolling pin, roll the dough into an even square with straight edges; the square will be about 9 to 10 inches across and the dough will be a scant 1/8-inch thick. Trim the edges of the dough with a pastry wheel, or use a long, thin, sharp knife and wipe the blade after each cut to keep the dough from sticking. Cut the dough into even squares or oblongs. Beat the egg whites until foamy. With a pastry brush, brush some of the white generously over each cookie. Sprinkle the almonds evenly over the egg white. Press down gently with the palms of both hands to press the nuts slightly into the dough. Carefully brush the remaining egg white over the almonds, it will keep them from falling off after the cookies have been baked. Transfer cookies to ungreased cookie sheets, placing them 1/2 to 1-inch apart. Bake at 350 degrees for about 20 minutes. Use the higher rack in oven. Bake until lightly browned; do not under-bake. Makes 9 large or 24 small oblong cookies.

Cinnamon Stars

A really different type of cookie.

1	teaspoon cinnamon	3	egg whites
1-1/2	cups confectioners' sugar sifted	1-1/2	cups unblanched almond nutmeats, grated

Mix cinnamon and 1-1/4 cups confectioners' sugar. Add unbeaten egg whites and mix well. To 1/4 cup of egg white mixture, add 1/4 cup confectioners' sugar and mix well; to the remaining egg white mixture, add nutmeats, mix well, turn on a board sprinkled with additional confectioners' sugar. Roll about 1/4-inch thick and cut with a floured 2-3/4-inch star cutter. Place on greased cookie sheet and brush with reserved egg white-confectioners' sugar mixture. Bake in a 300 degree oven for 20 minutes. Makes about 30 cookies.

Hazelnut Shorts

Love hazelnuts? Try these super cookies.

1	cup butter	2-1/2	cups sifted cake flour
1/2	cup sugar	1/2	pound hazelnuts, grated
1/4	teaspoon salt		(3 cups)
1	teaspoon vanilla		currant jelly

Cream butter. Add sugar gradually. Blend in salt, vanilla, flour and hazelnuts. Work dough with fingers to form a ball. Roll 1/4-inch thick on floured canvas. Cut with small cutters. Place on greased cookie sheets. Bake at 350 degrees 12 to 15 minutes. Spread bottom half of the cookies with jelly. Top with another cookie. Frost. Makes about 6 dozen small sandwich cookies.

Frosting:

1	tablespoon melted butter		cream
1	cup powdered sugar	1/3	cup grated pistachio nuts
1/2	teaspoon vanilla		

Combine butter, sugar, vanilla and cream to make frosting of spreading consistency. Frost cookies. Sprinkle with nuts.

Christmas Miniatures

Want a really pretty cookie? Be sure to try these different tender morsels.

1	cup butter	1/8	teaspoon salt
1/2	cup powdered sugar	1	cup cornstarch
1	teaspoons vanilla	1	cup sifted flour

Cream butter; add sugar gradually. Mix in remaining ingredients. Chill several hours. Roll about 1/2-inch thick on floured surface. Cut with miniature cookie cutters or cut into very small squares, rounds, bars, and triangles. Place on greased cookie sheets. Bake at 375 degrees for about 6 to 10 minutes. Depending on size. Cool. Tint decorating frosting red and green. Decorate cookies with small red frosting roses and green leaves. Makes about 7 dozen.

Coffee Crisps

It's coffee in the frosting that brings out the wonderful flavor of these crunchy frosted cookies.

1	cup margarine	3	cups sifted flour
1/2	teaspoon orange extract	1	teaspoon baking powder
1/4	teaspoon vanilla	1/2	teaspoon soda
1	cup sugar	1/4	teaspoon salt
1/4	cup orange juice		

Cream together, butter, sugar and flavorings until fluffy. Stir in orange juice. Blend in sifted dry ingredients. Chill 1 hour. Place chilled dough on a lightly floured surface and roll 1/4-inch thick. Cut with a 2-inch floured crescent cookie cutter. Place cookies on greased cookie sheets. Bake at 350 degrees, or until lightly browned. Cool on cooling racks.

Topping:

1	cup sugar	1	cup walnuts, chopped
3/4	cup coffee (cold)	1/2	cup honey

In a saucepan, bring sugar, coffee and honey to a boil; simmer 5 minutes. Brush tops of cookies with syrup. Sprinkle the chopped walnuts over the cookies. Remove to wire racks to cool completely. Makes about 7 dozen.

Rolled Sour Cream Cookies

Why not try something different with sour cream, it could be a winner.

2-2/3	cups sifted flour	1	cup butter
1/4	teaspoon baking soda	1	cup sugar
1	teaspoon baking powder	1	egg
1	teaspoon nutmeg	1/2	cup sour cream

Mix and sift flour, soda, baking powder and nutmeg. Cream butter well, add sugar gradually and continue creaming until light and fluffy; add well beaten egg and mix well. Add sifted dry ingredients alternately with sour cream, mixing just enough after each addition to combine ingredients. Chill in refrigerator for about 2 hours. Roll thin on floured pastry cover and cut with a floured 1-3/4-inch fluted round cutter. Bake on cookie sheets in a 375 degree preheated oven for about 9 minutes. Store in covered container. Makes 13 dozen.

Almond Butter Sticks

Tender and flaky almond flavored cookies.

1	cup butter, softened	2	teaspoons baking powder
8	ounce package cream cheese, softened	1/8	teaspoon salt
		1-1/2	cups sugar
2-1/4	cups flour	4-1/2	teaspoons almond extract

Combine all ingredients except sugar and almond extract in large mixer bowl; mix until a dough forms. Knead on floured surface until smooth. Roll out dough, half at a time, to 14 by 8-inch rectangles. Combine sugar and almond extract. Sprinkle each rectangle with 3 to 4 tablespoons sugar mixture. Fold one end of dough over center. Fold other end over to make 3 layers. Turning dough 1/4 way around, repeat rolling and folding as above 2 more times; sprinkling with 3 to 4 tablespoons sugar mixture each time. Roll out again to 14 by 8-inch rectangles. Cut into 3 by 1-1/2-inch strips. Place on ungreased cookie sheets. Bake at 400 degrees for 8 to 10 minutes. Remove from cookie sheets immediately. Cool on wire racks. Makes about 60 cookies.

Ragalach

Why not roll these in colored sugar to make them more festive.

1	cup butter	3/4	cup chopped walnuts
8	ounces cream cheese	1/3	cup sugar
2	cups sifted flour	1-1/2	teaspoons cinnamon
1/4	teaspoon salt		powdered sugar

Cream butter and cheese; blend in flour and salt. Shape into 14 balls; chill. Roll each ball into 6-inch circle on floured surface. Cut into 8 pie shaped wedges. Mix walnuts, sugar and cinnamon. Place about 1/4 teaspoonful of walnut mixture in center of each wedge. Start at wide edge; roll toward point; shape into a crescent. Place point down on ungreased cookie sheets. Bake at 350 degrees about 12 minutes. Cool; roll in powdered sugar. Makes about 11 dozen.

Cream Cheese Sugar Cookies

This recipe is too good to make only once a year.

1	cup sugar	1/2	teaspoon almond extract
1/2	teaspoon salt	1/2	teaspoon vanilla
1	cup butter or margarine, softened	1	egg yolk (reserve white)
3	ounce package cream cheese, softened	2-3/4	cups flour

In large bowl, combine all ingredients except flour; blend well. Stir in flour. Chill. Preheat oven to 375 degrees. On lightly floured surface, roll out dough, a third at a time, to 1/8-inch thickness. Cut into desired shapes with lightly floured cutters. Place 1-inch apart on ungreased cookie sheets. Sprinkle with sugar or, if desired, brush with slightly beaten reserved egg white before sprinkling with colored sugar. Bake about 7 to 10 minutes until golden brown. Cool. Frost and decorate, if desired. Makes about 5 to 6 dozen cookies.

Biscochitos

Using lard makes these cookies extra tender.

1	cup sugar	6	cups sifted flour
2	cups lard	3	teaspoons baking powder
1	teaspoon anise seed	1	teaspoon salt
2	eggs	1/4	cup brandy

Preheat oven to 350 degrees. Cream lard, sugar and anise seed. Beat eggs slightly and add to the lard mixture. Blend until light and fluffy. Sift flour, baking powder and salt and add to the lard mixture. Add liquid and knead until well mixed. Roll dough 1/2-inch thick and cut with cookie cutter. Roll top of each cookie in a mixture of cinnamon and sugar. Bake on cookie sheet at 350 degree temperature for 10 to 12 minutes. Makes about 10 dozen.

Peppermint Pinwheels

It's beginning to look a lot like Christmas, with these on a Christmas platter.

1	cup butter	1/2	teaspoon red food coloring
1	cup powdered sugar		
1	egg	1	egg white for topping
1-1/2	teaspoons almond extract	1	tablespoon water
1	teaspoon vanilla	1/4	cup sugar, for topping
2-1/2	cups flour	1/4	cup finely crushed peppermint candy
1	teaspoon salt		

Cream butter; add sugar gradually. Beat in egg and flavorings. Blend in sifted dry ingredients. Divide dough in half. Mix food coloring into 1/2 of dough. Chill dough until firm. Roll 1/2 of white dough into an 8-inch square on floured canvas. Roll 1/2 of red dough into an 8-inch square. Place white square on top of red square. Roll as for jellyroll. Repeat with remaining dough. Wrap in waxed paper; chill overnight. Cut into 1/8-inch slices. Place on greased cookie sheets. Bake at 375 degrees 8 to 10 minutes. Mix egg white and water; brush on hot cookies. Sprinkle with combined sugar and peppermint candy. Makes about 10 dozen.

Put cookies on a pretty tray or Christmas platter as a gift. Cover with colored plastic wrap and add a big bow or pieces of holly.

Cinnamon Maple Rings

A pinwheel cookie at its best.

2	cups flour	1/4	cup pure maple syrup, chilled
1/4	cup sugar		
1	cup butter, chilled and sliced into 8 pieces	2	to 4 tablespoons ice water

Mix flour and sugar in a medium bowl. Add butter and mix until the dough forms small, pea-size pellets. Add chilled maple syrup and 2 tablespoons water, and mix on low speed until dough can be formed into a ball. Do not over-mix. Separate dough into 2 balls and flatten into disks. Wrap dough tightly in plastic wrap. Refrigerate at least 2 hours. On a floured board, roll 1 piece of dough into a rectangle 10-inches wide, 15-inches long and 1/8-inch. Sprinkle dough with half of the cinnamon sugar filling. Starting with smaller side, roll dough up tightly into a cylinder. Dampen edge with water and seal. Repeat with remaining dough. Wrap each roll in plastic wrap and refrigerate for 1 hour. Using a sharp thin knife, cut 1/4-inch slices from each roll. Place slices on ungreased baking sheets, 1-inch apart. Brush tops lightly with 1/4 cup maple syrup. Bake in a 325 degree oven for 16 to 17 minutes. Immediately transfer cookies to a cool flat surface. Makes 4 dozen.

Filling:

1/4	cup white sugar	4	teaspoons cinnamon

Combine sugar and cinnamon in a small bowl.

Hoot Owl Cookies

Though not a Christmas cookie, it's fun to make as a Halloween treat.

3/4	cup butter	1-1/2	squares unsweetened chocolate, melted and cooled
1	cup brown sugar, firmly packed		
1	egg	1/4	teaspoon baking soda
1	teaspoon vanilla		

Cream butter and brown sugar; add egg and vanilla, beating well. Blend in dry ingredients gradually. Mix chocolate and soda together. Take out 1/3 of dough and blend in chocolate mixture. Chill dough for 1 hour. Roll out half of light dough to a 10x4-1/2-inch strip. Shape half of dark dough into a roll 10-inches long; place on strip of light dough. Mold sides of light dough around dark; wrap in aluminum foil. Repeat with remaining dough. Chill at least 2 hours. Cut into slices 1/8 to 1/4-inch thick and place 2 slices together on a greased baking sheet to resemble an owl. Pinch a corner of each slice to form ears. Place a chocolate chip in center of each slice for eyes; press a whole cashew nut between slices for a beak. Bake in a 350 degree oven for 8 to 12 minutes. Remove from baking sheets immediately. Store cooled cookies between layers of foil in a flat, tightly covered container. Makes about 4 dozen.

Hazelnut Crescents

Another great hazelnut lover's delight.

3	egg whites	3/4	cup unblanched almonds, grated (1-1/2 cups)
1/4	teaspoon salt		
1-3/4	cups powdered sugar	1/2	cup soda cracker crumbs
3/4	cup hazelnuts, grated (1-1/2 cups)	1	teaspoon vanilla

Beat egg whites and salt until foamy. Add sugar gradually. Beat until soft peaks are formed. Fold in nuts, crumbs and vanilla. Mix thoroughly. Roll 1/4-inch thick on canvas sprinkled with powdered sugar. Cut with crescent shaped cutter. Dip cutter in water for easier cutting. Place on greased cookie sheets. Spread top with Golden Icing before baking.

Golden Icing:

2   egg yolks
6   tablespoons powdered sugar

Beat egg yolks until lemon colored. Add sugar gradually. Beat until thick. Bake at 325 degrees 12 to 15 minutes. Makes about 5 dozen cookies depending on size.

Giving a cookie press, springerle or sandbakeleser as a gift? Add a batch of that type of cookie and your recipe.

Triple Treats

Nutmeg, vanilla and rum flavoring blend happily in these easy to mold cookies.

2	cups sifted flour	1	egg
3/4	teaspoon baking soda	1	tablespoon milk
1/2	teaspoon salt	1	teaspoon vanilla
1/2	cup butter or margarine	1	teaspoon rum extract
3/4	cup sugar	1	square unsweetened chocolate, melted

Sift together flour, soda, and salt. Cream butter. Gradually add sugar creaming well. Add egg, milk and vanilla. beat well. Blend in dry ingredients gradually; mix thoroughly. Remove 2/3 of dough from bowl to waxed paper or aluminum foil. Into remaining dough blend chocolate. Chill 1/2 to 1 hour. Roll out light dough on floured surface to a 12 by 6-inch rectangle. Roll out dark dough to a 12 by 4-inch strip. Cut light and dark dough into 12 by 2-inch strips. Stack the 5 strips, alternating light and dark. Pinch off marble-sized pieces of dough; shape into balls. Arrange 3 together with sides touching on greased baking sheet; flatten slightly. Bake at 375 degrees for 10 to 12 minutes.

Ischler Hearts

These cookies are laced with apricot jam and dipped into a rich chocolate glaze.

1-1/2 cups butter	1-1/2 teaspoons grated orange zest
3 ounces cream cheese	
1-1/2 cups granulated sugar	1-1/2 cups ground blanched almonds
1 egg, lightly beaten	
2 cups flour	1/2 cup apricot jam
1/2 teaspoon salt	

Cream the butter until smooth and soft; beat in the cream cheese, sugar and egg, blending well. Sift the flour and salt together and stir into the creamed mixture. Stir in the orange zest; fold in the almonds. Divide the dough into halves. Roll out 1 portion of the dough on a sugared work surface to 1/8-inch thickness, using more sugar as necessary to prevent the dough from sticking. With a 1-1/2-inch heart-shaped cookie cutter, stamp out the cookies and transfer to the buttered cookie sheets. Repeat with remaining dough and scraps. Bake at 350 degrees for 8 to 10 minutes, or until they are firm and the bottoms are a light golden brown. Remove to racks to cool completely. Warm the apricot jam and spread a thin layer on half of the cookies. Cover each with a plain cookie.

Glaze:

8 squares (8 ounces) semisweet chocolate	1/3 cup heavy cream
	1 teaspoon rum extract
3 tablespoons butter	

Melt the chocolate, butter and heavy cream in the top of a double boiler or in a heavy saucepan over very low heat. Cool slightly; stir in the rum extract. Dip each cookie lengthwise halfway into the chocolate mixture and place on cookie sheets lined with wax paper. Refrigerate for 1 hour, or until set. Store the cookies between layers of waxed paper in the refrigerator. Makes about 25 to 30 cookies.

Rum Mocha Treasures

You don't need a map to find this treasure, just follow the directions below.

3/4	cup butter	1	teaspoon baking powder
1	cup sugar	1/2	teaspoon baking soda
1	egg	1/4	cup cold strong coffee
2	cups sifted flour		about 1 pound rum
3/4	cup cocoa		flavored chocolate wafers
1/2	teaspoon salt		

Cream butter; add sugar gradually; beat in egg. Blend in sifted dry ingredients and coffee alternately; chill. Roll dough 1/8-inch thick on floured canvas; cut with 1-1/2-inch cutter. Arrange half the cookies on ungreased cookie sheets. Top each cookie with a chocolate wafer. Cover wafers with remaining half of cookies, sandwich fashion. Bake at 350 degrees for about 8 minutes. Cool; frost with pastel butter frosting.

Brazil Nut Diamonds

Brazil nuts make this a really different tasting cookie.

1-1/3	cups sifted flour	1/2	cup sugar
1-1/2	cups grated, blanched Brazil nutmeats	1	teaspoon vanilla confectioners' sugar
2/3	cup butter		

Mix flour and nutmeats. Cream butter well, add sugar gradually and continue creaming until light and fluffy. Add vanilla and mix. Add flour mixture gradually and mix well. Pat dough 1/8-inch thick on floured board and cut with a floured diamond-shaped cutter. Bake on baking sheets in a preheated 350 degree oven for about 10 minutes. If desired, sprinkle with confectioners' sugar. Store in covered container. Makes about 30 cookies.

Peanut Cutouts

A faint orange flavor adds a distinctive flavor to these tasty rounds.

1	cup margarine	1	teaspoon baking powder
2	cups sugar	1/2	teaspoon salt
2	eggs	1	cup peanuts, finely ground
1/4	cup milk	2	teaspoons grated orange rind
3-1/2	cups flour		
1/4	teaspoon baking soda		chocolate Jimmies

Cream margarine; add sugar to margarine and cream lightly. Beat in eggs one at a time. Sift flour, soda and salt together. Add alternately with milk only until flour has disappeared and dough is smooth. Fold nuts and orange rind in. Roll dough about 1/4-inch thick on flour dusted cloth. Cut with a round cookie cutter. Brush top with mixture of 2 tablespoons milk, dash of salt and 1 beaten egg. Sprinkle cookies with chocolate Jimmies. Place on cookie sheets. Bake a 375 degrees for 12 to 15 minutes. Makes 72 to 80 cookies.

Walnut Walkaways

What a good flavor in these extra tender cookies.

1	package yeast	1/2	cup sugar
1/4	warm water	1	teaspoon orange zest
2	cups flour	1	teaspoon lemon zest
1/8	teaspoon salt	1/2	cup finely chopped walnuts
3/4	cup butter		
1	egg		confectioners' sugar
3	ounce package cream cheese, softened		

Soften yeast in warm water. Combine flour and salt in mixing bowl. Cut in butter until mixture resembles coarse crumbs. Add yeast and egg; mix just until blended. Roll out dough, half at a time, on floured surface to a 13 by 9-inch rectangle. Beat cream cheese, sugar, and orange and lemon zest until light and fluffy. Spread half on each rectangle; sprinkle with walnuts. Starting with 13-inch side, roll up jellyroll fashion. Place, seam-side down, on lightly greased cookie sheet. Cut each roll halfway through lengthwise. Bake at 375 degrees for 20 to 25 minutes. Cool. Sprinkle with confectioners' sugar. Cut diagonally into 1-inch slices. Makes about 24 cookies.

Sweet Pastry Pockets

If you desire a different change in cookie tastes, do try these with a cream cheese and coconut filling in sheet pastry cookie dough.

2	cups sifted flour	1	egg, separated
1/2	teaspoon salt	2	teaspoons grated orange rind
3/4	cup butter		
2	tablespoons powdered sugar	1/4	cup orange juice sugar

Combine flour and salt. Cream butter with powdered sugar and egg yolk. Blend in orange rind and dry ingredients; mix well. Add orange juice; mix until a stiff dough forms. Roll out, half at a time, on well floured surface to 1/8-inch thickness. Cut out with floured 2-1/2-inch cutter. Place 1/2 teaspoon filling in center of each; moisten edges with water. Fold in half; seal edges. Place on ungreased cookie sheet. Repeat with remaining dough. Make 1-1/2-inch cut in top of each for an escape of steam. Brush with slightly beaten egg white. Sprinkle with sugar. Bake at 400 degrees for 8 to 10 minutes until light golden brown. Makes 36 cookies.

Filling:

3/4	cup brown sugar, packed	1	teaspoon vanilla
3	ounces cream cheese	1/2	cup flaked coconut
1/8	teaspoon salt		

Cream brown sugar and cream cheese. Add salt and vanilla; beat well. Stir in coconut. Chill while preparing dough.

Note:

For a dessert pastry, cut into 3-inch rounds. Place about 1 teaspoon filling in center of each. Makes about 24.

Drop Cookies

There's nothing quite as pleasing
when a friend drops by for tea;
as a plate of just baked cookies
that demand your recipe.

Old-Fashioned Soft Sugar Cookies

These tender cake-like cookies are flavored with nutmeg and lemon.

2-1/2	cups flour	2	eggs
1	teaspoon baking soda	1/2	teaspoon vanilla
1	teaspoon nutmeg	1/2	teaspoon grated lemon rind
1/4	teaspoon salt		
1/2	cup butter, softened	1	cup sour cream
1-1/2	cups sugar	1/4	cup raisins

Preheat oven to 375 degrees. In mixer combine butter and sugar, and beat until well blended. Beat in eggs, one at a time, mixing until fluffy after each addition. Add vanilla and lemon rind and mix to blend thoroughly. Add sifted dry ingredients alternately with sour cream, mixing until smooth after each addition. Drop by tablespoons, placed well apart, onto well-greased baking sheets. Sprinkle each cookie lightly with granulated sugar. Place 1 or more raisins in the center of each. Bake until cookies are golden brown, about 12 to 14 minutes. Remove at once to wire racks to cool. Makes about 5 dozen 2-3/4-inch cookies.

Old-Fashioned Cookies

Add anything to these you want to, frosted or unfrosted. A recipe mom made 75 years ago.

1	cup sugar	2	teaspoons baking powder
1	cup brown sugar	1	teaspoon baking soda
1	cup butter, softened	1	teaspoon salt
3	eggs	1	cup milk
4	cups sifted flour	1	tablespoon vanilla

Preheat oven to 400 degrees. In large bowl, cream together both sugars, and butter. Beat in eggs. Sift together dry ingredients. Stir into bowl alternately with milk, then add vanilla. Drop by teaspoonfuls onto ungreased cookie sheets, about 2-inches apart. Bake 7 to 10 minutes, or until just beginning to brown. Do not overbake. Remove from sheets while still warm. Makes about 10 dozen.

Date Lemon Sugar Cookies

A soft flavorful sugar cookie, which is good for everyone.

1/2	cup margarine	2-1/4	cups flour
1/2	cup sugar	1/2	teaspoon baking soda
2	teaspoons lemon extract	1/2	cup chopped dates
1/4	cup egg whites	1/2	cup water, room temperature
1	tablespoon lemon juice		
2	tablespoons grated fresh lemon rind		

Preheat oven to 350 degrees. Spray cookie sheets with cooking spray or line with aluminum foil. Set aside. Cream margarine, sugar, and lemon extract together until light and fluffy. Add egg whites, lemon juice, and rind and mix at medium speed for 30 seconds, scraping down the bowl before and after the addition. Stir flour, baking soda, and dates together to blend and add, along with the water, to the egg mixture. Mix at medium speed to blend. Drop the dough onto the prepared cookie sheets by 1-1/2 tablespoonfuls. Using the back of a tablespoon dipped in cold water, gently press each cookie down about 1/3-inch thick. Bake for 10 to 12 minutes or until lightly browned and firm. Cool on wire racks. Makes about 2 dozen cookies.

Eggnog Cookies

A festive cookie to enjoy with your eggnog.

2-1/4	cups flour	3/4	cup butter, softened
1	teaspoon baking powder	1/2	cup eggnog
1/2	teaspoon cinnamon	1	teaspoon vanilla
1/2	teaspoon nutmeg	2	large egg yolks
1-1/4	cups sugar	1	tablespoon nutmeg

In a large bowl cream butter and sugar with an electric mixer to form a grainy paste. Add eggnog, vanilla and egg yolks and beat at medium speed until smooth. Sift together flour, baking powder, cinnamon and nutmeg. Add the flour mixture and beat at low speed just until combined. Drop by rounded teaspoonfuls onto ungreased baking sheets, 1-inch apart. Sprinkle lightly with nutmeg. Bake in 300 degree oven for 23 to 25 minutes or until bottoms turn light brown. Makes 3 dozen.

Potato Chip Cookies

A very rich butter cookie you'll just love.

1	cup butter	1-1/2	cups flour
1/2	cup sugar	1/2	cup nuts, chopped
1	egg yolk	1/2	cup potato chips, crushed
1	teaspoon vanilla		

Cream butter and sugar. Mix in slightly beaten egg yolk. Add vanilla. Stir in flour, nuts and potato chips. Drop by rounded teaspoonfuls onto greased cookie sheet. Bake approximately 15 minutes at 350 degrees. After removing from oven toss in powdered sugar. For the holidays you may wish to decorate with half a maraschino cherry pressed in the center before baking. Makes about 3 dozen.

Maple Pecan Cookies

Maple syrup and pecans compliment each other in these low-cal cookies.

4	tablespoons margarine	2	cups flour
1/2	cup brown sugar	1	tablespoon dry buttermilk
1/2	cup maple syrup		
1/4	cup egg whites	1/4	teaspoon salt
1	teaspoon maple flavoring	1/2	cup chopped pecans

Preheat oven to 350 degrees. Spray cookie sheets with cooking spray or line with aluminum foil. Set aside. Beat margarine, brown sugar, and maple syrup together until creamy. Add egg whites and flavoring and mix at medium speed for 30 seconds, scraping down the bowl before and after the addition. Stir flour, dry buttermilk, baking soda, salt, and pecans together to blend and add to the egg mixture. Mix at medium speed to blend. Drop the batter onto the prepared cookie sheets by the tablespoonful. Bake for 10 to 12 minutes or until lightly browned. Cool on wire racks. Makes about 2-1/2 dozen cookies.

Tea Time Macaroons

No need for nuts - A truly inexpensive delight.

1/2	cup peanut butter	1/4	teaspoon salt
2	egg whites	3/4	cup sugar

Stir peanut butter to soften it. Add salt to egg whites and beat until a peak of egg white stands upright when beater is pulled out. Add sugar gradually, beating meanwhile. Add peanut butter and mix gently. Drop by teaspoonfuls on lightly greased baking sheets. Bake in a preheated 325 degree oven about 19 minutes. Store in airtight container. Makes about 2 dozen.

Macaroonies

A sweet morsel to serve beside a dish of sherbet.

2	eggs	1	16-ounce package chocolate morsels or chips
1/8	teaspoon salt		
3/4	cup sugar		
1/2	cup flour	1	teaspoon grated lemon rind
1	tablespoon butter, melted		
2	cups flaked coconut	1	teaspoon vanilla

Beat eggs and salt until foamy. Gradually add sugar. Continue beating until thick and ivory colored, 5 to 7 minutes. Fold in flour and butter. Stir in coconut, chocolate morsels, lemon rind and vanilla. Drop dough by rounded teaspoons onto lightly greased and floured cookie sheet. Bake at 325 degrees for about 12 to 15 minutes until delicately browned. Cool 1 minute. Remove from cookie sheet.

Chewy Christmas Macaroons

Mixed candied fruit gives these coconut macaroons a festive look.

4	egg whites, at room temperature	3	tablespoons flour
	pinch salt	3-1/2	cups sweetened flaked coconut
1	cup sugar	1	cup finely chopped, mixed candied fruit
1	tablespoon lemon juice		

In mixer bowl beat whites with salt to from peaks. Add 1/2 cup of sugar, 1 tablespoon at a time. Add lemon juice, 1 teaspoon at a time. Beat 5 minutes at high speed; set aside. In a bowl, combine flour and remaining 1/2 cup sugar. Stir until well blended. Fold flour mixture into meringue; fold in coconut and all but 2 tablespoons candied fruit. Drop mixture by rounded tablespoons, place 1-1/2-inches apart onto greased and floured cookie sheets, garnish each cookie with some of reserved candied fruit. Bake in 300 degree oven about 30 minutes or until lightly colored and feel firm when touched gently. Transfer to wire racks to cool. Store in airtight containers. Makes about 3 dozen.

Pistachio Angels

Perfect for dieters in the crowd.

3	egg whites, room temperature		green food coloring
1/8	teaspoon salt	3/4	cup finely chopped pistachio nuts or blanched almonds
1	cup sugar		
1/2	teaspoon almond extract		

Line 2 cookie sheets with foil; set aside. In large mixer bowl with mixer at high speed, beat egg whites and salt until frothy. Gradually add sugar, 2 tablespoons at a time. Add extract and continue beating for about 5 minutes until sugar is dissolved and mixture holds stiff peaks. Beat in enough food coloring to tint a pale green. Fold in nuts. Drop by rounded teaspoonfuls about 2-inches apart onto cookie sheets. Bake 30 minutes in a 300 degree oven. Cool completely on cookie sheets set on wire racks. Peel away from foil when cooled. Makes about 40 cookies, about 35 calories each.

Brown Sugar Kisses

Longing for a kiss? Your sure to get one when you serve these to your family.

1	egg white	2	cups pecan halves, broken
3/4	cup brown sugar		
1/2	teaspoon vanilla		

Beat egg whites in a small bowl of electric mixer until stiff but not dry; add sugar gradually; continue beating about 3 minutes; fold in vanilla and pecans. Drop level tablespoons of batter onto greased cookie sheet. Bake at 300 degrees 6 to 8 minutes. Makes about 48 kisses. Store in covered container.

Mint Chocolate Meringues

A feathery light, crunchy cookie with a surprise burst of mint chocolate.

3	egg whites, room temperature	3/4	cup coarsely chopped Andes mints or other chocolate covered mint patties
1	cup superfine sugar		

Line cookie sheets with parchment paper. Beat the egg whites in a mixer bowl until foamy. Gradually beat in the sugar, 1 tablespoon at a time, and continue beating until the peaks are very stiff and glossy. Gently fold in the chopped candies. Drop the meringue, in mounds of about 2 teaspoons, about 1-inch apart on the paper-lined cookie sheets. Bake at 275 degrees for 45 to 60 minutes until the meringues are quite dry but still slightly chewy inside. Let cool completely. Makes about 3 dozen meringues.

Chocolate-Pecan Meringues

Clouds of chocolate meringue perch atop clustered pecan halves to make these puffy and delicate cookies.

72	pecan halves	2/3	cup sugar
2	egg whites (1/4 cup)	1	teaspoon vanilla
1/4	teaspoon cream of tartar	3	tablespoons unsweetened cocoa
1/8	teaspoon salt		

Place parchment paper or brown wrapping paper on baking sheets. On parchment make clusters of 3 pecans each, spacing clusters 2-inches apart. Preheat oven to 300 degrees. In mixer bowl combine egg whites, cream of tartar, and salt. Beat at high speed until foamy. Gradually add sugar, beating until egg-white mixture is stiff and glossy. Reduce speed and beat in vanilla and cocoa until cocoa is completely incorporated. Drop a rounded teaspoonful of the cocoa mixture over each cluster of pecans. Bake until meringues are firm to the touch 25 to 30 minutes. Remove to wire racks to cool. Makes 2 dozen 2-inch cookies.

Chocolate-Pistachio Macaroons

A totally different taste - try it you'll like it.

6	large egg whites, room temperature	2	cups chopped toasted pistachio nuts
2	cups sugar	1/2	cup European-style unsweetened cocoa powder
2	teaspoons vanilla		

Preheat oven to 250 degrees. Line 3 large baking sheets with cooking parchment. In large bowl of electric mixer, at low speed, beat egg whites until frothy. At high speed, gradually beat in sugar, 2 tablespoons at a time, beating until stiff peaks form when beaters are raised from bowl. Add vanilla; beat until blended. Place cocoa in fine sieve; sift over meringue. With rubber spatula, fold in cocoa and all but 1/4 cup pistachios until no white streaks remain. Drop heaping 1 tablespoon meringue, 1/2-inch apart, onto prepared baking sheets; sprinkle with reserved pistachios. Bake 20 to 25 minutes or until macaroons are dry and cracked slightly on top. Cool on paper on wire rack; gently peel away paper. Store macaroons in airtight container. Makes about 4 dozen.

Little Chocolate Drops

Tiny morsels straight from heaven.

3	egg whites	1	bar German sweet chocolate, grated
1/8	teaspoon salt		
1/2	cup sugar	3/4	cup unblanched almonds, grated

Beat egg whites with salt to form moist peaks. Add sugar gradually, beating constantly. After all sugar has been added, beat another 2 minutes. Fold in grated almonds and chocolate. Drop by teaspoonful on a well-greased cookie sheet. Bake at 275 degrees for 35 to 40 minutes. Makes about 30 cookies.

Chocolate Dipped Kisses

An unforgettable experience for the sweet tooth.

3	egg whites	4	squares unsweetened chocolate, ground
1	tablespoon vinegar		
1/4	teaspoon salt	1	cup chocolate bits, melted
1	cup sugar		
1	teaspoon vanilla	1/2	cup finely chopped nuts
1-1/2	cups blanched almonds, ground		

Beat egg whites with vinegar and salt until soft peaks form. Add sugar gradually; beat until mixture is stiff and glossy. Blend in vanilla; fold in almonds and ground chocolate. Drop rounded teaspoonfuls, 1-inch apart, onto greased cookie sheets; form into oval shapes. Bake at 250 degrees about 30 minutes; cool. Dip half of each cookie into the melted chocolate bits; sprinkle with nuts. Makes about 8 dozen.

Macaroon Top Hats

A nice addition for a tray of assorted cookies.

1-1/2	cups sifted flour	1	whole egg
1/2	teaspoon baking powder	1	egg yolk
1/4	teaspoon salt	1	teaspoon grated lemon rind
1/2	cup butter		
1/2	cup granulated sugar		

Sift flour, baking powder and salt together. Cream butter. Add sugar gradually. Beat in egg and egg yolk. Blend in lemon rind and sifted dry ingredients. Drop rounded teaspoonfuls of dough onto ungreased cookie sheets. Flatten to 1-1/2-inches in diameter with glass dipped in sugar. Place 1/2 teaspoonful of topping in center of each cookie. Top with almond half. Bake at 350 degrees for about 12 minutes. Makes 4 dozen.

Almond Topping:

1	egg white	1/2	cup blanched toasted almonds, chopped
1/8	teaspoon salt		granulated sugar
1/2	cup granulated sugar		toasted almond halves for top
1/4	teaspoon cinnamon		

Beat egg white and salt. Add sugar gradually. Beat until stiff. Fold in cinnamon and almonds.

Cake Mix Chewies

So easy a child can make them.

1	package yellow cake mix	2	eggs, beaten
1	cup brown sugar	1	cup chopped walnuts or flaked coconut
2	tablespoons soft butter		
2	tablespoons honey		

Mix ingredients thoroughly. Drop by spoonfuls on ungreased baking sheets and bake in a preheated 375 degree oven about 10 minutes. Makes about 6-1/2 dozen.

Wheatie Coconut Macaroons

We all must eat our Wheaties - what better way.

3/4	cup shortening	2	cups sifted flour
1	cup sugar	1	teaspoon baking soda
1	cup brown sugar	1/2	teaspoon baking powder
2	eggs	1/2	teaspoon salt
1	cup coconut	1	teaspoon vanilla
1	cup broken nutmeats	2	cups Wheaties

Cream shortening and sugars. Add eggs and beat thoroughly. Add coconut and nuts. Sift flour, soda, baking powder and salt and add to batter. Stir in vanilla and Wheaties. Drop by spoonful onto slightly greased baking sheets. Bake for 12 minutes in preheated 375 degree oven. Makes about 6 dozen cookies.

Stachelschweinchen

Almond macaroons at their best.

3	egg whites	1-1/4	cups (about) blanched
1	pinch salt		slivered almonds, divided
1/2	cup sugar		

In mixing bowl (not plastic), beat egg whites and salt until whites are stiff. Gradually beat sugar into beaten whites. Add 3/4 cup of the almonds, reserving remaining 1/2 cup for decoration. Drop small mounds by tablespoonfuls onto cookie sheet lined with wax paper (or use non-stick or very lightly greased baking sheet). Decorate each mound with about 6 slivered almonds to create spiky effect. Bake at 325 degrees about 25 minutes or until golden brown. Cool to slightly warm before removing from cookie sheet. Makes about 24 macaroons.

Note:
Stored in an airtight container, macaroons will keep for 2 to 3 weeks.

Mammy's Plantation Drops

Try this Easy Way of putting cookies together.

3	egg whites	1/2	cup minced dates
1	cup sugar	1/2	cup minced almonds
1	teaspoon flour	1/2	cup coconut
1	teaspoon cornstarch		

Beat egg whites until stiff using high speed on electric mixer. Gradually add sugar. Beat well. Place in top of double boiler. Cook, stirring constantly, about 5 minutes. Remove from heat. Add flour, cornstarch, dates, almonds and coconut. Drop from teaspoon onto greased cookie sheets. Bake at 300 degrees for about 20 minutes. Makes about 4 dozen.

Meringue Fudge Drops

A must for every cookie lover.

2	egg whites	1/2	cup sugar
1/8	teaspoon cream of tartar	1/4	teaspoon almond extract
1/8	teaspoon salt		

Beat egg whites until foamy. Add cream of tartar and salt. Beat until soft peaks are formed. Add sugar a tablespoonful at a time. Beat until smooth and satiny. Add extract. Mix well. Drop from teaspoon onto ungreased cookie sheets covered with brown paper. Shape into mounds the size of a small walnut. Use a spoon to make a depression in center of each cookie. Bake at 300 degrees about 30 minutes. Remove from paper. Makes about 5 dozen.

Fudge Filling:

1/4	cup butter	2	tablespoons powdered sugar
1/2	cup chocolate bits	2	tablespoons chopped pistachio nuts
2	egg yolks		

Melt butter and chocolate in saucepan. Beat egg yolks slightly. Stir in sugar. Blend into chocolate. Cook at a very low heat 1 minute. <u>Stir constantly</u>. Remove from heat. Stir until smooth and cool. Fill meringues with a teaspoonful of filling. Sprinkle with pistachio nuts.

Coconut Almond Haystacks

The easiest cookie you will ever make.

3/4 cup sweetened condensed milk	1 cup dry shredded or dry flaked coconut
1 cup coarsely chopped toasted blanched almonds	1-1/2 teaspoons vanilla

Combine all ingredients in large bowl. Drop about 1 tablespoon of mixture onto well-greased cookie sheets. Bake at 300 degrees about 10 minutes. Cookies brown quickly. Makes about 4-1/2 dozen 2-inch cookies.

Coconut Gingers

These coconut balls will disappear like snowballs in the sun.

3/4 cup butter	2-1/2 cups cake flour
1/2 cup sugar	1/2 teaspoon salt
1/4 cup corn syrup	1/8 teaspoon baking soda
1/4 cup molasses	2 teaspoons baking powder
1 egg, beaten	3/4 teaspoon ginger
1 tablespoon lemon juice	3/4 cup shredded coconut

Cream butter and sugar. Add corn syrup, molasses, beaten egg and lemon juice. Sift dry ingredients together and add. Mix well and add the coconut. Drop by teaspoonfuls on a greased baking sheet and bake in a 350 degree oven for 10 to 15 minutes. Frost and roll in shredded coconut. Makes about 4 dozen.

When shipping cookies, wrap two together with plastic wrap. Layer with popcorn. Fill box so cookies can't bounce around.

Coconut Maples

Maple syrup cookies may be frosted and rolled in coconut.

1/2	cup butter	1/2	teaspoon salt
1/2	cup brown sugar	1/8	teaspoon baking soda
1/2	cup maple syrup	2	teaspoons baking powder
1	egg, beaten	1/2	teaspoon ginger
2	cups cake flour	1	cup shredded coconut

Sift the flour, salt, soda, baking powder and ginger together and cut in butter as for pastry. Combine the sifted brown sugar, maple syrup and beaten egg. Combine mixtures. Add coconut. Drop from a teaspoon on a buttered baking sheet and bake in a 350 degree oven for 10 to 15 minutes.

Coconut Mounds

The slight taste of cinnamon makes these a delight to eat.

1/3	cup butter	2	cups cake flour
3/4	cup brown sugar	1/4	teaspoon salt
1	egg	2	teaspoons baking powder
1/3	cup milk	1/2	teaspoon cinnamon
1	teaspoon vanilla	1	cup shredded coconut

Mix butter and sugar together. Beat egg, add milk and vanilla. Sift together dry ingredients and add to butter and sugar mixture alternately with milk and vanilla. Add the shredded coconut. Drop from a teaspoon on a greased baking sheet and bake in a 350 degree oven for 10 to 15 minutes. Spread with any frosting and roll in shredded coconut. Makes 3-1/2 dozen, 2-inch in diameter cookies.

Coconut Sponge Drops

Coconut and citrus flavoring make this an outstanding cookie.

2-1/2	cups sifted flour	2	eggs
1/4	teaspoon salt	1-3/4	cups chopped shredded coconut
1/2	teaspoon soda		
3/4	cup butter	1	teaspoon grated orange rind
1/2	cup sugar		
1/2	cup dark corn syrup	1/2	cup orange juice

Sift flour, salt and soda together. Cream butter. Add sugar gradually. Add syrup. Cream well. Add eggs one at a time. Beat well after each addition. Add coconut and orange rind. Blend. Add dry ingredients and orange juice alternately to creamed mixture. Drop a level tablespoonful onto greased cookie sheets. Bake at 350 degrees 10 to 12 minutes. Cool. Makes 5 dozen. Frost with Orange Frosting.

Orange Frosting:

2-1/4	cups powdered sugar	3	tablespoons orange juice
3	tablespoons melted butter	1	tablespoon lemon juice

Combine all ingredients. Blend until smooth.

Lemon Drops

In a hurry? Then these easy drops are for you.

1	package lemon cake mix	1	egg
2	cups Cool Whip	1/2	cup powdered sugar

Preheat oven to 350 degrees. Grease cookie sheets. Combine cake mix, topping, and egg in large bowl. Mix well. Drop by teaspoon into powdered sugar, roll to coat. Place 1-1/2-inches apart on cookie sheet. Bake 15 minutes. Makes about 48.

Sweet Treats

A treat anytime of the year.

1/2	cup brown sugar, packed	1	cup miniature chocolate bits
1/4	cup melted butter		
1/2	cup cream	1	cup finely chopped pecans
1-1/2	cups graham cracker crumbs		

Mix sugar, butter and cream together until sugar is dissolved. Blend in cracker crumbs, chocolate bits and pecans. Drop rounded teaspoonfuls of dough into small paper candy liners. Place on ungreased cookie sheets. Bake at 375 degrees about 10 minutes. Cool and frost with Browned Butter Frosting. Makes about 5 dozen.

Browned Butter Frosting:

2	tablespoons butter	1	tablespoon hot water cream
1-1/2	cups powdered sugar		

Brown butter in saucepan; remove from heat; stir in sugar and water. Add enough cream to make frosting of spreading consistency.

Almond Cookies

The traditional cookie served in Chinese restaurants.

1	cup lard	2	teaspoons baking powder
1-1/3	cups sugar	1	teaspoon baking soda
1/4	cup egg whites	1/2	teaspoon salt
2	teaspoons almond extract	1/2	cup water
4	cups flour	36	almonds

Preheat oven to 350 degrees. Grease cookie sheets. Cream lard and sugar together until light and fluffy. Add egg whites and almond extract and mix at medium speed until creamy. Stir flour, baking powder, baking soda, and salt together to blend and add to the egg mixture, along with the water. Mix at medium speed to blend. Drop dough onto the prepared cookie sheets by 1-1/2 tablespoonfuls. Gently press down on each cookie with the back of a tablespoon dipped in cold water. Then press an almond in the center of each cookie. Bake for 12 to 15 minutes or until very lightly browned and firm. Cool on wire racks. Makes about 3 dozen cookies.

Brown Almond Drop Cookies

Pecans or walnuts may be substituted in these good tasting cookies.

1/2	cup margarine	1-1/2	cups flour
3	ounces unsweetened chocolate	1/4	teaspoon salt
1-1/2	cups sugar	1	cup chopped toasted almonds
3	eggs		

Melt butter and chocolate. Remove from heat. (Do not boil.) Stir in sugar and mix well. Add eggs one at a time, beat well after each addition. Blend in the flour and nuts. Drop by rounded teaspoonful onto greased cookie pans. Bake in a 350 degree oven for 12 to 15 minutes. Makes about 3-1/2 dozen cookies.

Golden Nut Drops

Lemon Icing brings out the old-fashioned taste of carrot cookies.

2	cups sifted flour	1/4	cup brown sugar, sifted and packed
1-1/2	teaspoons baking powder		
1/2	teaspoon salt	1	egg
1	cup chopped nuts	2	jars (4-3/4 ounces each) strained carrot baby food
3/4	cup butter		
1/2	cup sugar	1	teaspoon vanilla

Mix and sift flour, baking powder and salt; add nuts and mix. Cream butter, add sugars gradually and cream until fluffy. Add well beaten egg and mix. Add carrot and vanilla and mix. Drop by spoonfuls on ungreased baking sheets. Bake in a preheated 400 degree oven about 10 minutes. Cool slightly. Frost with Lemon Icing. Store in airtight container.

Lemon Icing:

1-1/2	cups sifted confectioners' sugar	3	teaspoons grated lemon rind
		3	tablespoons lemon juice

Combine ingredients. Makes about 5 dozen.

Pumpkin Whoopie Pies

A fun serving huge, soft sandwich cookie that is chewy-soft with a creamy center.

4-2/3	cups flour	1	cup oil
1	tablespoon cream of tartar	2-1/3	cups dark brown sugar
2	teaspoons baking soda	1-1/4	cups pumpkin
1	teaspoon baking powder	1	large egg
1/4	teaspoon salt	2	large egg yolks
1	tablespoon cinnamon	1	tablespoon vanilla
1-1/2	teaspoons ginger	1/4	teaspoon lemon zest
1-1/2	teaspoons allspice	1-1/3	cups quick cooking oats
1	cup butter		

Beat butter and oil until light and fluffy. Add brown sugar, beating well. Add egg, yolks, pumpkin, vanilla and zest. Beat in dry ingredients. Stir in oats. Drop about 2 tablespoons of dough on well-greased cookie sheet, space 4-inches apart. Swirl in circular motion to shape evenly in a 2-1/2-inch round. Bake for 10 to 12 minutes in a 350 degree oven. Let cookies stand on sheets about 3 minutes before removing.

Filling:

12	ounces cream cheese	1/4	teaspoon lemon zest
2	large egg whites	2-3/4	cups powdered sugar
1/4	teaspoon vanilla		

Beat together cream cheese, egg whites, zest, vanilla and half of powdered sugar; add remaining powdered sugar gradually. Beat until smooth. Refrigerate 2 hours. Spoon 2 tablespoons filling in center of flat side of half the cookies; place remaining cookies flat side down over filling, gently press down so filling spreads just to edges. Let cookies stand at least 30 minutes so filling sets. Store refrigerated in an airtight container up to 1 week. Freeze for longer storage. Makes 20 large cookies.

Rinse measuring cup or spoons with warm water before measuring honey or molasses. It will slide right out.

Spell-Binders

A perfect name for a perfect cookie, loaded with goodies.

1-1/2	cups flour	1	egg
1-1/2	teaspoons baking powder	1	cup quick cooking oats
		1	cup flaked coconut
1	teaspoon baking soda	1	cup Spanish salted peanuts
1	cup brown sugar, firmly packed		
		1/2	cup corn flakes, finely crushed
1	cup soft butter		

Combine flour, baking powder and soda. Gradually add sugar to butter in mixing bowl, creaming until light and fluffy. Add egg; beat well. Gradually add dry ingredients, blending well after each addition. Stir in oats, coconut, peanuts and corn flakes. Drop by rounded teaspoonfuls onto ungreased cookie sheets. Flatten slightly with bottom of glass dipped in additional crushed corn flakes. Bake at 350 degrees for 12 to 15 minutes. Drizzle with Icing. Makes about 48 cookies.

Icing:

2	tablespoons butter	1	tablespoon hot water
1	cup confectioners' sugar	1	teaspoon vanilla

Melt butter; add confectioners' sugar, hot water and vanilla, beat until consistency of a glaze. If necessary, thin with a few drops of hot water.

Cowboy Cookies

Drop or sliced, these are good both ways.

1	cup soft margarine	1/2	teaspoon salt
3/4	cup brown sugar, packed	1-1/2	cups quick cooking oatmeal
3/4	cup sugar		
2	eggs	1/2	cup coarsely chopped nuts
1	teaspoon vanilla		
2	cups flour	6	ounces chocolate chips
1/2	teaspoon baking soda	1	cup raisins

Preheat oven to 350 degrees. Cream margarine, add sugars and beat well. Add the eggs and vanilla; stir to blend. Add dry ingredients at one time, mix to blend thoroughly. Last stir in oatmeal, nuts, chocolate chips and raisins. Mix well. Drop by spoonfuls on cookie sheet and bake for 13 to 15 minutes. This dough freezes well; just form into a roll and freeze. Slice later and bake for 12 to 13 minutes. Makes about 4 dozen large cookies.

Triplets

There's a trio of flavors in each novel cookie.

2-1/2	cups sifted flour	1	teaspoon cinnamon
2	teaspoons baking powder	1/2	cup finely cut dates
1	teaspoon salt	1	teaspoon almond extract
1	cup shortening	1	square (1-ounce) unsweetened chocolate, melted
1/2	cup sugar		
1/2	cup brown sugar, firmly packed		
		1	tablespoon water
2	eggs	1/2	cup cut coconut
1	teaspoon vanilla		maraschino cherries
1/2	cup milk		

Cream shortening and sugar well; add eggs and vanilla, beat well. Blend in half of dry ingredients, then milk, then rest of dry ingredients. Divide dough in 3 parts; add cinnamon and dates to 1 part, and chocolate and water to 1 part. Drop a small teaspoonful of each dough onto greased baking sheet so balls just touch, forming a triangle. Top almond balls with a sliver of maraschino cherry. Bake in a 400 degree oven for 10 to 13 minutes. Remove from sheets immediately. Makes about 4 dozen cookies.

Odds And Ends Cookies

Anything goes into these, experiment on your own.

1/2	cup shortening	3/4	cup milk
1/2	cup peanut butter	1/2	cup chopped nuts
2	cups brown sugar	1/4	cup mincemeat or any kind of jam
2	eggs, beaten		
1	teaspoon vanilla	1/2	cup raisins
2	cups sifted flour	1	cup quick cooking oats
3	teaspoons baking powder	1-1/4	cups any 1 or 2 kinds dry cereal
1/2	teaspoon salt		

Cream together the shortening and peanut butter. Add brown sugar and cream thoroughly. Add eggs and beat until light and fluffy. Add vanilla. Sift together the flour, baking powder and salt and add alternately to the creamed mixture with the milk. Stir in remaining ingredients. Drop by spoonful on greased cookie sheets and bake at 350 degrees for 15 minutes. Makes 6 or 7 dozen cookies.

Mom's Favorite Christmas Cookies

A pretty pink brings out the festive color to these cookies.

3	cups flour	1	(6-ounce) jar maraschino cherries, chopped, juice reserved
1	teaspoon baking soda		
1/2	teaspoon salt		
1	cup shortening	1	(8-ounce) package dates, coarsely chopped
1-1/2	cups sugar		
3	eggs	1/2	cup walnuts, coarsely chopped

In a large bowl sift together flour, salt, and baking soda. Set aside. In a small bowl, mix cherries, dates and walnuts together; pour the juice over the mixture. Set aside. Cream together shortening and sugar, add the eggs and blend well. Add the cherry mixture and mix until blended. Add the creamed cherry batter to the flour mixture and blend well. Drop by rounded teaspoonfuls on lightly greased cookie sheet. Bake for 25 to 30 minutes in a 300 degree oven. Remove cookies to rack to cool. Freezes well. Makes 72 cookies.

Pistachio Orange Drops

Cardamom and pistachios are added to these tender cakey drops.

2	cups sifted flour	1/3	cup firmly packed brown sugar
1	teaspoon baking powder		
1/2	teaspoon baking soda	2	tablespoons orange juice
1/2	teaspoon salt	2	tablespoons grated orange rind
1	teaspoon cardamom		
1/2	cup butter or margarine	1	teaspoon almond extract
1/3	cup sugar	1/2	cup pistachio nuts
1	egg, unbeaten		

Cream together butter and sugars. Add egg; beat well. Add half of sifted dry ingredients mixing thoroughly. Combine orange juice with enough water to make 1/3 cup. Add orange rind and almond extract. Add to mixture alternately with remaining flour. Blend thoroughly. Add nuts; mix well, drop by teaspoonfuls onto greased cookie sheets. Bake at 375 degrees for 15 to 17 minutes. Cool. Store tightly covered.

Fruited-Orange Cookies

No one needs to know these are such healthy cookies.

2	cups sifted flour	1/4	cup chopped nuts
1/2	teaspoon baking soda	1	teaspoon grated orange rind
1	teaspoon salt		
1/2	cup butter	1	egg
3/4	cup sugar	1/4	cup orange juice
1	cup dates, raisins or figs, cut into pieces	1/2	cup sour cream

Mix and sift flour, soda and salt. Cream butter well, add sugar gradually and continue creaming until light and fluffy; add fruit, nutmeats and orange rind and mix well. Add sifted dry ingredients alternately with liquids, mixing just enough after each addition to combine ingredients. Drop spoonfuls on baking sheets. Bake at 375 degrees for about 12 minutes. Makes about 3 dozen.

Chewy Orange Drops

Lets taste the good old-fashioned orange slices again.

1	cup snipped orange slices (shaped jelly candies)	1	egg
1/2	cup coconut	1	teaspoon vanilla
1/2	cup margarine or butter	1-1/4	cups flour
1/2	cup sugar	2	teaspoons finely shredded orange peel
1/8	teaspoon baking soda		

Use kitchen shears to snip the jelly candies into tiny pieces; set aside. Toast coconut; set aside. In a large mixing bowl beat margarine or butter with an electric mixer on medium to high speed for 30 seconds. Add sugar and baking soda; beat until combined. Beat in egg and vanilla. Beat in as much of the flour as you can with the mixer. Stir in any remaining flour with a wooden spoon. Stir in jelly candies, coconut, and orange peel. Drop by rounded teaspoons, 2-inches apart onto an ungreased cookie sheet. Bake in a 375 degree oven for 8 to 10 minutes or until edges are golden. Remove from cookie sheet; cool on a wire rack. Makes 24.

Bake ginger cookies and let your children cut them out in different shapes. Let them put the name of each child on them for their class at school and make a cookie tree. Any rolled-out cookie can be made into a Christmas Tree ornament. Cut a string for each cookie. Before baking the cookies, press each down on both ends of string forming a loop.

Glazed Apple-Spice Drops

There's spicy apple cider in these moist, cake-like Glazed Apple-Spice Drops. Cider is also in the glaze.

1-3/4	cups flour	1-1/2	cups firmly packed brown sugar
1	teaspoon baking soda		
1	teaspoon cinnamon	1	egg
1/2	teaspoon nutmeg	1/4	cup cider or apple juice
1/4	teaspoon salt	1	large apple, peeled, cored, and finely chopped
1/4	teaspoon cloves		
1/2	cup butter or margarine, softened	1	cup chopped walnuts

Preheat oven to 400 degrees. In mixer bowl combine butter and brown sugar, and beat until well blended. Beat in egg until fluffy. Add dry sifted ingredients alternately with cider, mixing until smooth after each addition. Stir in apple and walnuts. Drop by tablespoons, placed about 2-inches apart, onto lightly greased baking sheets. Bake until cookies are golden brown, about 10 minutes. Remove to wire racks; while warm, spread lightly with Cider Glaze. Makes about 4 dozen 3-inch cookies.

Cider Glaze:

1	cup confectioners' sugar	1/2	teaspoon vanilla
1	tablespoon butter or margarine, softened	1-1/2	to 2 tablespoons cider or apple juice

In a small bowl combine confectioners' sugar and butter. Add vanilla, then cider, and blend until mixture has a good spreading consistency.

Golden Yam Drop Cookies

These tender drop cookies can be made with shredded yam, sweet potato or carrots.

1	cup powdered sugar	1-1/2	cups shredded yam
3/4	cup margarine, softened	1	cup chopped nuts or coconut
1	cup flour		
1/2	teaspoon nutmeg	1/2	cup powdered sugar
1	teaspoon vanilla	1	teaspoon nutmeg

Preheat oven to 350 degrees. In large bowl, cream powdered sugar and margarine. Stir in next 5 ingredients; mix well. Drop by teaspoonfuls, 2-inches apart, onto ungreased cookie sheets. Bake 12 to 18 minutes until lightly browned. Remove from cookie sheets. Combine 1/2 cup powdered sugar and 1 teaspoon nutmeg. Sift generously over cookies. Makes 2 to 3 dozen cookies.

Oriental Tea Treats

Crisp and chewy brown sugar cookies with an Oriental accent from almonds, candied ginger and tea.

1	cup blanched almonds	1/2	cup butter
1/4	cup crystallized ginger	1-3/4	cups brown sugar, firmly packed
2-3/4	cups sifted flour		
1/2	teaspoon baking soda	1/4	cup tea
1/4	teaspoon salt	1	teaspoon vanilla
1/2	cup shortening		

Chop nuts and crystallized ginger very fine. Cream shortening, butter and brown sugar. Cream well; add sifted dry ingredients alternately with tea. Blend well. Stir in nuts, ginger and vanilla. Shape into balls, using a teaspoon. Place 1-1/2-inches apart on ungreased cookie sheets. Bake at 350 degrees about 12 to 15 minutes. Makes 6 to 7 dozen.

Pumpkin Spice Cookies

Welcome fall with these scrumptious cookies.

2-1/2	cups flour	1/2	cup white sugar
1/2	teaspoon baking soda	3/4	cup butter, softened
1/4	teaspoon salt	1	large egg
2	teaspoons pumpkin pie spice	1	cup pumpkin
		1	teaspoon vanilla
1	cup dark brown sugar, packed	1	cup raisins
		1/2	cup walnuts, chopped

In large bowl of an electric mixer beat together the sugars and butter. Add egg, pumpkin and vanilla. Beat at medium speed until light and fluffy. Sift together flour, soda, salt and pumpkin pie spice. Add to mixture with raisins and walnuts. Blend at low speed just until combined. Drop by rounded tablespoons onto ungreased cookie sheets, 1-1/2-inches apart. Bake in a 350 degree oven 22 to 24 minutes until slightly browned along edges. Makes 3 dozen cookies.

Frosted Holiday Cookies

There isn't anything anyone could add to these, except a satisfied look when eating them.

1/2	cup butter	1	teaspoon baking soda
1-1/4	cups brown sugar, packed	1	cup applesauce
1	egg	1/2	cup chopped walnuts
1-3/4	cups sifted flour	1/2	cup chopped filberts
1	teaspoon salt	3/4	cup dates, cut-up
1/2	teaspoon cinnamon	1/2	cup cut dried prunes
1	teaspoon cloves	1/2	cup diced, mixed, candied fruit
1/8	teaspoon nutmeg		

Cream butter; add sugar gradually; beat in eggs. Blend in sifted dry ingredients and applesauce. Mix in remaining ingredients. Drop rounded tablespoonfuls onto greased cookie sheets. Bake at 375 degrees 12 to 15 minutes. Cool; frost with browned butter frosting. Decorate with pieces of candied cherries and citron if desired. Makes about 8-1/2 dozen.

Christmas Lizzies

The ingredients fit in with the festive season.

1/2	pound candied green pineapple, chopped	1/2	cup sugar
1	pound candied red cherries, chopped	2	eggs
		1/2	teaspoon baking soda
		1	teaspoon cinnamon
2	(8-ounce) packages chopped dates	1/4	teaspoon cloves
		1/4	teaspoon nutmeg
2	cups chopped pecans	1-1/2	tablespoons milk
1-1/2	cups flour, divided	3	tablespoons bourbon
1/4	cup butter or margarine, softened		

Combine fruit and pecans; dredge in 1 cup flour, and set aside. Cream butter; add sugar, beating at medium speed of an electric mixer. Add eggs, and beat well. Combine remaining 1/2 cup flour, soda, and spices; add to creamed mixture, mixing well. Stir in milk and bourbon. Add fruit mixture, and mix well. Batter will be stiff. Chill dough at least 1 hour. Drop chilled dough by heaping teaspoonfuls onto lightly greased cookie sheets. Bake at 300 degrees for 20 to 25 minutes or until lightly browned. Cool on wire racks. Makes about 8 dozen.

Nuggets

These are special with raisins, nuts and chocolate. Who needs anything more.

2	cups margarine	1-1/2	teaspoons salt
2	cups brown sugar, packed	1/2	cup sour cream
1	teaspoon cinnamon	1/2	cup sweet chocolate, grated
1/4	teaspoon nutmeg		
2	eggs	1-1/2	cups chopped walnuts or pecans
3	cups flour		
1-1/2	teaspoons baking powder	1	cup seedless raisins

In a large bowl, combine shortening, sugar and spices. Cream butter mixture until light and lemony. Add eggs and beat again. Add dry ingredients to the mixture, alternating with sour cream. Add chocolate and blend well. Add nuts and raisins, mix well. Drop by teaspoonfuls onto greased cookie sheet. Bake in a 350 degree oven for 15 minutes. Remove from pan and cool. Makes 4-1/2 dozen.

Applesauce Cookies

Good moist spicy flavor.

1	cup shortening	1	teaspoon salt
2	cups brown sugar, packed	1	teaspoon cinnamon
2	eggs	1	teaspoon nutmeg
1/2	cup cold coffee	1	teaspoon cloves
2	cups well-drained thick applesauce	1	cup raisins
		1/2	cup coarsely chopped nuts
3-1/2	cups flour, sifted		
1	teaspoon soda		

Mix shortening, sugar and eggs thoroughly. Stir in coffee and applesauce. Mix dry ingredients and stir into applesauce mixture. Chill at least 2 hours. Heat oven at 400 degrees. Drop rounded tablespoonfuls of dough about 2-inches apart on lightly greased baking sheet. Bake 9 to 12 minutes, or until almost no imprint remains when touched lightly. If desired, frost when cool with lemon butter icing. Makes about 7 to 8 dozen cookies.

Powder-Puff Tidbits

These can be served 2 ways, each prettier than the other.

1	cup shortening	1/2	teaspoon salt
1	cup brown sugar	2	cups quick cooking oatmeal
1	cup sugar		
2	eggs	6	ounces chocolate chips
1	teaspoon vanilla	1	cup coconut, finely chopped
2	cups flour		
1	teaspoon baking soda	14	to 16 maraschino cherries, finely chopped
1/2	teaspoon baking powder		

Cream together shortening and sugars. Beat eggs and vanilla, mix well. Sift together flour, baking soda, baking powder and salt. Add oatmeal together with flour to egg mixture and blend well. Melt chocolate, add with coconut and cherries to dough. Drop from teaspoon onto greased cookie sheets. Bake at 375 degrees for 10 to 12 minutes. When cool leave single or put 2 cookies together with jam. Sift confectioners' sugar over tops. Makes 15 or 16 dozen tidbits.

Scottish Reels

These feature a unique flavor of chocolate, brown sugar, cream cheese and pecans.

2	cups sifted flour	2	eggs
1	teaspoon baking powder	2	squares (2 ounces) unsweetened chocolate, melted
1/2	teaspoon baking soda		
1/2	teaspoon salt		
1-1/2	ounces cream cheese	2	teaspoons vanilla
1/2	cup shortening	1	cup chopped pecans
1/2	cup butter or margarine	1	cup oatmeal
1	cup brown sugar, firmly packed	1/4	cup confectioners' sugar
1/2	cup sifted confectioners' sugar		

Sift dry ingredients. Cream shortening, cream cheese, brown sugar and confectioners' sugar; add eggs and vanilla, beat well. Blend in dry ingredients. Stir in pecans. Chill 1 hour. Combine oatmeal and confectioners' sugar. Drop dough by tablespoonfuls into oatmeal mixture. Coat thoroughly. Place on greased cookie sheet, flatten to 1/2-inch with bottom of glass. Bake in a 350 degree oven for 12 to 15 minutes. Cool. Frost tops with Chocolate Frosting. Makes about 4 dozen cookies.

Chocolate Frosting:

1	(6-ounce) package chocolate chips	1-1/2	cups sifted confectioners' sugar
1-1/2	ounces cream cheese	6	to 7 tablespoons cream

Melt chocolate in top of double boiler over hot water. Blend in cream cheese and confectioners' sugar. Add cream, beating until smooth and of spreading consistency.

Almond - Oatmeal Cookies

Toasted almonds give an extra good flavor to these oatmeal cookies.

1-1/2	cups quick-cooking oatmeal	1/8	teaspoon salt
1/2	cup flour	1/2	cup sugar
1/2	cup ground toasted almonds	1/2	cup brown sugar
		1/2	cup margarine
		1/2	teaspoon vanilla
1/2	teaspoon baking soda	1/2	cup sliced almonds
1/4	teaspoon baking powder		

Mix oats, flour, ground almonds, baking powder, baking soda and salt. In a large bowl beat sugars, margarine, egg and vanilla. Stir in flour mixture, then sliced almonds. Drop rounded teaspoonfuls about 2-inches apart on ungreased cookie sheets. Bake 10 to 11 minutes until light brown in a 375 degree oven. Cool on cookie sheets 2 minutes before removing from cookie sheets. Makes 36 cookies.

Caramel Oatmeal Cookies

A chewy delicious treat.

1	cup butter	1-1/2	cups sifted flour
1/2	cup brown sugar, packed	1	teaspoon soda
1/2	cup granulated sugar	1/2	teaspoon salt
2	eggs	1	cup caramel bits
1	tablespoon water	2	cups uncooked oatmeal
1	teaspoon vanilla	1/2	cup chopped walnuts

Cream butter. Add sugars gradually. Add eggs, water and vanilla. Mix well. Add sifted dry ingredients. Blend in caramel bits, oatmeal and walnuts. Drop from teaspoon onto greased cookie sheets. Bake at 375 degrees 10 to 12 minutes. Makes about 8 dozen 2-inch cookies.

Oatmeal Lace Cookies

Cookies that look like snowflakes and so easy to make a child can make them.

1/2	cup flour	2	tablespoons heavy cream
1/2	cup sugar	2	tablespoons light corn syrup
1/4	teaspoon baking powder		
1/8	teaspoon salt	1/3	cup melted butter
1/2	cup quick-cooking oats	1	tablespoon vanilla

Preheat oven to 375 degrees. Line a cookie sheet with foil and brush or spray lightly with oil. In a medium sized bowl, combine flour, sugar, baking powder, and salt with a whisk. Stir in remaining ingredients with a fork. Using a 1/4-inch teaspoon measuring spoon, drop batter onto cookie sheet 3 to 4-inches apart. Bake 6 to 8 minutes, until lightly browned. Let stand a few seconds before removing from sheet. Makes about 5 dozen.

Holiday Fruit Drops

Elegant! Butterscotch flavored - studded with nuts and fruits.

1	cup soft shortening	1	teaspoon salt
2	cups brown sugar, packed	1-1/2	cups broken pecan meats
2	eggs	2	cups candied cherries, halved
1/2	cup sour milk or buttermilk		
3-1/2	cups sifted flour	2	cups cut-up dates
1	teaspoon soda		

Mix the sugar shortening and eggs thoroughly. Stir in the sour milk. Sift together dry ingredients and stir into batter. Add nuts, cherries and dates. Mix well. Chill at least 1 hour. Drop teaspoonful about 2-inches apart on lightly greased baking sheets. Put half pecan in center. Bake at 400 degrees for about 8 to 10 minutes. Makes about 6 dozen 2-1/2-inch cookies.

Cape Cod Oatmeal Cookies

A fine, chewy oatmeal cookie, wholesome and nourishing.

1-1/2	cups flour	1/2	cup melted margarine
1/2	teaspoon baking soda	1	tablespoon molasses
1	teaspoon cinnamon	1/4	cup milk
1/2	teaspoon salt	1-/3/4	cups uncooked oatmeal
1	egg, lightly beaten	1/2	cup raisins
1	cup sugar	1/2	cup chopped nuts

Preheat the oven to 350 degrees. Mix the flour, baking soda, cinnamon, and salt together in a large bowl. Stir in the remaining ingredients. Arrange by teaspoonfuls on unbuttered cookie sheets and bake until the edges are brown, about 10 to 12 minutes. Makes about 70 cookies.

Applesauce Oatmeal Cookies

Applesauce gives a moist tender texture to every one's favorite, the oatmeal cookie.

1/2	cup shortening	1-3/4	cups sifted flour
1	cup sugar	1/2	teaspoon baking powder
1	egg	1	teaspoon baking soda
1/2	cup finely chopped, pitted dates or seedless raisins	1/2	teaspoon salt
		1	teaspoon cinnamon
		1/2	teaspoon cloves
1/2	cup chopped walnuts or pecans	1/2	teaspoon nutmeg
		1	cup applesauce
1	cup quick-cooking oats		

Set oven to 375 degrees. Grease cookie sheets lightly. Put shortening into large mixing bowl and cream until smooth. Gradually add sugar; continue beating until fluffy. Add egg and beat well. Then add dates, nuts and oats. Stir until evenly distributed in mixture. Add sifted dry ingredients alternately with the applesauce. Stir after each addition, just until blended. Drop the batter by rounded teaspoonfuls, about 2-inches apart on prepared cookie sheets. Bake 12 to 15 minutes or until the edges of cookies are browned. Remove from pans with a wide spatula and cool the cookies on wire racks. Makes about 3 dozen.

Banana Oatmeal Cookies

Use very ripe bananas to get that extra good flavor.

1-1/2	cups sifted flour	1	egg
1	cup sugar	1	cup mashed ripe bananas
1/2	teaspoon baking soda	1/2	cup chopped pecans or walnuts
1	teaspoon salt		
3/4	teaspoon cinnamon	1-3/4	cups quick-cooking oats
1/4	teaspoon nutmeg		pecan or walnut halves
3/4	cup shortening		

Sift dry ingredients in large mixing bowl. Add shortening and cut in with a pastry blender or 2 knives until mixture is crumbly. Put egg in small bowl and beat with a rotary beater until light and foamy. Add mashed banana and stir well. Add banana mixture, chopped nuts and oats to shortening mixture and stir just until thoroughly blended. Drop dough by teaspoonfuls, about 2-inches apart on greased cookie sheets. Top each with half pecan or walnut. Bake at 400 degrees for 12 to 15 minutes or until edges of cookies are golden brown. Cool on wire racks. Makes about 3-1/2 dozen.

Peanut Butter Carrot Cookies

Adding carrots, whole wheat flour and oats to peanut butter cookies makes them extra healthful.

3/4	cup brown sugar	3/4	cup whole wheat flour
1/2	cup salad oil	1/2	cup instant nonfat dry milk
1/2	cup peanut butter	1/2	cup raisins
1	egg	3/4	teaspoon salt
1	cup shredded carrot	1/2	teaspoon cinnamon
1	cup oats, uncooked	1/2	teaspoon baking powder

Mix together first 4 ingredients. Add remaining ingredients and mix. Drop by 1-1/2 teaspoonfuls on ungreased cookie sheets. Bake in a preheated 350 degree oven about 15 minutes. Makes about 6-1/2 dozen cookies.

Orange-Glazed Banana Cookies

A great taste of bananas and walnuts.

2-1/2	cups sifted flour	1	cup light brown sugar, firmly packed
2	teaspoons baking powder		
1/4	teaspoon baking soda	2	eggs
1/2	teaspoon salt	1	cup mashed ripe bananas
1/2	teaspoon cinnamon	1	teaspoon vanilla
1/4	teaspoon cloves	1/2	cup coarsely chopped walnuts
1/2	cup butter or margarine, softened		

Preheat oven to 400 degrees. Lightly grease cookie sheets. Sift flour with baking powder, baking soda, salt, cinnamon, and cloves; set aside. In large bowl of electric mixer, at medium speed, beat butter, sugar, and eggs until light and fluffy. Beat in bananas and vanilla until smooth. Gradually beat in flour mixture until well combined. Stir in nuts. Drop by rounded teaspoonfuls, 2-inches apart, onto prepared cookie sheets. Bake 12 to 15 minutes, or until golden brown. Remove to wire rack; cool partially. Meanwhile, make glaze.

Orange Glaze:

3	cups sifted confectioners' sugar	3	to 4 tablespoons milk
1	tablespoon grated orange peel		

In a medium bowl, combine sugar, orange peel, and milk; stir until smooth. Spread top of slightly warm cookies with glaze. Makes about 4-1/2 dozen.

Black Walnut Cookies

Tastes like old-fashioned sour cream cookies. Serve with applesauce.

1/2	cup shortening	1	teaspoon cinnamon
3/4	cup sugar	1/2	teaspoon salt
1	egg	1/4	teaspoon baking soda
1/2	teaspoon vanilla	1/2	cup sour cream
2	cups sifted flour	1/2	cup chopped black walnuts
1	teaspoon baking powder		

Cream shortening and sugar until light and fluffy. Beat in egg and vanilla. Sift together dry ingredients. Add to creamed mixture, alternately with sour cream. Stir in walnuts. Drop by teaspoonfuls on greased baking sheet. Press flat with bottom of drinking glass, dipping glass into sugar before pressing each cookie. Bake in a 375 degree oven for 9 to 12 minutes. Cool on racks. Makes 4-1/2 dozen.

Cocoa Oatmeal Drop Cookies

A little different taste by using syrup and cocoa in these great oatmeal cookies.

3/4	cup butter or margarine	1/2	teaspoon cinnamon
1	cup dark brown sugar	1/2	teaspoon allspice
3	tablespoons dark corn syrup	2	tablespoons cocoa
		3/4	cup milk
1	cup flour	2	cups regular oats
1/2	teaspoon salt	1/2	cup raisins
2	teaspoons baking powder	1/2	cup chopped nuts

In a large bowl, cream together the butter and sugar until light. Add the syrup. Sift together the dry ingredients and combine alternately with milk to the butter mixture. Add oatmeal, raisin, and nuts, and blend well. Chill for about 45 minutes. Drop by teaspoonfuls onto a greased cookie sheet and bake in a 375 degree oven for 8 to 10 minutes, until lightly brown. Makes 2-1/2 dozen.

Light-Brown Oatmeal Cookies

Everyone loves oatmeal cookies - these have a faint taste of molasses.

1	cup butter or margarine	1	tablespoon molasses
1-1/2	cups light brown sugar	1	egg, slightly beaten
2-1/4	cups oatmeal (uncooked)	1	teaspoon vanilla
1/2	teaspoon salt		milk
3	tablespoons flour		pecan halves

Melt butter, remove from heat. Beat brown sugar and butter. Add butter and sugar mixture to oatmeal. Let stand overnight at room temperature. Sift flour and salt together. Add egg and vanilla alternately with molasses. Mix well with oatmeal. Drop level teaspoons of dough 2-inches apart on heavily greased and floured cookie sheets. Brush tops lightly with milk. Press a pecan half on the center of each cookie. Bake at 375 degrees for 5 to 7 minutes, or until brown around edges. After removing from oven, let cookies remain on pan a few minutes until firm. Then immediately remove with spatula to cooling rack. Makes about 100 drop cookies.

Oatmeal Cherry Cookies

Red maraschino cherries add color and flavor to these favorite oatmeal cookies.

1/2	cup shortening	1/2	teaspoon salt
1/2	cup butter	1	jar (8 ounces) red
1	cup dark brown sugar		maraschino cherries,
1	cup sugar		drained and chopped
2	eggs	1/2	cup flaked coconut
1	teaspoon vanilla	2	cups quick rolled oats
1-1/2	cups sifted flour	1	jar (8 ounces)
1	teaspoon baking powder		maraschino cherries,
1/2	teaspoon soda		for decoration

Cream butter and sugars until fluffy. Beat in eggs and vanilla. Sift dry ingredients together and add to creamed mixture with cherries, coconut and rolled oats. Mix well. Chill 1 hour. Drop by tablespoonful onto ungreased cookie sheets. Place a piece of maraschino atop each cookie. Bake in a 375 degree oven about 10 to 12 minutes. Remove from racks and cool. Makes about 6 dozen cookies.

Carrot Oatmeal Cookies

What a pleasant surprise! Carrots added to our favorite cookies.

2	cups sifted flour	1	cup raisins
1	teaspoon baking powder	1	cup chopped nuts
1/4	teaspoon soda	1/2	cup shortening
1/2	teaspoon salt	1	cup brown sugar
1	teaspoon cinnamon	1/3	cup milk
1/2	teaspoon nutmeg	2	well beaten eggs
2	cups quick cooking oats	1	cup grated raw carrot

Sift together flour, baking powder, soda, salt and spices. Add oatmeal, raisins and nutmeats. Mix well. Cream shortening, add brown sugar and milk. Beat thoroughly. Add eggs, beating again, then add carrots and mix well. Add dry ingredients, and stir until everything is mixed well. Drop by teaspoonful onto a greased baking sheet. Flatten out with a floured fork. Bake 15 minutes in a preheated oven at 350 degrees. Do not store until cold. Makes about 5 dozen.

Apple Butter Cookies

What a good old-fashioned taste to these chewy cookies.

1/4	cup butter	1/2	teaspoon baking powder
1	cup brown sugar	1/2	teaspoon soda
1	egg	1/2	teaspoon salt
1/2	cup quick cooking oats	2	tablespoons milk
1/2	cup apple butter	1/2	cup chopped nuts
1	cup flour	1/2	cup raisins

Cream butter and sugar. Beat in egg, oats, and apple butter. Combine dry ingredients, gradually add to creamed mixture along with the milk; beat until blended. Stir in nuts and raisins. Chill well. Drop by teaspoonfuls onto lightly greased cookie sheets. Bake at 350 degrees for 15 minutes. Makes 30 cookies.

Val's Oatmeal Cookies

The combination of spices and oatmeal make this an outstanding tasty cookie.

1-1/4	cups margarine	1	teaspoon salt
1/2	cup sugar	1	teaspoon cinnamon
3/4	cup brown sugar	1/2	teaspoon nutmeg
1	egg	3	cups oatmeal
1-1/4	teaspoons vanilla	1/2	cup raisins
1-1/2	cups flour	1/2	cup chopped nuts or coconut
1	teaspoon baking soda		

Cream together margarine and sugars. Beat in egg and vanilla. Sift dry ingredients together. Add to batter, mixing well. Stir in oatmeal, raisins and nuts. Drop by tablespoonfuls on ungreased cookie sheets. Bake in a 375 degree oven for 10 to 12 minutes. Makes 4 dozen. For smaller cookies, drop by teaspoonfuls and bake 8 to 10 minutes.

Hawaiian Cookies

Aloha! Serve with a tall cool glass of orange juice.

1	cup margarine	2	teaspoons baking soda
1	cup brown sugar, packed	1	teaspoon salt
1	cup sugar	1-1/2	cups quick oats
2	eggs	2	cups flaked coconut
1	teaspoon vanilla	1	12-ounce package butterscotch chips
2	cups flour		
2	teaspoons baking powder		

Cream the margarine and sugars until light and fluffy. Beat in eggs and vanilla. Combine flour, baking powder, soda and salt; add to creamed mixture; mix well. Stir in oats, coconut and chips. Drop by rounded teaspoonfuls on greased cookie sheets. Bake at 350 degrees for about 10 to 12 minutes. Makes about 8 dozen.

Ginger Jumbos

They'll remind you of big puffs of gingerbread.

2-1/4	cups sifted flour	1/3	cup sugar
2	teaspoons baking soda	2/3	cup molasses
1	teaspoon cinnamon	1	egg
1/2	teaspoon ginger	1/2	cup milk
1/4	teaspoon salt	1-1/2	teaspoons vinegar
1/2	cup butter or margarine		walnut halves

Cream butter or margarine with sugar until fluffy in large bowl; beat in molasses and egg. Combine milk and vinegar in 1-cup measure. Sift dry ingredients, adding alternately with milk mixture, a third at a time, into molasses mixture, blending well after each to make a thick batter. Drop by rounded tablespoonfuls, 2-inches apart, on greased cookie sheets; top each with a walnut half. Bake in a 400 degree oven for about 8 minutes, or until centers spring back when lightly pressed with fingertip. Remove from cookie sheets; cool completely on wire racks. Makes about 2 dozen jumbos.

Ginger Drops

These cookies are good when dunked in cold milk on a hot day.

3	cup sifted flour	3/4	cup shortening
2	teaspoons baking soda	3/4	cup butter or margarine, softened
2	teaspoons cinnamon	2	cups sugar
1	teaspoon cloves	2	eggs
2	tablespoons ginger	1/2	cup light molasses

Preheat oven to 375 degrees. Sift flour with baking soda, cinnamon, cloves, and ginger; set aside. In large bowl of electric mixer, at medium speed, beat butter, shortening, sugar, and eggs until light and fluffy. Add molasses; beat until thoroughly combined. At low speed, beat in flour mixture until well combined. Drop by teaspoonfuls, 3-inches apart, onto ungreased cookie sheets. Bake 10 to 12 minutes. Remove to wire rack; cool. Makes about 7 dozen.

Ginger Creams

When the aroma fills the kitchen you won't be able to wait to sample these.

1/3	cup shortening	1/2	teaspoon salt
1/2	cup sugar	1/2	teaspoon baking soda
1	egg	1	teaspoon ginger
1/2	cup molasses	1/2	teaspoon nutmeg
1/2	cup water	1/2	teaspoon cloves
2	cups sifted flour	1/2	teaspoon cinnamon

Mix shortening, sugar, egg, molasses, and water thoroughly. Stir dry ingredients together and blend in. Chill dough. Heat oven to 400 degrees. Drop dough by teaspoonfuls about 2-inches apart on lightly greased baking sheet. (Cookies will spread slightly during baking.) Bake about 8 minutes, or until almost no imprint remains when touched lightly. While slightly warm, frost with vanilla frosting.

Molasses Prune Drops

Prunes give a moist texture to these spicy drops.

1-3/4	cups water	1/4	cup light brown sugar
1	cup dried prunes	1/4	cup sugar
1-1/3	cups sifted flour	1	egg
2	teaspoons baking powder	2	tablespoons molasses
1/8	teaspoon salt	3	tablespoons milk
1/8	teaspoon baking soda	1/4	cup walnuts, coarsely chopped
1/4	teaspoon cinnamon		
1/4	cup butter, softened		

In small saucepan, combine prunes and water. Cook uncovered 30 minutes. Drain; remove pits; cut prunes into eighths. Cream butter and sugars until light. Add egg, molasses, and milk; beat until light and fluffy. Beat in sifted dry ingredients until well combined. Stir in nuts and prunes. Drop by spoonfuls onto lightly greased cookie sheet. Bake 15 minutes in a 350 degree oven. Let cool 5 minutes on cookie sheet. Remove to wire rack. Makes about 4 dozen.

Crispies

This cookie has a lot of snap, crackle and pop.

2	cups flour	3/4	cup butter, softened
1/4	teaspoon salt	1	large egg
1/2	teaspoon baking soda	2	teaspoons vanilla
1/2	cup dark brown sugar, packed	1	cup crispy rice cereal
1/2	cup white sugar	1-1/2	cups crispy rice chocolate bar, coarsely chopped

In a large bowl beat butter and sugars. Add egg and vanilla, beating at medium speed until light and fluffy. Sift dry ingredients together and add to mixture. Blend in rice cereal and chocolate chunks at low speed just until combined. Drop by rounded tablespoons onto ungreased cookie sheets, 2-inches apart. Bake in a 300 degree oven for 22 to 24 minutes. Makes 3 dozen cookies.

Honey Crunch Cookies

Buzz around the kitchen and make these for your honey.

2	cups flour	2	eggs
2	teaspoons baking powder	1	cup shredded coconut
1/2	teaspoon salt	1	cup butterscotch chips
1	cup butter	4	cups crisp rice cereal
1	cup honey		

Cream butter. Add honey a little at a time. Mix well. Add eggs, one at a time, beating well after each addition. Mixture will appear to separate. Gradually add sifted dry ingredients; mix until moistened. Fold in coconut, chips and cereal. Drop by teaspoonfuls onto greased cookie sheets. Bake at 350 degrees for about 12 minutes. Remove to rack. Makes about 5 dozen cookies.

Peanut Jumbles

Peanut butter and peanuts make these big cookies extra special.

2/3	cup shortening	1	teaspoon vanilla
1/2	cup peanut butter	2	cups flour
2/3	cup granulated sugar	2	teaspoons baking powder
2/3	cup brown sugar, packed	1	teaspoon salt
2	eggs	1	cup chopped peanuts
1/2	cup milk		

Mix shortening, peanut butter, sugars and eggs thoroughly. Stir in milk and vanilla. Blend dry ingredients; stir into shortening mixture. Stir in peanuts. Drop rounded teaspoonfuls of dough 2-inches apart on greased baking sheet. Bake at 375 degrees for about 10 to 12 minutes. Makes 5 dozen.

Ranch Cookies

A healthy cookie Grandma would approve of.

3/4	cup whole wheat flour	1/2	cup creamy peanut butter
3/4	cup flour	1/4	cup honey
1/2	teaspoon baking powder	2	large eggs
1	cup oats	2	teaspoons vanilla
1	cup light brown sugar, packed	1	cup raisins
1/2	cup butter, softened	1/2	cup sunflower seeds

In medium bowl mix together flours, baking powder and oats. In a large bowl beat sugar and butter with an electric mixer at medium speed. Add the peanut butter, honey, eggs and vanilla. Add the flour mixture, raisins and sunflower seeds. Blend at low speed just until combined. Drop by rounded tablespoonfuls onto ungreased baking sheets, 2-inches apart. Bake in a 300 degree oven for 23 to 25 minutes until bottoms are golden brown. Makes 3 dozen cookies.

Chewy Peanut Butter Cookie

An unusual soft and chewy cookie that keeps well.

2	cups flour	1-1/4	cups white sugar
1/2	teaspoon baking soda	1	cup butter, softened
1/4	teaspoon salt	3	large eggs
1-1/4	cups dark brown sugar, firmly packed	1	cup creamy peanut butter
		2	teaspoons vanilla

In a large bowl blend sugars using an electric mixer set at medium speed. Add butter and mix to form a grainy paste. Add eggs, peanut butter and vanilla, and mix at medium speed until light and fluffy. Add the sifted flour ingredients and mix at low speed until just mixed. Drop by rounded tablespoons onto an ungreased cookie sheet, 1-1/2-inches apart. With a wet fork gently press crisscross pattern on top of cookies. Bake in a 300 degree oven for 18 to 22 minutes until cookies are slightly brown along edges. Makes 3-1/2 dozen.

Salted Peanut Crisps

These are best when using little Spanish peanuts, Um' Good.

1	cup soft margarine	3	cups sifted flour
1-1/2	cups brown sugar	1/2	teaspoon baking soda
2	eggs	1	teaspoon salt
2	teaspoons vanilla	2	cups salted peanuts

Mix thoroughly, margarine, sugar, eggs and vanilla. Sift dry ingredients together. Mix into mixture, stir in peanuts. Drop rounded teaspoonfuls about 2-inches apart onto greased cookie sheet. Flatten with wet glass dipped in sugar. Bake at 375 degrees for 10 minutes. Makes 6 dozen.

Bear Track Cookies

Kids love these unusual looking cookies.

1	cup butter	2-1/3	cups sifted flour
2/3	cup sugar	2	teaspoons baking powder
2	eggs	1	teaspoon salt
1/2	cup chocolate flavored syrup	1/4	cup milk
1	teaspoon vanilla	1/2	cup peanut halves, approximately

Cream butter; add sugar gradually; beat in eggs. Blend in chocolate syrup, vanilla, sifted dry ingredients and milk. Drop by heaping teaspoonfuls onto greased cookie sheets. Insert 4 peanut halves into 1 side of each cookie to resemble claws. Bake at 375 degrees about 10 minutes. Makes about 4-1/2 dozen.

Sour Cream Cashew Drops

Like cashews? These are for you.

1/2	cup butter	3/4	teaspoon soda
1	cup brown sugar, packed	1/4	teaspoon salt
1	egg	1/2	cup sour cream
1	teaspoon vanilla	1-1/2	cups chopped salted cashews
2	cups sifted flour		
3/4	teaspoon baking powder		

Cream butter. Add sugar gradually. Add egg and vanilla. Blend in sifted dry ingredients, sour cream and cashews. Drop from teaspoon onto greased cookie sheets. Bake at 375 degrees about 10 minutes. Cool. Frost. Makes about 8 dozen 1-1/2-inch cookies.

Easy Butterscotch Frosting:

3	tablespoons butter	1-1/2	tablespoons hot water
2	cups powdered sugar		cream

Brown butter in a saucepan. Remove from heat. Stir in sugar, water and enough cream to make frosting of spreading consistency.

Cashews and Coconut Cookies

Coconut, cashews and dates. What a great combination.

2-1/4	cups flour	2	teaspoons vanilla
1/2	teaspoon baking soda	1/2	cup sweetened shredded coconut
1/4	teaspoon salt		
3/4	cup light brown sugar, packed	1	cup chopped raw cashews
		1	cup chopped dates
1/2	cup white sugar	1/2	cup sweetened shredded coconut, reserved for topping
3/4	cup butter, softened		
2	large eggs		

Sift together dry ingredients. In a medium bowl of an electric mixer mix together butter and sugars. Add eggs and vanilla, and beat until smooth. Add flour mixture, coconut, cashews and dates. Blend at low speed. Drop by rounded tablespoonfuls onto ungreased baking sheets, 2-inches apart. Sprinkle tops lightly with reserved coconut. Bake in a 300 degree oven for 23 to 25 minutes or until bottoms turn golden brown. Makes 2-1/2 dozen.

Reese's Chewy Chocolate Cookies

A great tasting chewy chocolate cookie with a slight taste of peanut butter.

1-1/4	cups butter, softened	3/4	cup cocoa
2	cups sugar	1	teaspoon baking soda
2	eggs	1/2	teaspoon salt
2	teaspoons vanilla	1-2/3	cups Reese's peanut butter chips
2	cups flour		

Heat oven to 350 degrees. In large mixer bowl, beat butter and sugar until light and fluffy. Add eggs and vanilla; beat well. Stir together flour, cocoa, baking soda, and salt; gradually blend into butter mixture. Stir in chips. Drop by rounded teaspoonfuls onto ungreased cookie sheet. Bake 8 to 9 minutes. They will puff while baking and flatten while cooling. Cool slightly; remove from cookie sheet to wire rack. Cool completely. Makes about 4-1/2 dozen.

Chocolate Chip Cookies

Every one's favorite, young and old alike.

3/4	cup shortening	3/4	teaspoon baking soda
1/4	cup sugar	1	teaspoon salt
1	cup brown sugar	1	cup chopped pecans
1	egg	1	package (6-ounce) semi-sweet chocolate chips
2	tablespoons milk		
1-1/2	teaspoons vanilla		
1-3/4	cups flour		

Heat oven to 375 degrees. Mix shortening, sugars, egg, milk and vanilla thoroughly. Stir dry ingredients together; blend in. Mix in nuts and chocolate chips. Drop tablespoonfuls of dough about 3-inches apart on ungreased baking sheet. Bake 8 to 10 minutes in a 375 degree oven or until delicately browned. (Cookies should still be soft.) Cool slightly before removing from baking sheet. Makes about 4 dozen cookies.

Chocolate Chip Bars:

Make dough for chocolate chip cookies except spread in greased oblong pan, 13 by 9-1/2 by 2-inches. Bake in a 375 degree oven for 20 to 25 minutes. Makes 24 bars.

Mother's Milk Chocolate Pecan Drops

Sons, daughters and dads - love mother's cookies.

1/2	cup flour	1/2	teaspoon vanilla
1	tablespoon cornstarch	1	cup milk chocolate chips, melted and cooled
1/8	teaspoon salt		
1/2	cup margarine, room temperature	1/2	cup pecans, chopped
1/2	cup plus 2 tablespoons confectioners' sugar		

Mix flour, cornstarch and salt. Beat butter and sugar with electric mixer until fluffy. Beat in vanilla. Gradually beat in flour mixture until blended. Stir in chocolate, then nuts. Drop heaping teaspoonfuls 1-1/2-inches apart onto ungreased cookie sheet. Heat oven to 250 degrees, bake 40 to 45 minutes until tops look dry and bottoms are very lightly browned. Remove to wire racks to cool.

Double Chocolate Potato Drop Cookies

These cookies made with mashed potatoes are excellent keepers.

1-1/2	cups sifted flour	1	egg
1/2	teaspoon salt	2	ounces unsweetened chocolate, melted and cooled
1/2	teaspoon baking soda		
1/2	cup butter		
1	cup brown sugar, sifted packed	1/2	cup mashed potatoes
		1/2	cup chopped nuts
1	teaspoon vanilla	3/4	cup buttermilk

Mix and sift flour, salt and soda. Cream butter, add sugar gradually and cream until fluffy. Add vanilla and egg and mix. Add chocolate, mashed potatoes, nuts and mix. Add sifted dry ingredients alternately with buttermilk, mixing just enough after each addition to combine ingredients. Drop by spoonfuls on ungreased baking sheets. Bake in a preheated 375 degree oven for 12 to 13 minutes. Frost immediately with icing. Store in airtight container. Makes 54 cookies.

Chocolate Icing:

1	tablespoon butter	1	cup sifted confectioners' sugar
1	ounce unsweetened chocolate	2-1/2	tablespoons hot water (approximately)

Melt butter and chocolate in a saucepan. Remove from heat and add sugar and water and beat until mixture is smooth.

Brownie Drops

Sweet chocolate gives a more delicate flavor to these brownies.

2	bars "Baker's" sweet chocolate	1/4	teaspoon baking powder
		1/4	teaspoon cinnamon
1	tablespoon butter	1/8	teaspoon salt
2	eggs	1/2	teaspoon vanilla
3/4	cup sugar	3/4	cup finely chopped pecans
1/4	cup flour		

Melt chocolate and butter. Stir. Cool. Beat eggs until foamy, then add sugar, 2 tablespoons at a time, beat until thickened (5 minutes in electric mixer). Blend in chocolate. Add flour, baking powder, salt and cinnamon; blend. Stir in vanilla and nuts. Drop by teaspoonfuls onto greased baking sheet. Bake in a 350 degree oven for 8 to 10 minutes. Makes about 36 cookies.

Chocolate-Malted Cookies

Malted milk powder is a new taste to cookies, try it!

1-1/4	cups sifted flour	1	cup light-brown sugar, firmly packed
1	cup instant sweetened, chocolate-flavored malted-milk powder	1	egg
		1	teaspoon vanilla
1	teaspoon baking powder	1/4	cup undiluted evaporated milk
1/4	teaspoon salt		
1/2	cup soft butter or margarine	1	cup coarsely chopped walnuts

Sift together flour, malted-milk powder, baking powder, and salt; set aside. In large bowl, with portable electric mixer at medium speed, or wooden spoon, beat butter, sugar, egg, and vanilla until fluffy. Beat in milk until smooth. Gradually stir in flour mixture, mixing until well combined. Stir in nuts. Refrigerate, covered, at least 1 hour. Preheat oven to 350 degrees. Lightly grease cookie sheets. Drop batter by rounded teaspoonfuls, 2-inches apart, onto prepared cookie sheets. Bake 10 to 12 minutes, or until set, not brown. Remove to wire rack; cool completely. Makes about 4-1/2 dozen.

Cherry Chocolate Chip Cookies

Cherries make a welcome change to the old stand by chocolate chip cookies.

1-1/4	cups sifted flour	1	egg
1/2	teaspoon salt	1	jar (4 ounces) maraschino cherries, drained and chopped
1/2	teaspoon soda		
1/2	cup margarine		
1/2	cup sugar	1/4	cup chopped walnuts
1/4	cup dark brown sugar	6	ounces chocolate chips

Sift together flour, salt and soda. Cream butter with sugars. Beat in egg. Stir in cherries, walnuts, chocolate chips and dry ingredients. Drop rounded teaspoons of batter on ungreased baking sheets, about 1-inch apart. Bake in a 375 degree oven 8 to 10 minutes. Let stand 1 minute, then remove from baking sheet.

The Best Chocolate Chip Cookies

They're large and chock-full of chocolate and nuts. Bake them one way if you like your cookies soft and chewy, another way if you prefer them crisp.

1	cup butter or margarine, softened	2	teaspoons baking soda
		1-1/2	teaspoons salt
1/2	cup shortening	1	teaspoon cinnamon, optional
1-1/3	cups sugar		
1	cup firmly packed brown sugar	1/2	cup oats
		2	(12-ounce) packages, semi-sweet chocolate chips
4	eggs		
1	tablespoon vanilla		
1	teaspoon lemon juice	2	cups chopped walnuts
3	cups flour		

Beat butter, shortening, sugar and brown sugar in electric mixer on high speed until very light and fluffy (about 5-minutes). Add eggs, one at a time, beating well after each addition. Beat in vanilla and lemon juice. Stir together flour, baking soda, salt, cinnamon (if used) and oats. Gradually add to butter mixture, blending thoroughly. Stir in chocolate chips and walnuts. Use a scant 1/4 cup of dough for each cookie. Drop dough onto lightly greased baking sheets, spacing cookies about 3-inches apart. For soft cookies, bake in a 325 degree oven for about 17 to 19 minutes or until light golden brown; for crisp cookies, bake in a 350 degree oven for about 16 to 18 minutes or until golden brown. Transfer to racks and let cool.

Chocolate Sundae Cookies

Guaranteed to be the first gobbled up at P.T.A. meetings.

2/3	cup brown sugar	2	squares unsweetened chocolate, melted
1/2	cup shortening		
1	egg	1/4	cup snipped maraschino cherries
1/2	teaspoon salt		
1/2	teaspoon baking soda	1/2	cup walnuts, chopped
1-1/2	cups sifted flour	2	dozen large marshmallows, cut in 1/2
1/4	cup cherry juice		
2	tablespoons milk		walnut halves

In mixing bowl cream sugar and shortening. Beat in egg. Add cherry juice, milk and melted chocolate. Add sifted dry ingredients. Add chopped cherries and nuts and stir in. Drop by teaspoonfuls onto greased cookie sheets and bake at 350 degrees for about 12 minutes. After removing from oven immediately push marshmallow into center of cookie. Cool, frost with glossy chocolate frosting while a little warm. Add walnut half on top of each cookie.

Note:
Prior to frosting, return to oven for 1 minute to soften marshmallow, if desired.

Frosting:

2	squares (1-ounce each) unsweetened chocolate	1/3	cup butter
		1-1/3	cups powdered sugar
1	egg	1	teaspoon vanilla

Melt chocolate and butter. Sift powdered sugar, and add egg, melted chocolate and butter. Add vanilla and mix well. Frost chocolate cookies while still warm.

Chocolate Coffee Drops

A treat for your coffee break.

2-1/4	cups flour	2	tablespoons instant coffee
1	tablespoon baking powder	2/3	cup shortening
		1	cup dark brown sugar
1	teaspoon salt	1	egg
2	teaspoons nutmeg	1	teaspoon vanilla
2	teaspoons cinnamon	1	12-ounce package mini-chocolate chips
2	tablespoons boiling water	1/2	cup chopped nuts

Stir together dry ingredients. Pour boiling water over coffee. Let cool. Cream shortening and sugar until light and fluffy. Beat in egg and vanilla. Add flour mixture alternately with coffee. Stir in chocolate chips and nuts. Drop by level tablespoons on greased cookie sheet. Bake in a 375 degree oven 6 to 8 minutes. Makes about 4-1/2 dozen.

Florentines

Luscious chocolate-orange cookie.

3/4	cup whipping cream	1/2	pound candied orange peel, very finely chopped
1/4	cup sugar		
1/4	cup sifted flour	2	bars (4 ounce each) German sweet chocolate
1/2	cup slivered almonds (blanched or toasted), very finely chopped		

Stir cream and sugar together until well blended. Stir in flour, almonds and orange peel. Drop dough by scant teaspoonfuls on heavily greased and floured baking sheet. Flatten cookie with knife or spatula. Bake in a 350 degree oven for 10 to 12 minutes or just until cookies brown lightly around edges. Leave cookies on baking sheet for a few minutes to firm up. Melt chocolate bars over hot water. Turn cookies upside down; spread with chocolate. Allow to dry several hours or overnight at room temperature until chocolate becomes firm. Store in refrigerator. Makes about 5 dozen cookies.

Creamy Chocolate Cookies

This is the perfect chocolate cookie, creamy and moist with a brownie-like texture.

6	ounces unsweetened chocolate	1/2	teaspoon salt
2	tablespoons butter	3	eggs
1/4	cup flour	1-1/4	cups sugar
1/2	teaspoon baking powder	6	ounces semisweet chocolate chips (1 cup)

Melt the chocolate with the butter in a saucepan over very low heat. Mix together the flour, baking powder, and salt. In a mixing bowl beat the eggs, then add the sugar, and continue beating until light and well blended. Add the chocolate mixture to the egg mixture and beat well. Add the flour mixture and mix until well blended. Stir in the chocolate chips and then chill the mixture in the refrigerator for at least 1 hour. Preheat the oven to 350 degrees. Grease a cookie sheet. Drop by teaspoonfuls onto the cookie sheet and bake for 5 to 6 minutes. Do not overbake; these cookies are best if slightly under-baked. Remove to rack to cool. Makes about 4 dozen cookies.

Why not have a "Cookie Exchange". Ask about eight people to bring two batches of cookies. Be sure everyone baked different kinds. Keep out two or three of each batch to sample at your "Exchange Tea Party". Bring along a pretty box to take home your share. A great way to get an easy assortment of cookies.

Bittersweet Chocolate-Chip Rounds

Sandy-textured and crisp, these big cookies have bittersweet chocolate chunks dotted throughout.

2	cups butter, softened	2	pounds bittersweet bar chocolate, cut into 1/3-inch pieces
2	cups sugar		
1	tablespoon plus 1 teaspoon vanilla	1	cup coarsely chopped walnuts
4	cups flour		
1	teaspoon salt		

Preheat oven to 350 degrees. In a large bowl of an electric mixer, cream the butter for 2 to 3 minutes, or until light. On low speed, beat in the sugar in 2 additions, beating for 1 to 2 minutes and scraping down the sides of the bowl after each portion of sugar is added. Beat in the vanilla. On low speed, blend in the flour in 3 additions, beating just until the flour particles are absorbed. With the final portion of flour, add the salt. By hand, stir in the chocolate pieces and walnuts. Drop rounded tablespoon mounds of dough 2-1/2-inches apart onto parchment paper-lined cookie sheets. Bake cookies, a sheet at a time, on the middle-level rack of the oven for 10 to 12 minutes, or until the tops feel firm and the cookies are a light golden color all over. With a wide spatula remove the cookies to a cooling rack. When cooled, store in an airtight container.

Note:
Dark Swiss Lindt Excellence chocolate gives these cookies a deep taste of chocolate that melts smoothly on the tongue.

Chocolate Drop Cookies

Two types of cookies - one batter.

1/2	cup butter	1	teaspoon vanilla
1	cup sugar	1-3/4	cups sifted flour
1	egg	1/2	teaspoon soda
2	squares unsweetened chocolate, melted and cooled	1/2	teaspoon salt
		1	cup chopped nuts, if desired
3/4	cup buttermilk		

Mix shortening, sugar, egg, and chocolate thoroughly. Stir in buttermilk and vanilla. Sift together flour, soda, and salt; blend in. Mix in nuts. Chill at least 1 hour. Heat oven to 400 degrees. Drop rounded teaspoonfuls of dough about 2-inches apart on lightly greased baking sheet. Bake for about 8 to 10 minutes or until no imprint remains when touched lightly. If desired, frost cooled cookies with browned butter glaze or chocolate icing. Sprinkle with chopped nuts or flaked coconut. Makes about 3-1/2 dozen 2-1/2-inch cookies.

Note:
Divide dough in half, add 1 cup of maraschino cherries to one-half, 3/4 cup nuts to other half.

White Chocolate Cookies

Toasted macadamia nuts give a special taste to these cookies.

1/2	cup butter or margarine	1/2	teaspoon salt
1/2	cup shortening	2	tablespoons vanilla
3/4	cup sugar	10	ounces white chocolate, coarsely chopped
1/2	cup brown sugar, packed		
1	egg	1/2	cup coarsely chopped macadamia nuts, lightly toasted
1-3/4	cups flour		
1	teaspoon baking soda		

In a large bowl, cream butter and shortening. Gradually add sugars, beating until light and fluffy. Add egg; mix well. Combine flour, soda and salt; add to creamed mixture. Blend in vanilla. Stir in chocolate and nuts. Cover and chill dough for 1 hour. Drop by heaping tablespoonful about 3-inches apart on ungreased cookie sheets. Bake at 350 degrees for 12 to 14 minutes or until lightly browned. Let stand a few minutes before removing cookies to a wire rack to cool. Makes about 2-1/2 dozen cookies.

Chocolate Orange Puffs

Orange-flavored puffs filled with chocolate cream.

1/2	cup water	2	eggs
1/4	cup butter or margarine	2	to 3 tablespoons grated orange rind
1/8	teaspoon salt		
1/2	cup flour, sifted		Chocolate Cream Filling

Blend water, butter and salt; bring to a boil. Add flour; stir briskly until mixture leaves the pan and forms a smooth ball, about 1 minute. Remove from heat; add 1 egg at a time; beat well after each addition. Fold in orange rind. Drop dough by teaspoonfuls on ungreased baking sheet. Bake in a 450 degree oven for 12 to 15 minutes. Remove from baking sheet immediately; cool. Fill with filling. Refrigerate until served. Makes 4 to 5 dozen puffs.

Chocolate Cream Filling:

Melt 1/2 cup semisweet chocolate pieces over hot (no boiling) water. Add 2 tablespoons orange juice or water. Remove from heat and cool. Fold in 1/3 cup finely chopped almonds. Beat 1/2 cup whipping cream until stiff. Fold into chocolate mixture.

Chocolate Almond Bites

A tender melt in your mouth cookie.

1	8-ounce package semi-sweet chocolate baking bar	3/4	cup firmly packed brown sugar
2	eggs	1	cup almonds, chopped and toasted slivered or sliced almonds
1/4	teaspoon salt		
1	teaspoon vanilla		

Melt over hot (not boiling) water, chocolate baking bar, stirring until smooth. Remove from heat; cool for 5 minutes. In small mixer bowl, beat eggs and salt at high speed until thick, about 3 minutes. Add brown sugar and beat at high speed until thickened, about 5 minutes. Beat in cooled chocolate and vanilla until smooth. Stir in chopped almonds. Drop mixture by rounded measuring teaspoonfuls onto greased cookie sheets. Insert 1 almond slice into top of each cookie. Bake 8 to 10 minutes in 325° oven or until shiny and set. Cool on cookie sheets for 2 minutes. Remove from cookie sheets; cool.

Chocolate Bonnets

Like a chocolate macaroon cookie topped with a coconut meringue.

1/2	cup butter, softened	1-3/4	cups flour
1/2	cup sugar	1/2	teaspoon baking powder
1/2	cup firmly packed brown sugar	1/4	teaspoon baking soda
2	egg yolks	1/4	teaspoon salt
1	teaspoon vanilla	1/3	cup milk
3	squares unsweetened chocolate, melted		

Cream butter and sugar. Add egg yolks and beat until fluffy. Add melted chocolate and vanilla to creamed mixture. Add sifted dry ingredients alternately with milk. Beat just until blended. Drop batter by rounded teaspoonfuls onto greased cookie sheets. Top each with 1/2 teaspoon meringue. Bake in a 375 degree oven for 6 to 8 minutes. Cool on wire racks. Makes about 4-1/2 dozen cookies.

Meringue:

2	egg whites	1	cup flaked coconut
1/8	teaspoon salt	1	tablespoon flour
1/4	cup sugar		

Beat salt and egg whites until stiff, gradually adding sugar. Fold in flour and coconut.

For large cookies, like Gingerbread men, use a pancake turner when placing cookies on cookie sheet.

Chocolate Cream Cushions

Fill these soft chocolate sandwich cookies with Butter Cream Filling or a filling of your choice.

6	tablespoons butter, softened	1-1/4	teaspoons baking powder
1	cup sugar	1/4	teaspoon salt
1	egg	5	tablespoons cocoa
1	teaspoon vanilla	1	cup milk
2	cups flour		Butter Cream Frosting

Cream butter and sugar; beat in egg and vanilla. Add sifted dry ingredients alternately with milk, beating just until smooth. Drop dough onto greased baking sheets, about 2-inches apart. Bake in a 400 degree oven for 10 minutes. Transfer to racks to cool completely. Spread bottoms of half the cookies with butter cream. Top with remaining cookies top side up. Makes about 2-1/2 dozen cookies.

Butter Cream Filling:

3/4	cup butter	6	tablespoons marshmallow creme
3/4	cup powdered sugar	1	teaspoon vanilla

Cream butter and sugar; add marshmallow creme and vanilla and beat until smooth.

Chocolate Marshmallow Cookies

These cookies are Mom's pride and joy. Their chocolatey goodness is devoured by young and old alike.

1	cup brown sugar	2	squares (1 ounce each) unsweetened chocolate
1	egg		
1/2	cup milk	1	teaspoon vanilla
1-1/2	cups flour	1/2	cup nuts, chopped
1/2	teaspoon soda		miniature marshmallows
1/2	cup butter		

Beat eggs slightly and add brown sugar. Mix with milk. Melt butter and chocolate together in a double boiler. When melted add to milk mixture. Stir in flour, baking soda and nuts. Mix thoroughly. Chill dough 1 hour. Then drop by teaspoonfuls onto a greased cookie sheet. Bake in oven at 375 degrees for about 10 to 12 minutes. Take from oven and place 1 or 2 small marshmallows on each cookie pressing in place. Return to oven for a few seconds. Remove from the cookie sheet. Frost while a little warm. Makes about 3 to 4 dozen.

Frosting:

2	squares (1-ounce each) unsweetened chocolate	1/3	cups butter
		1-1/3	cups powdered sugar
1	egg	1	teaspoon vanilla

Melt chocolate and butter. Sift powdered sugar, and add egg, melted chocolate and butter. Add vanilla and mix well. Frost chocolate cookies while still warm.

Chocolate-Coconut Mounds

The irresistible combination of 2 marvelous flavors loved by all who are coconut-chocolate fanciers.

7	ounces bittersweet bar chocolate, cut into pieces	2	teaspoons vanilla
1/2	cup unsalted butter, cut into tablespoon chunks	6	ounces bittersweet chocolate, chunked
1/4	teaspoon salt	1	cup chopped walnuts
1/4	cup sugar	14	ounces sweetened shredded coconut
3	large eggs, lightly beaten	1	cup chopped walnuts
2	extra large egg yolks, beaten		

Place the 7 ounces bittersweet chocolate and butter in the top of a double boiler. Let the chocolate and butter melt slowly, stirring occasionally. Remove the mixture from the heat. Pour the chocolate and butter mixture into a large mixing bowl. Preheat the oven to 325 degrees. When the chocolate has cooled to tepid, whisk in the salt and sugar. Pour in the beaten whole eggs and whisk again. Blend in the beaten yolks and vanilla. Whisk for 1 minute to combine everything together. By hand, stir in the cut-up bar chocolate and coconut. Drop the mixture by rounded tablespoons 2-inches apart onto parchment paper-lined cookie sheets. Bake the mounds on the middle-level rack of the oven for about 20 minutes, or until they are just firm to the touch. The insides will remain moist. Let the mounds settle on the baking sheet for 2 to 3 minutes, then with a wide spatula remove them to cooling racks. When cooled, store the mounds airtight, but do not stack them too high in the container. Makes about 3 dozen.

Chocolate-Chocolate Cookies

Good cookies made with Bisquick and instant chocolate pudding.

2	eggs, beaten	1	package instant chocolate pudding
1/3	cup cooking oil		
1/2	cup milk	6	ounce package chocolate chips
2	cups Bisquick		
1/2	cup sugar		chopped nuts, as desired

In bowl mix together beaten eggs, milk, oil, sugar, pudding mix and Bisquick. Stir in chocolate chips and nuts. Drop by spoonfuls onto ungreased cookie sheets. Bake at 350 degrees for 10 to 12 minutes.

Wicked Chocolate Drops

Do you love chocolate? These are for you, made with 32 ounces of chocolate.

5	ounces unsweetened chocolate, cut into small pieces	4	extra large or jumbo eggs, room temperature
11	ounces bittersweet chocolate, chopped coarsely	1-1/3	cups sugar
		2	teaspoons vanilla extract
		1	pound bittersweet chocolate, cut into 1/3-inch pieces
5	tablespoons unsalted butter, room temperature	4	cups walnuts, coarsely chopped into 1/3-inch pieces
1/2	cup flour		
1/2	teaspoon baking soda		
1/4	teaspoon salt		

Slowly melt unsweetened chocolate, the 11 ounces coarsely chopped bittersweet chocolate and butter. Stir from time to time. Remove mixture from heat and cool to tepid. In large bowl with an electric mixer on moderate high speed, beat eggs, sugar and vanilla until thick, about 3 to 5 minutes. On low speed, blend in chocolate mixture scraping down sides of bowl to keep mixture even. Add sifted ingredients and beat slowly until flour particles have been absorbed. By hand, stir in the 1 pound cut bittersweet chocolate pieces and walnuts. Drop by rounded tablespoons, 2-1/2-inches apart onto cookie sheets lined with parchment paper. Bake at 350 degrees on the middle rack of the oven for 10 to 13 minutes, or until cookies are just firm to touch. Insides will remain quite moist. Cool cookies on cookie sheet about 2 minutes. Then put on racks for final cooling.

Marbles

An absolute must for the holidays and special occasions.

1/2	cup butter, softened	1/2	cup sour cream
1/2	cup white sugar	2	cups flour
1/2	cup light brown sugar, packed	1/2	teaspoon baking powder
1	large egg	1/4	teaspoon salt
1	teaspoon vanilla	1	cup chocolate chips

In an electric mixer, beat butter and sugars. Add egg, sour cream and vanilla, beat at medium speed until light and fluffy. Add sifted dry ingredients and blend at low speed until just combined. Place chocolate chips in double boiler over hot but not boiling water. Stir constantly until melted. Cool chocolate for a few minutes and pour over cookie batter. Using a rubber spatula, lightly fold melted chocolate into the dough. Do not mix chocolate completely into cookie dough. Drop by rounded tablespoons, 2-inches apart onto ungreased cookie sheets. Bake in a 300 degree oven 23 to 25 minutes. Do not brown. Makes about 2-1/2 dozen cookies.

Chocolate Walnut Clusters

A walnut lover's dream cookie!

1/4	cup butter	1/2	cup flour
1/2	cup sugar	1/4	teaspoon baking powder
1	egg	1/2	teaspoon salt
1-1/2	teaspoons vanilla	2	cups broken walnut meats
1-1/2	squares unsweetened chocolate, melted		

Cream butter. Add sugar and cream well. Beat in egg, vanilla and chocolate. Blend in sifted dry ingredients and nuts. Drop from teaspoon onto greased cookie sheet. Bake in a 350 degree oven about 10 minutes. Makes 4 dozen cookies.

Chocolate Walnut Kraut Stacks

Sauerkraut gives a pleasing change of flavor to these cookies.

1-1/2	cups sifted flour	1	cup sugar
1/3	cup cocoa	1	egg
1	teaspoon baking powder	1	teaspoon vanilla
1/2	teaspoon baking soda	1	cup drained, finely chopped sauerkraut
1/4	teaspoon salt		
1/2	cup butter	1/2	cup chopped walnuts

Mix and sift flour, cocoa, baking powder, soda and salt. Cream butter, add sugar gradually and cream until fluffy. Add egg, vanilla, sauerkraut, nuts and mix; add sifted ingredients and mix. Chill well. Drop by 2 teaspoonfuls on lightly greased cookie sheets. Bake in a preheated 375 degree oven about 12 minutes. Cool. Frost with chocolate frosting and top with walnut halves. Makes about 5 dozen cookies.

Chocolate Lumps

Reminds me of small chocolate cream puffs. No bowls needed here.

1	cup milk	1/4	cup sugar
1/2	cup butter	4	eggs
1	cup flour	1-1/2	teaspoons vanilla
1/4	teaspoon salt	3	ounces chocolate chips

Put butter and milk in saucepan. Bring to boiling point. Remove from heat. Sift flour, salt and sugar together, and add all at once to butter and milk mixture, stir constantly. Return to heat, cook until mixture leaves sides of pan in smooth ball. Remove from heat. Add 1 egg at a time, beating well after each addition. Blend in vanilla, mix well. Drop dough by 1/2 teaspoons 2-inches apart, onto ungreased cookie sheet. Place 1 chocolate chip on each cookie. Then cover with teaspoon of dough. Bake in a 375 degree oven about 15 to 20 minutes. Let cool, sprinkle with confectioners' sugar. Makes about 24 lumps.

Chocolate Surprise Cookies

What's the surprise? Dates and chocolate chunks.

1	cup butter	1	teaspoon soda
3/4	cup light brown sugar	2	tablespoons warm water
3/4	cup granulated sugar	1	cup broken walnuts
3	eggs	1/2	pound milk chocolate, cut in chunks
2-1/2	cups flour		
1	cup chopped dates		

Cream butter. Add sugar gradually and beat until light and fluffy. Add eggs one at a time. Beat well after the addition of each. Add flour alternately to creamed mixture with dates that have been combined with soda and warm water. Fold in walnuts and chunks of chocolate. Drop by teaspoonfuls on greased cookie sheet. Bake at 350 degrees for about 15 minutes. Makes about 8 dozen cookies.

Candy Cookies

For lovers of chocolate covered raisins.

1/2	cup shortening	1/2	teaspoon salt
1/2	cup brown sugar, packed	1/2	teaspoon baking soda
1/4	cup sugar	3/4	cup packaged chocolate-covered raisins
1	egg		
1/2	teaspoon vanilla	1/4	cup coarsely chopped walnuts
1	cup plus 2 tablespoons sifted flour		

Beat shortening with brown sugar and granulated sugar until light and fluffy. Beat in egg and vanilla. Sift flour with salt and baking soda. At low speed, beat them into shortening-sugar mixture until batter is smooth. Then fold in raisins and walnuts. Drop cookie batter by teaspoonfuls onto a greased cookie sheet. Bake cookies about 10 to 12 minutes in a 375 degree oven or until they are lightly browned. Remove to a wire rack to cool. Makes 2-1/2 dozen.

Mocha Cookies

Chocolate and coffee flavors combined give these cookies an outstanding taste.

4	ounces unsweetened chocolate, chopped	1/2	teaspoon salt
3	cups semisweet chocolate chips	4	large eggs, room temperature
1/2	cup butter, cut into bits	1-1/2	cups sugar
1/2	cup flour	1-1/2	tablespoons instant coffee
1/2	teaspoon baking powder	2	teaspoons vanilla

Melt the unsweetened chocolate, 1-1/2 cups of chocolate chips, and the butter, stirring until the mixture is smooth. In a small bowl, stir together the flour, baking powder, and salt. In a bowl, beat the eggs with sugar until the mixture is thick and pale, beat in the coffee and vanilla. Fold the chocolate mixture into the egg mixture. Fold in the flour mixture and stir in the remaining 1-1/2 cups chocolate chips. Let the batter stand for 15 minutes. Drop the batter by heaping tablespoons onto baking sheets lined with parchment paper. Bake in a 350 degree oven for 8 to 10 minutes or until they are puffed and shiny and cracked on top. Let the cookies cool on the baking sheets, transfer them to racks and let them cool completely. Makes about 36 cookies.

Chocolate Cracklers

Share at a cookie exchange-these perky cookies fill the bill.

1	6-ounce package semisweet chocolate morsels	1	cup sugar
		1/2	cup butter, softened
		1-1/2	teaspoons vanilla
1	cup flour	2	eggs
1/2	teaspoon baking powder	1-1/2	cups chopped pecans
1/2	teaspoon salt		pecan halves, optional

Melt morsels over hot (not boiling) water; remove from heat. In small bowl, combine flour, baking powder and salt. In large bowl, combine sugar, butter and vanilla; beat until creamy. Beat in melted morsels and eggs. Blend in flour mixture. Stir in chopped pecans. Using a level tablespoonful for each cookie, drop dough onto lightly greased cookie sheets. Place pecan halves in centers of cookies, if desired. Bake at 375 degrees for 10 to 12 minutes. Cool on wire racks. Makes about 4 dozen cookies.

Anise Drops

Use of anise oil gives the cookies a very different taste.

2	eggs	1	drop anise oil
1-1/2	cups sifted confectioners' sugar	1	cup plus 1 tablespoon sifted flour

Beat eggs with beater until very thick; add sugar, about 2 tablespoons at a time, beating well after each addition. Add anise oil and flour gradually and mix. Drop as quickly as possible from teaspoon, forming cookies the size of a quarter, 1-1/2-inches apart, on greased baking sheets. Allow to stand, uncovered, about 12 hours in a cool place to dry. Bake in a preheated 300 degree oven about 18 minutes. Makes 4 dozen.

Note:
These cookies are best if allowed to ripen a month before using. Store in a covered container.

Self Frosting Anise Drops

Everyone likes these different tasting cookies.

2-1/4	cups sifted flour	2	cups sugar
1/2	teaspoon baking powder	1/2	teaspoon oil of anise or anise flavoring
1/4	teaspoon salt		
4	whole eggs		

Sift flour, baking powder and salt together several times. Beat eggs at a low speed of mixer until frothy. Turn mixer to a medium speed. Beat for 10 minutes. Beat in 1 tablespoon sugar at a time. This takes about 5 minutes. Turn mixer to a low speed. Add dry ingredients slowly. Beat 15 minutes longer. Blend in anise. Drop from teaspoon onto 5 or 6 well-greased cookie sheets. Allow to stand in a cool place several hours or overnight. Top of cookie should be dry to the touch. Bake at 325 degrees 12 to 14 minutes. Makes about 12 dozen 1-1/2-inch cookies.

Bachelor Buttons

Very excellent eating!

2	cups sifted flour	1/2	cup cut, candied cherries
2	teaspoons baking powder	3/4	cup butter
1/4	teaspoon salt	1	cup brown sugar, sifted and packed
1/2	cup dry shredded coconut		
1/2	cup shredded, blanched almond nutmeats	1	egg
		1/2	teaspoon vanilla extract

Mix and sift flour, baking powder, and salt. Add coconut, nutmeats and cherries and mix well. Cream butter well, add sugar gradually and continue creaming until light and fluffy; add well beaten egg and extract and mix well. Add flour mixture gradually and mix. Drop by spoonfuls on baking sheets. Bake in preheated oven. Store in airtight container. Bake at 375 degrees for about 9 minutes. Makes about 4-2/3 dozen.

Marmalade Drops

The marmalade give these a unique flavor.

1	cup orange marmalade	2	cups flour
1	teaspoon soda	1	teaspoon salt
1/2	cup shortening	1/2	cup chocolate bits (or raisins)
1	egg		
1	teaspoon vanilla	1/2	cup broken nuts

Combine marmalade, soda, shortening and egg. Beat with medium speed of electric mixer until light and fluffy. Add vanilla. Add sifted dry ingredients using low speed of electric mixer. Fold in chocolate chips and nuts. Drop from teaspoon onto greased cookie sheets. Bake at 350 degrees for about 10 minutes. Makes about 5-1/2 dozen.

Frosted Pecan Drops

These icing-drizzled wafers are both chewy and crisp.

- 1-1/2 cups flour
- 1-1/2 teaspoons baking powder
- 1/4 teaspoon salt
- 1/2 cup butter or margarine, softened
- 1-1/2 cups firmly packed brown sugar
- 1 egg
- 1 teaspoon vanilla
- 1 cup pecans, coarsely chopped

Preheat oven to 350 degrees. In mixer bowl combine butter and brown sugar. Beat until well blended, then beat in egg until fluffy. Add vanilla and mix to blend, stir in sifted dry ingredient mixture until just blended. Drop by rounded teaspoons, place slightly apart, onto lightly greased baking sheets. Flatten each cookie slightly with a fork. Sprinkle with pecans, using about 3/4 teaspoon of nuts for each cookie. Bake until golden brown about 10 minutes. Transfer at once to wire racks. Drizzle cooled cookies generously with icing. Makes about 4 dozen 2-1/2-inch cookies.

Praline Icing:

- 1 cup firmly packed brown sugar
- 1/2 cup whipping cream
- 1 cup confectioners' sugar

In a 1-1/2- to 2-quart saucepan, combine brown sugar and whipping cream. Place over medium-high heat, stirring until sugar dissolves and cream comes to boil. Boil, stirring constantly, for 1 minute. Remove from heat and blend in confectioners' sugar. Beat until smooth, then use at once.

Refrigerated Cookies

*Half the fun of christmas
is shopping thoughtfully;
for gifts that bring a glow to those
who find them "neath" the tree.*

Cookie Jar Cookies

Children love to cut out cookies with this easy to handle dough.

1	cup butter	3/4	teaspoon salt
1-1/.4	cups sugar	1/4	teaspoon nutmeg
1	egg	1/3	cup water
2-1/2	cups sifted flour		sugar
1	teaspoon soda		raisins

Cream butter. Add sugar gradually. Beat in egg. Blend in sifted dry ingredients and water alternately. Refrigerate overnight. Roll part of the dough 3/8-inch thick on floured canvas. Cut with large round cutter. Cookies spread. Place 2-inches apart on ungreased cookie sheets. Sprinkle with sugar. Decorate with 3 or 4 raisins. Bake at 400 degrees for about 10 to 12 minutes. Makes about 2 to 3 dozen depending on size.

Slice O' Spice

Crisp and snappy, butter cookies dipped in sugar-cinnamon before baking.

3	cups sifted flour	2	eggs
1	teaspoon baking soda	1	teaspoon vanilla
1	teaspoon cream of tartar	1	cup quick cooking oats
1/2	teaspoon salt	1/2	cup sugar
1/2	cup butter or margarine	4	teaspoons cinnamon
1/2	cup shortening		
2	cups brown sugar, firmly packed		

Sift together flour, baking soda, cream of tartar and salt. Cream butter and shortening in mixing bowl. Gradually add brown sugar, creaming well. Blend in eggs and vanilla. Stir in dry ingredients. Add oats; mix thoroughly. If desired, chill dough 1 hour for easy handling. Divide dough into 3 parts; place on heavy-duty foil and shape into rolls 12-inches long. Wrap in foil and chill 5 to 6 hours or overnight until firm enough to slice. Cut into 1/4-inch slices. Dip each slice into a mixture of sugar and cinnamon to coat both sides. Place on greased baking sheets. Bake in a 350 degree oven for 9 to 12 minutes until golden brown. Makes about 9 dozen cookies.

Peanut Butter Swirls

Rolled like a jellyroll with chocolate inside.

1-1/4	cups sifted flour	1/2	cup chunk-style peanut butter
1/2	teaspoon salt	1	egg
1/2	teaspoon baking soda	2	tablespoons milk
1/2	cup butter	1	package (6 ounces)
1	cup sugar		semisweet chocolate bits

Mix and sift flour, salt and baking soda. Cream butter well, add sugar gradually and continue creaming until light and fluffy; add peanut butter, egg and milk and beat well. Add sifted dry ingredients and mix well. Place dough on lightly floured waxed paper; roll into a rectangle, 15x8-inches. Melt chocolate over hot water and spread over dough. Roll as for jellyroll lifting waxed paper slightly with each turn. Freeze. Slice about 1/4-inch thick and bake on baking sheets in a 375 degree oven for about 8 minutes. Makes about 5 dozen.

Chewy Cranberry Gingers

Cranberry sauce in a chewy ginger cookie.

2-1/3	cups sifted flour	3/4	cup shortening
2	teaspoons baking soda	1	egg, unbeaten
1/2	teaspoon salt	1/4	cup molasses
1	teaspoon cinnamon	1/2	cup canned whole
1/2	teaspoon ginger		cranberry sauce
1	cup sugar		

Cream shortening and sugar. Add egg and molasses. Beat well, stir in sifted dry ingredients. Mix in whole cranberry sauce. Cover bowl and refrigerate overnight. (Dough will be soft.) Drop dough by teaspoonfuls into sugar, coat thoroughly. Form into balls. Place about 3-inches apart on greased cookie sheets. Bake in a 375 degree oven about 12 to 15 minutes. Remove from sheets while warm. Makes about 4 dozen cookies.

Molasses Crisps

The molasses flavor of these thin, tender cookies is so subtle that you may need to taste them twice to detect it.

1-1/2	cups flour	3/4	cup sugar
1	teaspoon baking soda	1/2	teaspoon vanilla
1/2	cup butter or margarine, softened	1/4	cup light molasses
1/2	cup vegetable shortening	1	cup finely chopped walnuts

In mixer bowl beat butter, shortening, and sugar until well combined; blend in vanilla and beat until fluffy. Add dry sifted ingredients alternately with molasses, mixing to blend after each addition. Stir in walnuts. Divide dough in half, transfer each half to a sheet of waxed paper or plastic wrap. Shape each half into a 2-inch diameter log and wrap tightly. Refrigerate overnight. Preheat oven to 350 degrees. Carefully cut logs into 1/4-inch thick slices; arrange slices, about 1-1/2-inches apart, on lightly greased baking sheets. Bake until cookies are golden brown, about 10 to 12 minutes. Let stand on baking sheets for about 2 minutes, then transfer to wire racks to cool. Makes about sixty-six 2-1/2-inch cookies.

Spiced Nut Cookies

Because these cookies are baked to dryness of a rusk, they keep well for weeks. Store them in a tightly covered tin so you can enjoy them whenever your cup or glass holds a few last swallows for dunking.

2-1/2	cups flour	1	teaspoon vanilla extract
1-1/2	teaspoons baking powder	3	eggs
1	teaspoon cinnamon	1	cup unblanched whole hazelnuts or almonds
1/2	teaspoon nutmeg		
1/4	teaspoon salt	1	cup coarsely chopped walnuts
1/4	teaspoon allspice		
1/4	cup butter or margarine, softened	1/3	cup pine nuts
1	cup sugar plus sugar for sprinkling		

In a medium bowl stir together flour, baking powder, cinnamon, nutmeg, salt, and allspice to combine thoroughly; set aside. In a mixer bowl combine butter and the 1 cup sugar; beat until well mixed. Blend in vanilla. Separate 1 egg, reserving white in a small bowl. To butter mixture add egg yolk, then remaining 2 eggs, one at a time, beating well after each addition. Gradually beat flour mixture into butter mixture until dough is smooth and well blended. Divide dough in half and enclose each portion in plastic wrap. Refrigerate until firm, overnight. While dough is chilling, stir hazelnuts, walnuts, and pine nuts together in a small bowl. Preheat oven to 350 degrees. On a lightly floured surface, roll out 1 portion of dough to an 8x12-inch rectangle. Sprinkle with half of nut mixture. Starting with a 12-inch side, roll rectangle compactly, jellyroll style. Pinch edge and ends to seal. Place, sealed side down, on a lightly greased baking sheet. Repeat with other portion of dough. In a small bowl beat reserved egg white until slightly bubbly; brush egg white over each roll. Sprinkle rolls lightly with sugar. Bake until golden brown, 35 to 40 minutes. Let rolls cool on baking sheet on a wire rack for about 5 minutes. Transfer rolls to a board; with a serrated knife cut rolls on the diagonal into 1/2-inch thick slices. Place slices, cut sides down, on baking sheets and return to oven. Bake until crispy toasted, about 15 to 20 minutes. Transfer to wire racks to cool completely. Makes about 4 dozen cookies.

Gingersnaps

A cookie Grandma used to make.

1	cup sour cream	1/2	teaspoon cloves
1	cup light molasses	1/2	teaspoon baking soda
1/2	cup brown sugar	1/4	teaspoon salt
1	teaspoon cinnamon	4	cups flour
1/2	teaspoon ginger		

Stir together sour cream, molasses and brown sugar. Sift together dry ingredients and add, blending well. Dough should be soft. Chill overnight. Roll dough on lightly floured board. Cut with floured cutters. Bake on greased baking sheet 8 to 10 minutes at 375 degrees. Makes 5 to 6 dozen.

Soft Ginger Cookies

Of all the ginger cookies, these are family favorites.

6	cups sifted flour	3/4	cup shortening
2	teaspoons salt	1	cup sugar
1-1/2	teaspoons soda	1	cup dark molasses
1	tablespoon ground ginger	2	eggs
1	teaspoon ground cloves	1	cup water
1	teaspoon allspice		butter cream frosting
1	teaspoon cinnamon		

Sift together flour, salt, soda, ginger, cloves, allspice and cinnamon. Cream together shortening and sugar until light and fluffy. Beat in molasses and eggs one at a time. Add flour mixture to creamed mixture alternately with water. Beat well after each addition. Batter will resemble thick cake batter. Divide batter in half and wrap in aluminum foil. Chill in freezer at least 12 hours or until very cold and stiff. Roll out dough 3/8-inch thick on well floured board or pastry cloth. Cut with 2-1/2-inch cookie cutters. Place on greased and floured baking sheets. Bake in moderate oven, 350 degrees, 15 to 18 minutes or until lightly browned around edges. When cool, decorate with butter cream frosting, if desired. Makes about 4-1/2 dozen cookies.

Ginger Pinks

Pink peppermint candy patties melt in the oven to form an attractive filling between crisp molasses ginger cookies.

1/2	cup shortening	1/2	teaspoon cinnamon
1/2	cup sugar	1/2	teaspoon ginger
1/2	cup molasses	1/4	teaspoon nutmeg
3-1/4	cups flour	1/2	cup buttermilk
1-1/2	teaspoons soda	4	dozen pink peppermint patties
1/2	teaspoon salt		

Cream sugar and shortening well. Beat in molasses. Stir in half the dry ingredients, which have been sifted together. Mix well. Add buttermilk and remaining flour mixture. Refrigerate several hours. Roll out on floured board to 1/8-inch thickness. Cut with 2-1/4-inch round cutter; place on greased cookie sheets. Bake in moderate oven, 350 degrees, for 6 minutes. Remove from oven. Using 4 dozen pink peppermint patties, top half of partially-baked cookies with a patty. Bake all cookies 2 to 3 minutes longer until golden brown. Remove from oven; immediately top the mint-covered cookies with the plain ones. Press slightly to seal. Remove from sheets; cool. Makes about 4 dozen sandwich cookies.

Molasses Cookies

Best molasses cookie I ever made. But I must confess, it came off the label on the Brer Rabbit molasses jar.

3/4	cup butter	2	teaspoons baking soda
1	cup sugar	1	teaspoon cinnamon
1	egg	1/2	teaspoon cloves
1/4	cup light molasses	1/2	teaspoon ginger
2	cups flour	1/2	teaspoon salt

Preheat oven to 375 degrees. Cream together butter and sugar. Beat in egg and molasses. Sift together remaining ingredients, then stir into molasses mixture. Refrigerate several hours. Form into 1-inch balls and place 2-inches apart on a greased or foil-lined cookie sheet. Bake 8 to 10 minutes. (They will crack a little on top when done.) Makes about 5 dozen.

Spicy Refrigerator Cookies

Start with Bisquick and turn out a good cookie to have in your freezer for a rainy day.

3-1/2	cups Bisquick	1/4	cup fresh orange juice
1	cup sugar	1/2	cup chopped nuts
1/4	cup salad oil	1/2	cup sugar
1/8	teaspoon salt	1	teaspoon cinnamon
1	egg		
3	tablespoons grated orange rind		

Combine Bisquick, 1 cup sugar, salad oil, salt, egg and orange rind and juice; beat vigorously by hand for 1 minute. Add nuts and mix. Form dough into rolls, about 2-inches in diameter; freeze or chill thoroughly. Slice about 1/8-inch thick; sprinkle with combined 1/2 cup sugar and cinnamon. Bake on ungreased cookie sheets in a 425 degree oven for about 8 minutes. Makes about 5 dozen cookies.

Swedish Ginger Cookies

An excellent recipe to make cut-outs for your children.

1	cup dark syrup	1	teaspoon cloves
1	cup sugar	1	teaspoon cinnamon
1	cup butter, melted	1	teaspoon soda
3/4	cup cream	1/4	cup cream
1	teaspoon ginger	6	cups bread flour

Bring syrup to boiling point and boil 5 minutes. Cool. When cool, stir in sugar. Add melted butter, cream and spices. Mix well. Dissolve soda in 1/4 cup cream. Add to above mixture with flour. Mix thoroughly. Let stand in refrigerator overnight. Roll to about 1/8-inch thickness. Cut into desired shapes. Bake at 350 degrees for about 15 to 20 minutes. Makes about 10 dozen cookies.

Windmill Cookies

You have tried the commercial version, now try with real ingredients. What a difference.

1	cup butter	1	teaspoon nutmeg
2	cups brown sugar, packed		dash of cloves
1	teaspoon baking soda	1/2	teaspoon mace
1/2	cup hot water	3/4	cup blanched, slivered almonds
4	cups flour		
1	teaspoon cinnamon		

Mix together butter, brown sugar and baking soda dissolved in hot water. In separate bowl, mix together flour, cinnamon, nutmeg, cloves and mace. Combine with butter mixture. Add almonds. Roll dough into 2 loaves, each 3-1/2 by 10-inches. Chill overnight in refrigerator. Slice into 1/4-inch slices. Bake in a 350 degree oven for 15 to 20 minutes or until lightly browned. Makes about 3-1/2 to 4 dozen cookies.

Holiday time we like to be remembered. Bake-up some of these cookies and bring them to your friends and neighbors.

Mary Ann Cookies

An old-fashioned cookie you just can't beat. Color frosting if so desired.

2	teaspoons baking soda	1/2	teaspoon nutmeg
1/2	cup hot coffee	1/4	teaspoon cloves
1	cup shortening	3	cups plus 1 tablespoon flour
1	cup light molasses		
1	teaspoon salt		

Preheat oven to 350 degrees. To make cookies: dissolve baking soda in hot coffee. Place in a large bowl with shortening and molasses. Mix until well blended. Sift spices with flour, add to ingredients in mixing bowl, beating until well blended. Chill dough at least 2 hours or overnight. Roll out 1/4-inch thick on a lightly floured board. Cut out cookies using a clean, rounded, rectangular-shaped luncheon meat can. Bake 6 to 8 minutes or until lightly browned. Let cookies cool. Turn cooled cookies over and frost the underside. Let stand until frosting is dry. Makes about 2 dozen cookies.

Frosting:

1	envelope plain gelatin	3/4	cup powdered sugar
3/4	cup water	3/4	teaspoon baking powder
3/4	cup sugar	1	teaspoon vanilla

Soak gelatin in water in a saucepan to soften. Add sugar; bring to a boil. Simmer 10 minutes. Stir, add powdered sugar and heat until foamy. Add baking powder and vanilla, beating until thick.

German Christmas Cookies

These are a much-loved holiday tradition in Germany.

2-1/4	cups flour		
3/4	teaspoon black pepper	1/2	cup butter, room temperature
1/2	teaspoon salt		
1/2	teaspoon anise seed	1/2	cup light molasses
1/2	teaspoon cinnamon	1/2	cup sugar
1/4	teaspoon baking soda	1	large egg
1/4	teaspoon allspice	1	teaspoon water
1/8	teaspoon cloves	2/3	cup finely chopped pecans
1/8	teaspoon nutmeg		

Sift dry ingredients in medium bowl. Using an electric mixer, beat butter, molasses and 1/2 cup sugar in large bowl until fluffy. Beat in egg and 1 teaspoon water. Add dry ingredients and beat at low speed just until combined. Spoon dough into a 16-inch log on sheet of plastic wrap. Using plastic wrap as aid, smooth dough log. Wrap dough tightly and refrigerate until just firm, about 1 hour. Unwrap and press finely chopped pecans evenly into sides of cookie log. Wrap and refrigerate overnight. Position rack in center of oven and preheat to 350 degrees. Grease cookie sheets. Slice cookie log into 1/2-inch thick rounds. Transfer rounds to prepared sheets, spacing 1-1/2-inches apart. Bake cookies until brown around edges and firm to touch, about 16 minutes. Transfer cookies to rack and cool. Makes about 30 cookies.

Wagon Wheels

Inexpensive large chewy molasses cookies - good keepers.

1/2	cup soft shortening	1-1/2	teaspoons salt
1	cup sugar	1-1/2	teaspoons ginger
1	cup dark molasses	1/2	teaspoon cloves
1/2	cup water	1/2	teaspoon nutmeg
4	cups sifted flour	1/4	teaspoon allspice
1	teaspoon soda		

Mix shortening and sugar well. Stir in molasses and water. Blend in sifted dry ingredients. Chill dough several hours or overnight. Roll out 1/4-inch thick. Cut into 3-inch circles. Sprinkle with sugar. Place on well-greased baking sheet. Press a large raisin into center of each. Bake in a 375 degree oven until, when touched lightly with finger, almost no imprint remains, about 10 to 12 minutes. Leave on baking sheet a few minutes before removing to prevent breaking. If desired, make "spokes" of easy decorating icing, radiating out from centers of cooled cookies. Makes about 3 dozen cookies.

Pfeffernuesse Fruit Cakes

Those holidays come upon us so fast. Make these cookies early in the season, they mellow and improve.

1/2	cup sugar	1/4	teaspoon nutmeg
1/2	cup shortening	1/2	cup candied cherries
1/2	cup dark corn syrup	1/2	cup raisins
1/2	cup coffee	1/2	cup dates
3-1/4	cups sifted flour	1/2	cup walnuts
1-1/2	teaspoons baking soda	2	eggs
1/2	teaspoon cinnamon	1	teaspoon anise seed
1/4	teaspoon salt	1/2	teaspoon anise extract

In a 3-quart saucepan combine sugar, shortening, corn syrup and coffee; simmer 5 minutes. Cool. Sift together dry ingredients. Grind cherries, raisins, dates and walnuts. Set aside. Add unbeaten eggs, anise seed and anise extract to sugar-shortening mixture. Mix well. Stir in dry ingredients, then the fruit mixture; blend well. Chill at least 4 hours or overnight. Shape dough into 1-inch balls with well-floured hands. Place on greased cookie sheets. Bake at 350 degrees for 15 to 18 minutes. Dip warm cookies into glaze. Cool on racks until set. Store in tightly covered container.

Sugar Glaze:

1	cup sugar	1/4	teaspoon cream of tartar
1/2	cup water	1/2	cup powdered sugar

Combine sugar, water and cream of tartar in small saucepan. Boil until clear; cool. Stir in powdered sugar.

Pfeffernusse

The traditional pfeffernusse is dotted with brandy just before baking to cause it to and form a topknot. Make these cookies several weeks before Christmas.

2	eggs	1/2	teaspoon cinnamon
1/2	cup firmly packed brown sugar	1/4	teaspoon freshly ground pepper
1/2	cup sugar	1/4	teaspoon cloves
	grated rind of 1 lemon	1/4	teaspoon ginger
1/4	cup finely ground almonds	1/4	teaspoon cardamom
2	tablespoons minced candied fruit	1/8	to 1/4 cup brandy
			sifted confectioners' sugar for coating
2	cups sifted flour		
1/2	teaspoon baking powder		

In large mixing bowl beat eggs until light. Gradually add sugars; beat at high speed for about 10 minutes. Beat in lemon rind, almonds, and candied fruit on low speed, add dry sifted ingredients. Turn dough onto a lightly floured board. With your floured hands, pat dough to a thickness of 1/4-inch. Cut with a lightly floured, 1-inch round cutter. Place cookies 1-inch apart on greased and floured baking sheets. Let cookies stand uncovered in a cool place several hours or overnight. Preheat oven to 300 degrees. Turn over cookies. Use your finger to sprinkle a drop of brandy onto center of each. Bake until cookies puff and are no longer sticky inside, about 20 minutes. Break one open to make sure it is done in center. Transfer to wire racks and let cool slightly. When cookies are barely warm, shake them in a bag with confectioners' sugar. Store in an airtight container for at least 3 weeks before eating. Makes about 5 dozen cookies.

Adding a pinch of baking powder to powdered sugar icing will help it stay moist and not crack.

Holland Dutch Cookies

...ke bar cookies.

	...s butter	1-1/2	teaspoons baking soda
	...oons sugar	1/4	teaspoon salt
	..., beaten	1	teaspoon cinnamon
	cup molasses	1/4	teaspoon mace
	cup buttermilk	1/4	teaspoon cloves
1/2	cup ground pecans	1/4	cup mixed candied fruit, cut fine
1-3/4	cups flour		

Mix butter and sugar together until smooth and creamy. Add egg and mix in. Add molasses, buttermilk and pecans to egg mixture and beat until well blended. Sift all dry ingredients together and add to buttermilk combination. Add fruit and incorporate well into the dough. Spoon dough into a small, deep 8 by 8-inch square pan lined with waxed paper. Place in refrigerator overnight. Remove dough from pan, cut into square bars and then into 1/4-inch thick cookies. Place on lightly greased cookie sheets and bake in a 375 degree oven for 12 to 15 minutes. Makes about 48 cookies.

Frosted Anise Drops

A pretty cookie to decorate before or after baking.

4	cups sifted flour	2	eggs
1/2	teaspoon baking soda	1/2	cup dark molasses
1/2	teaspoon baking powder	1/4	cup hot water
1/4	teaspoon salt	1	tablespoon crushed anise seed
1	cup butter		
1-1/2	cups sugar		

Cream butter and sugar until creamy. Add eggs, molasses, hot water and anise seed. Add sifted dry ingredients and mix. Refrigerate overnight. Roll thin on floured board and cut with floured cutters. Bake on lightly greased cookie sheets in a preheated 375 degree oven about 8 minutes. Frost with Creamy Anise Frosting or ornamental frosting. If desired, these may be decorated before baking or after frosting. Makes about 6 dozen.

Creamy Anise Frosting:

3	tablespoons butter		food coloring, optional
1	cup sifted confectioners' sugar	1	tablespoon milk
		1	drop anise oil

Cream butter, add sugar gradually and cream until fluffy. Add milk and oil and beat well.

Holiday Cookies

Pretty and tasty with cherries, pecans and coconut an irresistible treat at Christmas time.

1	cup butter	3/4	cup finely chopped green and red cherries (candied or maraschino), chopped and drained well on paper towels
1	cup sugar		
1	teaspoon vanilla		
1/2	teaspoon rum extract		
2-1/2	cups sifted flour	1/2	cup finely chopped pecans
1/4	teaspoon mace	3/4	cup flaked coconut

Preheat oven to 375 degrees. Cream together butter and sugar. Stir in vanilla and rum extract. Stir in flour, mace, cherries, and pecans. Chill dough. Shape into rolls 1-inch in diameter. Roll in coconut. Wrap in waxed paper and chill overnight. Dough may be frozen at this stage and baked as needed. Slice 1/4-inch thick. Place on ungreased cookie sheets. Bake 5 to 7 minutes or until edges are golden. Makes 14 dozen 1-inch cookies.

Meringue-Filled Cookie Pastries

Unusual, because they're made from a yeast dough, meringue-filled cookie pastries are delicious with a steaming cup of coffee.

1	package dry yeast	2/3	cup sour cream
1/4	cup warm water	1	teaspoon vanilla
3	cups flour	3/4	cup firm butter or margarine
1/2	teaspoon salt	1/2	cup (approximately) confectioners' sugar
2	egg yolks		

In a medium bowl sprinkle yeast over the water. Let stand until yeast is soft, about 5 minutes. To yeast mixture add egg yolks, sour cream, and vanilla. Beat with a whisk until well blended. Using a pastry blender or 2 knives, cut butter into sifted dry ingredients until coarse crumbs form, add yeast mixture to flour mixture, stirring until flour is evenly moistened. Enclose dough in plastic wrap and refrigerate overnight. Preheat oven to 350 degrees. Work with a third of the dough at a time, keeping remainder in refrigerator. Sprinkle a board or pastry cloth with some of the confectioners' sugar, rubbing it in evenly. Roll out dough to a 10-inch square. Using a pastry wheel or knife, cut dough into 2-1/2-inch squares. Spoon about 1 teaspoon of Meringue Filling into center of each square. Bring up 2 opposite corners to overlap slightly in center, firmly pinching them together to seal. Place pastries about 2-inches apart on lightly greased baking sheets. Repeat with remaining dough. Bake until golden brown, about 18 to 20 minutes. Transfer to wire racks to cool. Sift a little more confectioners' sugar over cooled cookies, if desired. Makes about 4 dozen.

Meringue Filling:

2	egg whites	1/4	cup fine dry bread crumbs
1/2	cup sugar	1/4	cup very finely chopped walnuts
1	teaspoon vanilla		

Beat egg whites at high speed until stiff peaks form. Gradually add sugar, beating until meringue is stiff and glossy. Blend in vanilla. Combine bread crumbs and walnuts; fold into meringue.

Kipfel

A pretty cookie with a nut filling sprinkled with powdered sugar.

Dough:

1/2	pound butter	1	8-ounce package cream cheese
2	cups flour		
1/4	teaspoon salt		

Cut butter into dry ingredients, using pastry blender. Add room temperature cream cheese. Blend. Chill until firm. Prepare Nut Filling.

Nut Filling:

1	cup nuts, grated	1	teaspoon cinnamon
1	tablespoon fine bread crumbs	1	tablespoon lemon juice
1/2	cup sugar	1/2	cup cream

Combine ingredients. Cook until thick, stirring constantly. Cool.
When dough is firm, roll quite thin on floured canvas. Cut into 3-inch squares. Fill center with teaspoonful of Nut Filling or thick marmalade or jam may be used. Bring corners up to center. Press together. Place on ungreased cookie sheets. Bake at 450 degrees about 15 minutes. While warm, sprinkle with powdered sugar. Refrigerate until ready to use. Makes about 3 dozen.

Dipping the cookie cutter in slightly warmed salad oil will give you a much cleaner cut.

Mother's Special Cookies

A treasure! Passed on through generations and still a special treat.

1	cup butter	2-3/4	cups flour
1/2	cup sugar	1/2	teaspoon baking soda
1/2	cup brown sugar, packed	1/2	teaspoon salt
2	eggs	1	teaspoon vanilla

Cream butter and sugars until light and fluffy. Beat in eggs. Sift together flour, soda and salt; add to creamed mixture. Stir in vanilla. Chill. Shape into a roll 2-inches in diameter. Chill overnight. Slice; bake at 350 degrees for about 6 to 8 minutes. Frost with Caramel Icing.

Caramel Icing:

1/4	cup butter	2	cups sifted confectioners' sugar
1	cup brown sugar, packed		
1/4	cup milk		

Melt butter in saucepan. Stir in brown sugar; simmer for 2 minutes, stirring constantly. Add milk bring to a boil, stirring constantly. Cool. Beat in confectioners' sugar until thick enough to spread. Thin with hot water, if necessary. Makes about 4 dozen.

Cookies made with honey or fruit may be made a month ahead and stored in an airtight container to mellow.

Rum-Pecan Meltaways

During baking the surfaces of these sweet, tender cookies take on a crackled texture. Storing the cookies for a day or two in a covered tin allows the flavor to develop.

2	cups flour	1/2	teaspoon vanilla
1	teaspoon baking powder	2	tablespoons dark rum
1/2	teaspoon cream of tartar	1	egg yolk
1/2	cup butter, softened	2/3	cup pecan halves
1/4	cup shortening		(approximately)
2	cups confectioners' sugar		

In a bowl, stir together flour, baking powder, and cream of tartar to combine thoroughly; set aside. In mixer bowl combine butter and shortening; beat until fluffy. Add confectioners' sugar and beat until well blended. Stir in vanilla and rum, then egg yolk. Gradually add flour mixture, beating until well combined. Refrigerate about 3 hours. Shape dough into 1-inch balls. Place about 1-1/2-inches apart on ungreased cookie sheets. Flatten each cookie slightly with your fingertips; press a pecan half into the center. Bake in a 375 degree oven for 10 to 12 minutes until cookies are lightly browned and feel firm when touched gently. Let stand for about 2 minutes on cookie sheets, then transfer to wire racks to cool. Makes about 40 cookies.

Polish Pastries

Bet you've never made a more tender cookie.

1/2	pound cream cheese	1/4	cup raspberry or apricot
1	cup soft butter		preserves
2	cups sifted flour		nutmeats
	confectioners' sugar		

Mix cheese and butter; add flour and blend well. Chill overnight in refrigerator. Roll about 1/8-inch thick on cloth-covered board which has been sprinkled generously with confectioners' sugar. Cut into 3-inch squares. Cut through each point of each square leaving about 1-inch uncut in center; wet center with tip of finger dipped in water. Turn every other point toward center, pressing down well. Bake on baking sheets in a preheated 375 degree oven for about 12 minutes. Cool slightly; put 1/2 teaspoon of preserves in center of each pastry. Frost with confectioners' sugar frosting. Sprinkle pastries with chopped nutmeats. Makes 2 dozen.

Butter Crunch Confection-Cookies

Cut these 1/2-inch thick and serve with whipped cream as a delicious dessert.

1	package dates (8-ounce) chopped	1	can (4-ounce) coconut, toasted
1/2	cup water		Butter Crunch

Cook dates in water until thick. Cool. Fold in 2-1/4 cups Butter Crunch and toasted coconut. Roll into cylinder (2-inches wide). Roll in rest of Butter Crunch to coat outside. Refrigerate several hours or overnight. Slice about 1/4-inch thick for cookies. Makes 2 to 3 dozen cookies.

Butter Crunch:

1	cup butter or margarine	1	cup flour
1/4	cup brown sugar, packed	1/2	cup pecans or walnuts

Mix all ingredients with hands. Spread in ungreased oblong pan, 13 by 9-1/2 by 2-inch. Bake at 400 degrees for about 15 minutes. Take from oven; stir with spoon. Cool. Makes 2-1/2 cups.

Petticoat Tails

Extra rich and buttery - pretty for a tea party.

2	cups butter or margarine	2	teaspoons vanilla
2	cups sifted confectioners' sugar	4-1/2	cups flour
		1/2	teaspoon salt

Mix butter, sugar, and flavoring thoroughly. Mix flour and salt; stir in. Mix with hands. Mold in rolls about 2-inches across. Wrap in waxed paper; chill several hours or overnight. Cut slices about 1/8-inch thick. Place a little apart on ungreased baking sheet. Bake in a 400 degree oven for about 8 to 10 minutes, or until lightly browned. Makes about 10 dozen.

Coconut Shortbread Cookies

A buttery melt in your mouth coconut dream.

2	cups butter, room temperature	4	cups flour
1	cup sugar	1/2	cup flaked coconut
2	teaspoons vanilla		powdered sugar

In mixing bowl, combine butter, sugar and vanilla. Beat until well blended. Add flour gradually and beat until blended. Stir in coconut. Divide dough into 2 portions. Place each portion on sheet of waxed paper and roll into cylinder about 2-inches in diameter. Wrap in waxed paper. Chill 24 hours. Cut into 1/4-inch thick slices. Place on ungreased cookie sheet. Bake at 325 degrees for 15 minutes. Roll in powdered sugar while still warm. Makes about 9 dozen cookies.

Pecan Delights

Cookies topped with a dab of frosting and a pecan on top. What could be easier!

1/2	cup margarine	1/2	teaspoon baking soda
1	cup brown sugar	1/2	teaspoon cream of tartar
1	egg	1/4	teaspoon salt
1/4	teaspoon vanilla	1/2	cup chopped pecans
2	cups flour		nuts for decorations

Cream margarine and brown sugar until fluffy. Beat in egg and vanilla. Sift dry ingredients together and add to egg mixture in fourths. Mix well after each addition. Fold in nuts. Divide dough in half. Shape into 2 rolls. Wrap each in waxed paper. Chill. Slice thin onto ungreased cookie sheets. Bake in a 375 degree oven about 8 to 10 minutes. Cool. Frost with topping and press pecan half in center of each.

Pecan Delights Topping:

3	tablespoons butter, room temperature	1-1/2	tablespoons milk
1	cup confectioners' sugar	1/2	teaspoon vanilla

Beat confectioners' sugar with soft butter, with spoon. Add as much milk as needed to make frosting hold its shape when dropped from a spoon. Stir in vanilla. From tip of spoon, drop about 1/2 teaspoon of topping in center of each cookie. Press a pecan half into icing. Do not spread over cookie.

Marble Refrigerator Cookies

These are so pretty! But please, don't let them get brown.

1	cup butter	1	tablespoon corn syrup
1	teaspoon vanilla	2-1/2	cups flour
1	cup sifted confectioners' sugar	1	teaspoon salt
			food coloring

Cream butter, vanilla and confectioners' sugar well. Add corn syrup. Blend in dry ingredients. Divide dough in 4 parts. Color 1 part red, 1 yellow, and 1 green by adding 4 drops of food coloring to each part. Blend the color in each dough thoroughly with hands. Leave the fourth portion uncolored. Mix the 4 colors together carefully so each colored dough is mixed in but still distinctive. Make into rolls 2-inches in diameter. Place in refrigerator to stiffen. When cold, cut with a sharp knife into 1/8-inch slices. Place on cookie sheets. Bake in a 375 degree oven 8 to 10 minutes. Makes about 5 dozen cookies.

Swedish Chocolate Pinwheels

Always have a batch of these in your freezer to add to your cookie tray.

1-1/2	cups sifted flour	1	egg yolk
1/2	teaspoon baking powder	3	tablespoons milk
1/8	teaspoon salt	1	ounce unsweetened chocolate, melted and cooled
1/2	cup butter		
1	cup sugar		

Sift flour, baking powder and salt together. Cream well, add sugar, gradually and continue creaming until light and fluffy; add unbeaten egg yolk and beat well. Add sifted dry ingredients alternately with milk, mixing just enough after each addition to combine ingredients. Divide dough into 2 equal parts. To one part, add chocolate and mix well. Chill both doughs in refrigerator. Roll plain dough into a rectangle, 8 by 16-inches, on floured pastry cover. Roll chocolate dough into a rectangle of the same size. Place the chocolate dough on the plain dough and roll as for jellyroll (it should be about 1-1/4-inches in diameter). Chill in refrigerator overnight. Slice thin and bake on baking sheets in a 425 degree oven for 5 minutes. Store in covered container. Makes about 8 dozen.

Cinnamon Icebox Cookies

If you like cinnamon, you can't go wrong with these.

3	cups sifted flour	1	cup sugar
1/2	teaspoon baking powder	1/2	cup light brown sugar, firmly packed
1/2	teaspoon baking soda		
1/4	teaspoon salt	1/2	cup buttermilk
1	tablespoon cinnamon	1	cup finely chopped pecans or unblanched almonds
1/2	cup soft butter or margarine		

Sift flour with baking powder, baking soda, salt and cinnamon; set aside. In large bowl, with wooden spoon, or electric mixer at medium speed, beat butter until light. Gradually beat in sugars until light and fluffy. At low speed, beat in buttermilk until smooth. Gradually beat in half of flour mixture. Mix in rest with hands, to form a stiff dough. Add nuts, mixing to combine well. On lightly floured surface, divide dough in half. With hands, shape each half into a roll 7-inches long. Wrap each roll in plastic or foil; refrigerate until firm, about 8 hours, or overnight, before slicing and baking. Preheat oven to 375 degrees. With a sharp knife, cut in slices. Place slices 2-inches apart, on ungreased cookie sheets. Bake 8 to 10 minutes, or until golden. Remove to wire rack; cool. Makes about 9 dozen.

When decorating cookies, keep all bits of candied fruit, colored sugars, nuts, etc. in muffin pans or paper cups.

Aristocrats

They are a two-in-one treat; nut or chocolate dough, formed into a log, is encased in vanilla dough and rolled in sugar. The thin sliced cookies reveal their pattern, which always charms guests.

14	tablespoons unsalted butter, softened	1-1/2	ounces bittersweet chocolate, finely minced
2/3	cup sugar		coarse sugar or
2	eggs		decorating sugar or
1	teaspoon vanilla		crushed sugar cubes
2-1/2	cups flour		for coating
1/3	cup finely minced almonds or pecans		

Cream butter and sugar until light. Add 1 egg and vanilla. Beat well. Add flour and blend. Divide dough in half; enclose one-half in waxed paper or plastic wrap and refrigerate. Divide other half in half again. Add almonds to one part, kneading to blend well; add chocolate to other part and knead to blend well. With your lightly floured hands, roll each part into a 10-inch long log. On a lightly floured board, roll refrigerated dough into a 9-inch by 11-inch rectangle. Beat remaining egg and lightly brush on dough. Cut dough in half to make 2 rectangles, each 4-1/2-inches by 11-inches. Position nut log in center of 1 rectangle and chocolate log in center of other. Wrap logs securely with plain dough, pressing seams together and sealing ends. Lightly brush each log all over with beaten egg; roll in coarse sugar. Wrap each log in aluminum foil; refrigerate several hours. Cut each log into 36 slices. Place, about 1-inch apart, on ungreased cookie sheets. Bake at 400 degrees for about 10 minutes or until bottoms are lightly browned. Transfer to wire racks to cool. Store in airtight containers. Makes about 6 dozen.

Peanut Butter Pillows

Peanut butter is sandwiched between 2 butter icebox cookies. They are crisp; the filling is soft.

1-1/2	cups sifted flour	1/2	cup granulated sugar
1/2	teaspoon baking soda	1/4	cup light corn syrup
1/4	teaspoon salt	1	tablespoon milk
1/4	pound butter		additional peanut butter
1/2	cup smooth (not chunky) peanut butter		for filling (a scant 1/2 cup)

Cream the butter. Add the peanut butter and sugar and beat until thoroughly mixed. Beat in the corn syrup and the milk. Blend in sifted dry ingredients and beat only until smooth. Turn the dough out onto a large board and knead it briefly and then, with your hands, form it into an even roll or oblong about 7-inches long and 2-1/4 to 2-1/2-inches in diameter. Wrap the dough in wax paper. Refrigerate overnight. With a sharp knife cut half of the roll of dough into slices 1/8-inch thick. Place slices 2-inches apart on unbuttered cookie sheets. Place 1 level measuring teaspoonful of the additional peanut butter in the center of each cookie. Then spread the peanut butter only slightly to flatten it, leaving 1/2 to 3/4-inch border. Slice the remaining half of the roll of dough and as you cut each slice, place it over one of the peanut-butter-topped cookies. Then seal the edges by pressing them lightly with the back of the tines of a fork, dipping the fork in flour as necessary to keep it from sticking. Bake at 350 degrees for 12 to 15 minutes. Bake until the cookies are lightly colored, then let stand on the sheet for about a minute. Transfer them to racks to cool. Makes about 16 to 20 pillows.

Almond Icebox Cookies

Cookies keep well and improve with age.

4	cups sifted flour	1	cup sugar
3	teaspoons cinnamon	1	cup dark brown sugar, firmly packed
1	teaspoon ginger		
1/2	teaspoon salt	3	extra large or jumbo eggs
1	teaspoon baking soda		
1/2	pound butter	8	to 10 ounces (2-1/2 to 3 cups) blanched and thinly sliced almonds
2	teaspoons instant coffee		
1/2	teaspoon almond extract		

Sift together the flour, cinnamon, ginger, salt, and baking soda and set aside. In the large bowl of an electric mixer, cream the butter. Add the coffee, almond extract, and both sugars and beat well. Add the eggs one at a time, beating until smooth after each addition. On low speed gradually add the sifted dry ingredients, scraping the bowl with a rubber spatula and beating only until smooth. The dough will be very stiff. It may be mixed using your hand at the end. Mix in almonds with your bare hands, divide dough in half. Shape each half of dough into a smooth oblong 12-inches long, 3-inches wide, and about 1-inch thick. Wrap the dough in waxed paper. Refrigerate overnight. Also can be frozen.

Note:
This slices better when it is frozen solid. Unwrap 1 roll of dough at a time. Place it on a cutting board. With a very sharp knife, cut the dough into 1/4-inch slices and place them 1 to 1-1/2-inches apart on ungreased cookie sheets. Bake at 350 degrees for about 12 minutes, reversing the position of the sheets top to bottom and front to back as necessary to insure even browning. Cookies are done when they are slightly colored and spring back if lightly pressed. Transfer to racks to cool. Makes about 90 cookies.

Icing won't become grainy if a pinch of salt is added to the sugar.

Orange-Flavored Snails

Anyone with memories of making butter and cinnamon tarts with their mother's leftover pie dough will enjoy these.

1-1/2	cups flour	1	egg
1/3	cup confectioners' sugar	1	tablespoon water
1	stick plus 1 tablespoon butter, cold, cut into pieces		

Put flour, confectioners' sugar, and butter in a food processor fitted with a steel blade until the mixture resembles coarse meal. Add egg with machine running, add tablespoon water by drops just until the dough starts to gather into a ball. Do not over process. Wrap dough in plastic wrap and refrigerate 2 hours.

Filling:

2	cups almonds	2	tablespoons finely grated orange zest
2/3	cup sugar, plus additional for coating	1/2	teaspoon almond extract

Place almonds, 2/3 cup sugar, orange zest and almond extract in food processor. Blend to a coarse paste. Divide dough in half and roll out each half on a floured surface into a rectangle about 1/8-inch thick. Sprinkle almond filling evenly over the dough rectangles. Using a rolling pin, press filling firmly into the dough. Roll up the dough like a jellyroll, starting from a long edge and rolling as tightly as possible. Freeze the rolls on trays overnight so that they will be easier to slice. Preheat oven to 350 degrees. Lightly grease cookie sheets. Cut the roll with a sharp knife into 1/4-inch slices and place on cookie sheets. Bake for 8 to 10 minutes. Immediately remove the cookies to wire racks to cool. When cooled to room temperature, roll each cookie in a shallow bowl of sugar to coat evenly. Makes about 4 dozen cookies.

Note:
The cookies may be made in the traditional way.

Ribbon Cookies

Why not make several batches of ribbon cookies, to freeze or refrigerate for an encore.

2-1/2	cups flour	1	ounce unsweetened chocolate, melted
1-1/2	teaspoons baking powder		
1/2	teaspoon salt	1/3	cup finely chopped pistachio nuts or diced toasted almonds
1	cup butter, softened		
1-1/2	cups sugar		
1	large egg	3	drops green food coloring
1	teaspoon vanilla		
1/4	cup red maraschino cherries, well drained and chopped		

Combine first 7 ingredients in a large mixing bowl. Mix at low speed until a dough forms, 2 to 3 minutes. Divide dough into 3 parts. Add cherries to one part, chocolate to second and nuts and food coloring to third. Line a 9 by 5-inch pan with waxed paper or foil. Place dough in pan in 3 layers. Cover; chill overnight. Remove from pan. Cut in lengthwise strips. Then cut each strip into 1/4-inch slices. Place on ungreased cookie sheets. Bake at 400 degrees for 8 to 10 minutes. Makes about 84 cookies.

Sugared Sherry Fingers

A glass of sherry with sherry cookies, a great combination.

1-1/2	cups flour	1/4	cup sugar
1/4	teaspoon salt	3-1/2	tablespoons medium-dry sherry
1	stick cold butter, cut into bits		
1/4	cup packed light brown sugar	1	large egg, beaten lightly sugar

Into a bowl sift together the flour and the salt. Cut in the butter, bit by bit, until the mixture resembles coarse meal. Stir in the brown sugar, sugar, and the sherry, and form the dough into a ball. Chill the dough, wrapped in plastic wrap overnight. On a lightly floured board roll out the dough 1/8-inch thick and cut into 2-1/2 by 1-inch fingers, re-rolling and cutting the scraps. Prick the fingers decoratively with a fork, brush them with the egg, and sprinkle them lightly with the additional sugar. Transfer the fingers with a spatula to a buttered baking sheet and bake them in the middle of a preheated 375 degree oven for 15 minutes, or until they are golden. Transfer the cookies immediately to a rack and let them cool. Makes about 36 cookies.

Simple Sesame Slices

The long slow baking makes these extra crunchy. A buttery sliced cookie with a delightful sesame flavor. A taste that's really different.

2	cups butter, room temperature	2	cups shredded coconut
1-1/2	cups sugar	1/2	cup finely chopped almonds
3	cups flour	1/2	cup sliced almonds
1	cup sesame seeds		

In a large bowl, cream butter. Gradually add sugar and continue beating until light and fluffy. Add flour and mix just until combined. Stir in sesame seeds, coconut and chopped almonds just until well mixed. Divide dough in thirds. Place 1 piece of dough on a long sheet of waxed paper. Shape in a long roll 2-inches in diameter. Press 1/3 of sliced almonds on top of roll. Repeat with remaining dough. Wrap and refrigerate overnight. Preheat oven to 300 degrees. Cut each roll in twenty-four 1/4-inch slices; place on ungreased baking sheets. Bake in preheated oven 25 to 30 minutes or until edges are golden brown and cookies are set. Cool 1 minute. Carefully remove cookies to wire racks to cool. Makes about 72 cookies.

Butter Nut Cookies

A delicate short cookie, perfect for holiday parties.

1	cup butter, softened	1-1/2	cups sifted flour
1	cup powdered sugar	1/2	teaspoon baking soda
1	teaspoon vanilla	1	cup quick-cooking oats
1/2	teaspoon almond flavoring	1	cup walnuts, finely chopped

Preheat oven to 325 degrees. In a mixing bowl, combine butter and powdered sugar with a wooden spoon or sturdy beater, then add vanilla and almond flavoring. Sift together flour and baking soda. Mix in well, along with oats. Refrigerate several hours. Roll dough into small balls the size of a marble; about 3/4-inch wide. Place chopped walnuts on a sheet of wax paper. Place balls on chopped nuts and flatten with a table fork to about 1-1/2-inches. Slide each cookie off fork onto an ungreased baking sheet, walnut side up, about an inch apart. Bake 15 minutes. Makes about 9 dozen.

Sugar Crisps

Flaky, tender, sugared twists that can be served as a cookie or dessert, serve at a tea or afternoon coffee.

1	package yeast	2	eggs, beaten
1/4	cup very warm water	1/2	cup sour cream
3-1/2	cups sifted flour	1	teaspoon vanilla
1-1/2	teaspoons salt	1-1/2	cups sugar
1/2	cup butter or margarine	2	teaspoons vanilla
1/2	cup shortening		

Soften yeast in warm water. Sift flour and salt into a mixing bowl. Cut in butter and shortening until particles are the size of small peas. Blend in eggs, sour cream, 1 teaspoon vanilla and softened yeast. Mix thoroughly. Cover; chill overnight. Combine the sugar, 2 teaspoons vanilla. Roll out half of chilled dough on pastry cloth which has been sprinkled with about 1/2 cup of the vanilla sugar. Roll out to a 16 by 8-inch rectangle. Sprinkle with about 1 tablespoon more vanilla sugar. Fold end of dough over center. Fold other end over to make 3 layers. Turn 1/4 way around and repeat rolling and folding twice, sprinkling board with additional vanilla sugar as needed. Roll out to a 16x8-inch rectangle about 1/4-inch thick. Cut into 4 by 1-inch strips. Twist each strip 2 or 3 times. Place on ungreased baking sheets. Repeat process with remaining dough and vanilla sugar. Bake at 375 degrees for 15 to 20 minutes until light golden brown. Makes 5 dozen.

Danish Sugar Cookies

Crisp, sugary edges and a ground almond dough make these special.

1	cup sugar	1	teaspoon vanilla
1/2	cup butter, cut into pieces	1	cup flour
1/2	cup whole blanched almonds, finely ground		sugar

Place the 1 cup sugar in a large bowl; cut in butter with a pastry blender or 2 knives until mixture forms fine particles. Stir in almonds and vanilla. Blend in flour, mixing with your hands if necessary, until well combined. Shape dough into a roll 1-1/2-inches in diameter. Sprinkle a little sugar (1 to 2 tablespoons) on a sheet of wax paper; then place roll of dough on paper and wrap snugly, coating outside of roll with sugar. Refrigerate until firm (at least 2 hours) or for up to 3 days. Unwrap dough. Using a sharp knife, cut into 1/8-inch thick slices. Place slices slightly apart on ungreased baking sheets. Bake in a 375 degree oven for about 8 to 10 minutes or until lightly browned. Let cool on baking sheets for about a minute, then transfer to racks and let cool completely. Makes about 5 dozen.

Striped Cookies

A gift of these cookies will bring pleasure to your friends.

2-1/2	cups sifted cake flour	1	egg
1	teaspoon baking powder	1	tablespoon milk
1/2	teaspoon salt	1	square unsweetened chocolate, melted
1/2	cup butter or margarine		milk
2/3	cup sugar		

Sift flour with baking powder and salt. Cream butter. Gradually add sugar. Beat until light and fluffy. Add egg and milk. Blend well. Add flour mixture, a small amount at a time, beating well after each addition. Divide dough in half. Blend chocolate into one half. If necessary chill or freeze both parts of dough until firm enough to roll. Roll each portion of dough on a lightly floured board into a 9 by 4-1/2-inch rectangle. Brush chocolate dough lightly with milk and top with plain dough. Using a long, sharp knife, cut rectangle lengthwise in 3 equal strips 1-1/2-inches wide. Stack strips, alternating colors, brushing each layer with milk and pressing together lightly. Carefully wrap in waxed paper. Freeze until firm enough to slice, or chill overnight in refrigerator. Cut into 1/8-inch slices, using a very sharp knife. Place on greased baking sheets. Bake at 400 degrees for 6 to 8 minutes or just until white portions begin to brown. Makes about 5-1/2 dozen.

Black And White Slices

Jaunty stripes of vanilla and chocolate-flavored dough give these little squares a festive appearance.

1/2	cup butter	1/8	teaspoon salt
1/2	cup sugar	3	tablespoons milk
1	egg yolk	1/2	teaspoon vanilla
1-1/2	cups flour	1	square unsweetened chocolate, melted
1-1/2	teaspoons baking powder		

Cream butter and sugar together. Add egg yolk and beat well. Add sifted dry ingredients alternately with milk and vanilla; blend in thoroughly after each addition. Divide dough in half; take 1 tablespoon dough from one half and add to the other half. Stir chocolate into smaller portion of dough, blending until well combined. Shape each portion of dough into a roll 1-1/2-inches in diameter. Wrap each roll in plastic wrap. Flatten sides to make square logs. Refrigerate overnight. Unwrap dough. Using a sharp knife, slice each log lengthwise into fourths. Then reassemble logs, using 2 dark slices and 2 light slices for each, alternating colors to make stripes. Gently press layers together to eliminate interior pockets. Cut logs crosswise into 1/8-inch slices (if layers start to separate, refrigerate until dough is firmer). Place slices about 1-inch apart on greased cookie sheets. Bake in a 350 degree oven for about 10 minutes. Transfer to rack to cool. Makes about 4 dozen.

Lemon-Pecan Wafers

Here's a good summertime cookie. Though rich with butter and nuts, it has a refreshing, lemony sparkle.

1/2	cup butter or margarine, softened	1	tablespoon lemon juice
1	cup sugar	2	cups flour
1	egg	1/8	teaspoon salt
1	tablespoon grated lemon peel	1	teaspoon baking powder
		1	cup chopped pecans

Beat butter and sugar until creamy; beat in egg, lemon peel, and lemon juice. Stir together flour, salt, and baking powder; gradually add to butter mixture, blending thoroughly. Stir in pecans, mixing with your hands if necessary to distribute nuts evenly. Shape dough into 2 rolls, each 1-1/2-inches in diameter; wrap in wax paper and refrigerate until firm (at least 2 hours) or for up to 3 days. Unwrap dough. Using a sharp knife, cut into 1/8-inch thick slices; place slices about 1-inch apart on greased baking sheets. Bake in a 350 degree oven for about 12 minutes or until edges are lightly browned. Transfer to racks and let cool. Makes about 6 dozen wafers.

Spiced Almond Thins

A crisp spice wafer with an appealing old-fashioned flavor.

1	cup butter or margarine, softened	1/2	teaspoon nutmeg
1	cup firmly packed brown sugar	1/4	teaspoon baking soda
		1/4	cup sour cream
2	cups flour	1/2	cup slivered blanched almonds
2	teaspoons cinnamon		

In the large bowl of an electric mixer, beat butter and sugar until creamy. In another bowl, stir together flour, cinnamon, and nutmeg. Stir baking soda into sour cream; add to butter mixture alternately with flour mixture, blending thoroughly. Stir in almonds until well combined. Shape dough into a 2-1/2-inch thick rectangular log; wrap in wax paper and refrigerate until firm (at least 2 hours) or for up to 3 days. Unwrap dough. Using a sharp knife, cut into 1/8-inch thick slices; place slices about 1-inch apart on ungreased baking sheets. Bake in a 350 degree oven for about 10 minutes or until golden brown. Let cool for about a minute on baking sheets, then transfer to racks and let cool completely. Makes about 5 dozen.

Pecan Turtles

These turtles are sure to beat the competition.

1/2	cup butter	1-1/4	cups sifted flour
1/3	cup brown sugar, packed	1/4	teaspoon soda
1	egg	1/4	teaspoon salt
1/4	teaspoon maple extract		large pecans
1/4	teaspoon vanilla	1	egg white, unbeaten

Cream butter; add sugar; beat in egg and extracts. Blend in sifted dry ingredients. Chill overnight. Place clusters of 3 pecans on greased cookie sheets. Shape dough into 1-inch balls. Dip 1 side of ball into egg white; place on cluster of pecans; flatten slightly. Bake at 350 degrees for about 12 minutes. Frost with Glossy Chocolate Frosting.

Glossy Chocolate Frosting:

1-1/2	squares unsweetened chocolate	2	egg yolks
1/2	cup butter	1	teaspoon vanilla
6	tablespoons powdered sugar		

Melt chocolate. Cool slightly. Cream butter. Add powdered sugar and egg yolks. Blend. Add vanilla and chocolate.

Black Walnut Charms

An apple butter and cream cheese filling make these cookies extra tasty.

1-1/2	cups flour	1	egg
1/2	teaspoon salt	1/4	cup butter, melted
1	cup firmly packed brown sugar	1/4	cup shortening, melted
		1	teaspoon vanilla

Beat egg until thick, blend in butter, shortening and vanilla. Mix well. Sift together flour and soda. Stir in brown sugar. Add dry ingredients gradually blending well. Chill 4 hours, drop by teaspoonfuls onto lightly greased cookie sheets; flatten slightly. Top with half teaspoon filling. Bake at 375 degrees for 9 to 11 minutes.

Apple Butter Filling:

3	or 4 ounces cream cheese	3	tablespoons apple butter
		1/4	cup chopped black walnuts

Combine ingredients and mix well.

Chocolate Nut Refrigerator Cookies

Pretty to look at, great to eat, what more could you ask for?

1-1/4	cups butter	1	cup finely chopped walnuts
1-1/2	cups powdered sugar		
1	egg	2	4-ounce bars sweet chocolate, melted
3	cups sifted cake flour		
1/2	cup cocoa		chopped walnuts for topping
1/4	teaspoon salt		

Cream butter; add sugar gradually; beat in egg. Blend in flour, cocoa and salt, chill several hours. Shape dough into 4 rolls, 1-1/2-inches in diameter. Roll shaped dough in 1 cup chopped walnut slices. Place on ungreased cookie sheets. Bake at 375 degrees for about 8 minutes. Cool; frost with melted chocolate; sprinkle with chopped walnuts, which may be tinted green. Makes about 10 dozen.

Scotch Scones

Guess these get their name from the few ingredients used.

3	tablespoons light brown sugar powdered sugar	1 2	cup butter cups sifted flour

Place brown sugar in 1-cup measure. Fill cup with powdered sugar. Cream butter. Add sugar gradually. Cream well. Add flour. Mix well. Form into 2-inch rolls about 5 or 6-inches long. Place in refrigerator overnight. Cut into slices. Place on greased cookie sheets. Bake at 375 degrees about 10 to 12 minutes. Makes about 4 dozen.

Oatmeal Refrigerator Cookies

Nice and chewy, with a molasses-lemon tang.

1/2	cup soft shortening	1-1/2	tablespoons molasses
1/2	cup sugar	1/2	teaspoon vanilla
1/2	cup brown sugar, packed	1	cup sifted flour
1	egg	1/2	teaspoon soda
1-1/2	teaspoons grated lemon rind	1/2	teaspoon salt
		1-1/2	cups rolled oats

Mix thoroughly, shortening, sugars, egg, grated lemon rind, molasses and vanilla. Sift together and stir in flour, soda and salt. Add rolled oats and mix thoroughly with hands. Press and mold into a long, smooth roll about 2-1/2-inches in diameter. Wrap in waxed paper, and chill until stiff (several hours). With thin sharp knife, cut in thin slices 1/8 to 1/16-inch thick. Place slices a little apart on ungreased baking sheet. Bake until lightly browned. Bake at 400 degrees for about 8 to 10 minutes. Makes about 4 dozen 2-1/2-inch cookies.

Store bar cookies right in the baking pan. Tightly covered with foil.

Malted Milk Rounds

Malted milk in cookies and frosting makes a delicious cookie.

4	cups flour	2	cups brown sugar, packed
3/4	cup malted milk powder	2	eggs
2	teaspoons baking powder	1/3	cup sour cream
1/2	teaspoon soda	2	teaspoons vanilla
1/2	teaspoon salt		Malt Frosting
1	cup butter or margarine		

Blend first 5 ingredients thoroughly. Cream butter; gradually add sugar. Blend in eggs; beat well. Add half the blended dry ingredients; mix thoroughly. Add sour cream and vanilla; stir in remaining dry ingredients. Chill overnight. Divide dough and roll 1/4-inch thick on well-floured pastry cloth. Cut with 2-1/2-inch cutter. Bake in a 375 degree oven for about 12 to 15 minutes on ungreased baking sheets. Cool about 2 minutes. Remove to racks. Cool; frost tops with Malt Frosting. Makes 5 dozen cookies.

Malt Frosting:

1/2	cup brown sugar, packed	1/2	teaspoon vanilla
1/4	cup butter or margarine	3	cups sifted confectioners' sugar
1/4	cup milk or cream		
1/3	cup malted milk powder (plain)		

Heat brown sugar, butter, and milk in a saucepan until sugar is melted. Remove from heat; stir in malted milk powder and vanilla. Blend in confectioners' sugar gradually until right consistency.

Chocolate Shot Cookies

Rolled in jimmies make these extra nice.

1-1/2	cups sifted flour	2	teaspoons vanilla
1/2	teaspoon baking soda	1	cup oatmeal
1	cup butter	1/2	cup jimmies or chocolate shot
1	cup sifted confectioners' sugar		

Mix and sift flour and soda. Cream butter well, add sugar gradually and continue creaming until light and fluffy. Add vanilla and mix well. Add oatmeal and mix. Add sifted dry ingredients gradually and mix. Form dough into a roll about 2-inches in diameter. Wrap in waxed paper and chill thoroughly in refrigerator. Coat side of roll with chocolate jimmies. Slice about 3/8-inch thick and bake on baking sheets in a 325 degree oven for about 22 minutes. Makes about 2-2/3 dozen.

Chocolate Tweed Cookies

Sprinkles not only outline each of these cookies but are also dotted throughout the crisp fabric of the cookies.

1-1/3	cups flour	1/2	cup firmly packed brown sugar
1/2	teaspoon baking powder	1/2	teaspoon vanilla
1/4	teaspoon salt	1	egg yolk
1/2	cup butter or margarine, softened	1/2	cup finely chopped walnuts
1/4	cup shortening	3/4	cup chocolate sprinkles
1/2	cup sugar		

Beat shortening, butter and sugars until light and fluffy. Beat in vanilla and egg yolk. Gradually add dry sifted ingredients, beating until just blended. Stir in walnuts and 1/4 cup of the chocolate sprinkles. Spread 1/4 cup of the remaining chocolate sprinkles on a piece of waxed paper or plastic wrap. Divide dough in half. Transfer half to the chocolate-sprinkled paper; shape into a 1-1/2-inch diameter log evenly coated with sprinkles. Repeat with remaining chocolate sprinkles and cookie dough. Wrap each log tightly and refrigerate overnight. Remove one roll of cookie dough at a time from refrigerator and cut cookies into 1/4-inch thick slices. Arrange slices about 1-inch apart on ungreased cookie sheets. Bake at 350 degrees until cookies are golden brown and feel firm when touched lightly, about 9 to 11 minutes. Let stand on cookie sheets for about 2 minutes, then transfer to wire racks to cool. Makes about 54 cookies.

Banana Whirls

A banana caramel filling in an almond flavored slice. What a treat.

3-1/4	cups sifted flour	1/2	cup brown sugar, firmly packed
1	teaspoon salt		
1/2	teaspoon soda	1/2	cup sugar
1-1/2	teaspoons cinnamon	2	eggs, unbeaten
1/2	cup shortening	1/2	cup almonds, finely chopped
1/2	cup butter		

Sift together dry ingredients. Cream shortening and butter. Gradually add brown sugar and sugar creaming well. Add the eggs; beat well. Blend in dry ingredients. Stir in almonds. Chill dough while preparing filling. Divide dough into 3 parts. Roll out 1 part on a sheet of floured foil to a 13 by 8-inch rectangle. Spread with 1/3 of filling. Roll as for jellyroll, starting with a 13-inch side. Wrap in foil and chill overnight. Repeat with remaining dough. Cut into 1/4-inch slices and place on greased baking sheets. Bake in a 375 degree oven 10 to 14 minutes until golden brown. Makes 4 dozen cookies.

Caramel Banana Filling:

1/4	cup butter	1/4	teaspoon salt
1/3	cup brown sugar, packed	2	medium bananas, mashed
1	cup quick cooking oats		

Melt butter in saucepan. Remove from heat. Stir in brown sugar, oats and salt. Stir in mashed bananas; chill 15 minutes.

Cherry-Cream-Cheese Slices

Chopped maraschino cherries lend a pastel pink tint and almond flavor to the dough of these appealing cookies.

1-1/2	cups flour	3/4	cup sugar
1-1/4	teaspoon baking powder	1	teaspoon vanilla
1-1/4	teaspoon baking soda	1	egg yolk
1/8	teaspoon salt	1/2	cup chopped maraschino cherries
1/2	cup butter or margarine, softened		
1	small package (3-ounce) cream cheese, softened		

In mixer combine butter and cream cheese; beat to blend well. Add sugar and beat until fluffy. Blend in vanilla and egg yolk. Gradually add sifted dry ingredients beating until just blended. Stir in cherries. Divide dough in half. Transfer each half to a sheet of waxed paper or plastic wrap. Using a spatula and the paper, shape each half into a 2-inch diameter log. Wrap each log tightly. Refrigerate overnight. Preheat oven to 350 degrees. Carefully slice logs into 1/4-inch thick slices; arrange slices, about 1-inch apart, on lightly greased baking sheets. Bake until cookies brown lightly, about 10 to 12 minutes. Transfer to wire racks to cool. Makes about forty-two 2-inch cookies.

Rich butter or meringue type cookies are best when baked several days before using.

Notes

Molded Cookies

*Years ago when I was small
and holidays drew near,
our kitchen was a special place
for planning christmas cheer.*

Powdered Sugar Cookies

How about starting a cookie sale at your child's school, with these tender morsels?

1/2	cup shortening	1/8	teaspoon salt
1/2	cup margarine	1	scant teaspoon baking soda
1	egg		
1	teaspoon vanilla	1	scant teaspoon cream of tartar
1	cup confectioners' sugar		
2	cups sifted flour		

Blend shortening, margarine, egg, and vanilla then add dry ingredients. Roll into balls, and bake on a greased cookie sheet in a 400 degree oven for 12 minutes. Makes 24 cookies.

Frosted Melting Moments

We all make melting moments - Now try this better than ever one.

1	cup butter	3/4	cup cornstarch
1/3	cup powdered sugar	1/8	teaspoon salt
1/4	teaspoon almond extract	1	cup sifted flour

Cream butter. Add sugar gradually. Add almond extract. Blend in sifted dry ingredients. Chill. Shape level teaspoonfuls of dough into balls. Place on ungreased cookie sheets. Bake at 375 degrees about 10 minutes. Cool. Makes about 6 dozen.

Frosting:

2	tablespoons butter	cream
1	cup powdered sugar	red and green food coloring
1/2	teaspoon vanilla	
1/4	teaspoon almond extract	

Melt butter in saucepan. Remove from heat. Stir in sugar and flavorings. Add cream to make frosting of spreading consistency. Tint half of frosting a delicate pink, other half green. Frost cookies.

Sugar Cookies

A real "Oldie" mom made for many years, satisfies every one's taste.

1/2	cup butter	2-1/4	cups flour
1/2	cup shortening	1/2	teaspoon baking powder
1	cup sugar	1/2	teaspoon baking soda
1	egg		additional sugar
1	teaspoon vanilla		

In mixing bowl, cream butter, shortening and sugar. Add egg and vanilla; mix well. Combine flour, baking powder and baking soda; gradually add to the creamed mixture. Shape into 1-inch balls. Roll in sugar. Place on greased cookie sheet; flatten with a glass. Bake at 350 degrees for about 10 to 12 minutes. Makes about 5 dozen.

Note:
Add cardamom or nutmeg to batter, if desired.

Lauren's Sugar Cookies

The taste everyone looks for in a sugar cookie.

1/2	cup sugar	1/2	teaspoon baking soda
1/2	cup powdered sugar	1/2	teaspoon cream of tartar
1/2	cup butter, softened	1/4	teaspoon salt
1/2	cup light oil	1/4	to 1/2 cup sugar
1	large egg		
2	cups plus 2 tablespoons flour		

Beat together the 2 sugars, butter and oil until creamy. Beat in egg. Combine flour, baking soda, cream of tartar, and salt with a whisk. Thoroughly blend into sugar and butter mixture. Place 1/4 to 1/2 cup sugar in a small bowl. Shape dough into 1-inch balls and roll in sugar to coat. Place 3 to 4-inches apart on ungreased cookie sheets. Using a small, flat-bottomed glass, flatten each ball to about 1/4-inch thickness, dipping glass in the sugar each time. Bake at 375 degrees until edges are lightly browned; about 10 to 12 minutes. Transfer cookies to racks to cool.

Cinnamon Sugar Butter Cookies

Spicy flavor and crunchy texture blend to make an all time favorite.

2-1/2	cups flour	1/2	cup white sugar
1/2	teaspoon baking soda	1	cup butter, softened
1/4	teaspoon salt	2	large eggs
1	cup dark brown sugar, packed	2	teaspoons vanilla

Sift together flour, soda and salt. In a large bowl blend sugars. Add the butter, and mix to form a grainy paste. Add the eggs and vanilla. Mix at medium speed until light and fluffy. Add the flour mixture and blend at low speed just until combined. Shape dough into 1-inch balls and roll each ball in cinnamon-sugar topping. Place on ungreased cookie sheets, 2-inches apart. Bake in a 300 degree oven for 18 to 20 minutes. Makes 3 dozen.

Topping:

3	tablespoons white sugar	1	tablespoon cinnamon

Combine ingredients in a small bowl.

Short 'nin' Bread

As the song states - All God's children love "Short 'nin Bread".

4	cups flour	1	egg yolk
1	cup light brown sugar	1	tablespoon water
1	pound butter		

Preheat oven to 325 degrees. Mix the flour and sugar. Cut the butter in slices over the flour mixture and work it in with your fingertips until blended into a paste. Pat on a floured surface to a thickness of 1/2-inch. Cut into squares and place on ungreased baking sheets. Paint each square with egg yolk blended with the water. Bake 20 to 25 minutes. Makes about 4 dozen.

Cardamom Butter Cookies

Cardamom is a ginger like spice used in Scandinavian baking.

2	cups cake flour	1/2	cup sliced almonds
1/8	teaspoon salt	6	tablespoons powdered sugar
3/4	cup butter, room temperature		sliced almonds
1/2	cup sugar		
5-1/2	teaspoons ground cardamom		

Preheat oven to 375 degrees. Grease cookie sheets. Combine flour and salt. Using electric mixer, beat butter, 1/2 cup sugar and 4 teaspoons ground cardamom until fluffy. Add flour mixture and beat at low speed. Stir in 1/2 cup sliced almonds. Combine powdered sugar and remaining 1-1/2 teaspoons ground cardamom in small bowl. Roll 1 tablespoon cookie dough into a ball. Roll in powdered sugar mixture to coat well. Place on prepared cookie sheet. Dip bottom of small glass into powdered sugar mixture and press cookie to 1/2-inch thickness with bottom of glass. Press 3 slices of almonds decoratively onto cookie. Repeat with remaining dough, powdered sugar and sliced almonds, spacing cookies at least 1-inch apart on sheets. Bake until cookies are light brown, about 14 minutes. Let cookies stand on sheets for 3 minutes. Transfer to rack and cool completely. Makes about 26 cookies.

Mix and Match Cookie Tarts

Why not make all 3. Excellent variety of tastes.

Crust:

1-1/2 cups sifted cake flour	3 ounces cream cheese
dash of salt	2 tablespoons milk
1/2 cup butter	

Mix flour and salt; cut in butter and cheese until particles are about the size of small peas. Sprinkle milk on flour mixture gradually and mix just enough to make particles stick together. Shape into a ball and divide into 2 parts. Refrigerate half while working with other part. Divide each half into 24 pieces; pat into muffin pans, 1-3/4 by 1-inch deep. Put about 2 teaspoons of desired filling into each. Bake in a preheated 400 degree oven about 20 minutes.

Nut-Coconut Filling:

1-1/3 cups flaked coconut
1-1/3 cups sweetened condensed milk
1 cup chopped nuts

Mix ingredients. Makes 2 cups for 48 tarts.

Almond Filling:

1-1/3 cups sweetened condensed milk
2/3 cup almond paste

Gradually add milk to almond paste to make a smooth mixture. Makes 2 cups for 48 tarts.

Coconut or Lemon-Coconut Filling:

1-1/3 cups flaked coconut
1-1/3 cups sweetened condensed milk
1/2 cup lemon juice, optional

Mix ingredients. Sprinkle top of cookies with additional coconut, if desired. Makes 2 cups for 48 tarts.

Kris Kringles

Norwegians are known for putting cardamom in their baked goods. It's a refreshing change of taste.

1/2	cup soft butter or margarine	1/4	to 1/2 teaspoon ground cardamom
1/2	cup sugar	1	tablespoon grated lemon peel
3	hard-cooked egg yolks, sieved	2	cups sifted flour
1	raw egg yolk	1	egg white

Preheat oven to 375 degrees. Lightly grease cookie sheets. In medium bowl, with wooden spoon, beat butter, sugar, egg yolks, cardamom, and lemon peel until well combined. Stir in flour; mix with hands to blend thoroughly. Dough will be stiff. Divide dough into 2 parts. On lightly floured surface roll out each part into a 7 by 6-inch rectangle. Cut each rectangle in half lengthwise; then cut crosswise into 12 strips. You will have 48 strips. With palms of hands, roll each strip 4-inches long. Form each into a ring; pinch ends together, to seal. Place on prepared cookie sheets, 1-inch apart. Brush with egg white beaten with 1 tablespoon water.

Topping:

1/2	cup chopped blanched almonds	2	tablespoons sugar

Combine almonds with sugar. Sprinkle over tops of cookies. Bake cookies about 10 to 12 minutes, or until golden-brown. Remove to wire rack; cool. Makes about 4 dozen.

Kringla

Pretzel shaped cookie from Norway.

1-1/2	cups sugar	4	cups sifted flour
1	egg, beaten	2	teaspoons soda
2-1/2	cups sour cream	1/4	teaspoon salt

Heat oven to 350 degrees. Mix sugar, egg, and cream. Mix flour, soda, and salt; blend thoroughly into cream mixture. Divide dough in half; form each half into a long roll. Refrigerate 1 roll until ready to use. Cut off a narrow slice of dough. Roll lightly with hands on lightly floured board into pencil-like strip 7 to 8-inches long. Form a modified figure 8 by pinching ends together tightly; bring pinched ends to center of the ring; tuck under, fastening securely. Place on lightly greased baking sheet. Repeat with remaining dough. Bake 12 to 15 minutes, or until lightly golden. Makes about 6 to 7 dozen cookies.

Frosted Cookie Canes

These frosted cookie canes are a favorite with youngsters everywhere.

1	cup butter	1/4	teaspoon salt
1/2	cup powdered sugar	2	cups flour
1	teaspoon vanilla	1/4	teaspoon baking powder

Cream butter; add sugar gradually; blend in vanilla, salt and sifted dry ingredients. Shape level teaspoonfuls of dough into pencil-like strips. Turn one end to resemble a cane and place on greased cookie sheets. Bake at 350 degrees about 10 minutes; frost when cool. Makes about 6 dozen.

Peppermint Frosting:

	cream	1/4	teaspoon peppermint extract
1-1/2	cups powdered sugar		
1	teaspoon vanilla		red food coloring

Add enough cream to sugar to make frosting of spreading consistency; add vanilla and peppermint extract. Divide in half; color one-half red. Decorate canes with alternate stripes of red and white.

Norwegian Christmas Wreaths

Make wreaths for your cookie exchange, always a winner.

2	hard-cooked egg yolks	1	cup soft butter
3	raw egg yolks	2	egg whites, slightly beaten
1	cup sugar	1/2	pound sugar cubes, ground
2-3/4	to 3 cups sifted flour		

Press hard-cooked yolks through a sieve. Beat well with raw yolks. Beat in sugar. Add flour alternately with butter to form a smooth soft dough. Refrigerate for 4 hours. Form pencil-thin strips about 6-inches long. Shape into wreaths, or circles, about 1-1/2-inches in diameter. Dip face of each wreath in beaten egg white, then into ground sugar. Place on ungreased cookie sheet. Bake at 400 degrees about 7 to 10 minutes, or until slightly browned. Makes about 80.

Berliner Kranze

Delicious and buttery, gay little wreaths.

1-1/2	cups butter	4	cups sifted flour
1	cup sugar	1	egg white
2	teaspoons grated orange rind	2	tablespoons sugar
2	eggs		red candied cherries
			green citron

Mix butter, 1 cup sugar, rind, and eggs thoroughly. Stir in flour. Chill dough. Heat oven to 400 degrees. Break off small pieces of dough and roll to pencil size about 6 inches long and 1/4-inch thick. (If rich dough splits apart or seems crumbly, let it warm or work in a few drops of liquid until the dough sticks together.) From each piece into a circle, bringing one end over and through in a single knot. Leave 1/2-inch end on each side. Place on ungreased baking sheet. Beat egg white until frothy; gradually beat in 2 tablespoons of sugar; brush tops with this meringue. Press bits of red candied cherries on center of knot for holly berries. Add little jagged leaves cut out of green citron. Bake about 10 to 12 minutes, or until set but not brown. Makes about 6 dozen 2-inch cookies.

Lemon Peel Sugar Cookie

An interesting tender sugar cookie with just a subtle hint of lemon.

2	cups sugar	3-1/4	cups flour
1	cup butter	1	teaspoon salt
1	tablespoon grated lemon peel	1	teaspoon baking soda
1/4	cup lemon juice	1	teaspoon cream of tartar
1	teaspoon vanilla		sugar
2	eggs		

In large bowl, blend first 6 ingredients until smooth. Stir in flour, salt, soda, and cream of tartar. Chill 1 hour. Preheat oven to 325 degrees. Form dough into 1-inch balls; roll each in sugar. Place 2-inches apart on a greased cookie sheet. Bake 15 to 20 minutes until light golden brown. (Cookies will be soft in center.) Cool 2 minutes; remove from cookie sheets. Makes 4 to 5 dozen cookies.

Orange Sun Bursts

The delicate orange flavor is followed through in the topping.

2-1/2	cups sifted flour	2	eggs
1	teaspoon baking powder	2	tablespoons orange juice
1	teaspoon baking soda	1	tablespoon grated orange rind
1/2	teaspoon salt		pecan halves, optional
3/4	cup butter		
3/4	cup sugar		

Mix and sift flour, baking powder, soda and salt. Cream butter, add sugar gradually and cream until fluffy; add eggs, one at a time, and beat well after each addition. Add juice and rind and mix. Add sifted ingredients gradually and mix just enough to combine ingredients. Using about 1 teaspoon per cookie, shape into balls; place on ungreased cookie sheet. Indent top of each cookie and add 1/4 teaspoon topping; then add a pecan half, if desired. Bake in a 400 degree oven about 8 minutes. Makes about 7 dozen.

Topping:

3/4	cup sugar	2-1/2	tablespoons orange juice (approximately)

Mix ingredients.

Cinnamon Almond Cookies

Wicker basket and Christmas ornaments make an attractive holiday setting for the popular cinnamon almond cookies.

1	cup butter	1/2	teaspoon baking soda
1/2	cup sugar	1	teaspoon cinnamon
1/2	cup brown sugar, packed	1	egg white
1	egg		sugar
1	teaspoon vanilla		blanched almonds
2	cups sifted flour		

Cream butter; add sugars gradually. Beat in egg and vanilla; blend in sifted dry ingredients; refrigerate. Shape dough into balls 1-inch in diameter and place on ungreased cookie sheets. Flatten slightly with bottom of glass covered with a damp cloth. Brush top of cookies with slightly beaten egg white; sprinkle with sugar; press an almond into cookie. Bake at 350 degrees about 12 minutes. Makes about 7 dozen.

Nut Strudel

A melt in your mouth pastry like cookie with a sugary nut filling.

1	8 ounce package cream cheese, softened	1	cup sugar
1/2	cup butter	1/3	cup milk
2	cups flour	1/2	pound ground nuts
			powdered sugar

Beat cream and butter until well combined. Add flour and mix well. Shape into a ball. Cover and chill dough for 1 to 2 hours. Roll out dough on a lightly floured surface to form an 18 by 12-inch rectangle. Cut lengthwise into 2 strips. Spread each with nut filling. Starting from long side, roll up each strip, jellyroll fashion. Cut rolls crosswise in half to fit on baking sheets. Place, seam side down, on ungreased cookie sheets. Cut into generous 1/2-inch thick slices without separating. Bake in a 350 degree oven for 15 to 20 minutes. Let cool slightly. Remove. Cool on wire racks. Dust with confectioners' sugar. Separate slices into individual cookies. Cover and refrigerate or freeze. Makes about 60 cookies.

Filling:

In a saucepan, cook sugar and milk over medium heat until the sugar dissolves, stirring occasionally. Stir in nuts. Remove from heat; cool until spreadable.

Molded Brown Sugar Cookies

A decorative cookie, great for a child's party.

1	cup light brown sugar	1	teaspoon vanilla
3	tablespoons corn syrup	1/2	cup butter, slightly softened
1/8	teaspoon salt		
1	large egg	2-2/3	cups flour

Mix sugar, syrup, egg and salt together. Let stand 5 minutes. Add butter and mix gently until smooth. Stir in flour. Refrigerate overnight. Brush speculas or ceramic molds with vegetable oil. Sprinkle with flour to coat evenly. Tap out excess flour. Break off a piece of dough and press firmly into mold. Keep dough cold. The cookie should be no thicker than mold. Tap mold firmly on counter top to loosen cookies. Tap it out on greased cookie sheet. Continue to mold rest of cookies. Be sure to re-flour molds after every cookie is removed. Place cookies 2-1/2-inches apart on baking sheet. Bake in a 350 degree oven for 10 to 14 minutes. Let cookies stand for several minutes before removing from cookie sheets. Store in airtight containers or freeze. Makes 8 large 6-inch cookies.

Tea Time Tassies

Versatile bite-size pastries. Vary the filling to suit your taste.

1	(3-ounce) package cream cheese	1	egg, slightly beaten
1/2	cup butter	1/2	cup chopped pecans
1	cup flour	1	tablespoon butter, melted
3/4	cup brown sugar, packed		dash of salt

Combine softened cream cheese and 1/2 cup butter. Cut in flour with pastry blender until mixture resembles coarse crumbs. Divide pastry into 24 portions. Press onto bottom and sides of greased miniature 2-inch muffin pans. Combine remaining ingredients. Fill cups half full. Bake at 350 degrees for 15 minutes reduce heat to 250 degrees continue baking for 10 minutes. Makes about 24 tassies.

Almond Crescents

Be sure to have copies of this recipe handy for your guests.

1	cup butter	2-1/2	cups sifted flour
3/4	cup sugar	1/8	teaspoon salt
4	hard-cooked egg yolks, sieved	1	egg white, slightly beaten
2	raw egg yolks	1/3	cup finely chopped almonds
2	teaspoons grated lemon rind	1/2	cup sugar
		1-1/4	teaspoons cinnamon

Cream butter; add 3/4 cup sugar gradually; beat in egg yolks and lemon rind. Blend in flour and salt. Chill. Shape level teaspoonfuls of dough into crescents. Dip into egg white, then roll in combined almonds, 1/2 cup sugar and cinnamon. Place on greased cookie sheets. Bake at 350 degrees about 14 minutes. Allow to stand on cookie sheet 1 minute before removing. Makes about 9 dozen.

Hazelnut Puff Balls

How easy these are! Icing and cookie in 2 easy steps.

4	egg whites	1/2	pound grated hazelnuts (3 cups)
1	pound powdered sugar	1	teaspoon grated lemon rind

Beat egg whites until stiff but not dry. Add sugar gradually; beat 5 minutes. Divide in half, use one-half for icing; set aside. Blend hazelnuts and lemon rind into one-half of mixture. Dip hands in powdered sugar; shape dough into small balls; place on greased cookie sheets; make a depression in center of each ball. Fill with icing; swirl top. Bake at 325 degrees for 15 to 18 minutes. Makes 7 to 10 dozen depending on size.

For a thinner, crisper rolled cookie try rolling the dough directly onto a greased and lightly floured cookie sheet. Cut the cookies out then pick up the scrap dough.

Hazelnut Sugar Dusties

People who like the distinctive flavor of hazelnuts always love these rich, tender cookies.

2/3	cup hazelnuts, ground	1	egg
3/4	cup unsalted butter, slightly softened	1/8	teaspoon salt
		1-3/4	cups flour
1/3	cup sugar	1/3	cup powdered sugar

Place butter in a large mixing bowl and beat with an electric mixer on medium speed until light and fluffy. Add sugar and continue beating until thoroughly incorporated and smooth. Beat in egg yolk and salt. Stir in hazelnuts. Gradually beat in the flour. Stir in the last of the flour with a wooden spoon. Pull off small pieces of dough and shape into 1-inch balls. Place on greased cookie sheets about 1-inch apart. Bake at 325 degrees for 15 to 17 minutes or until just barely brown at the edges. Remove cookie sheets from the oven and let stand for 1 to 2 minutes. Transfer cookies to wire racks and let stand until completely cooled. Place powdered sugar in a shallow bowl and dredge cooled cookies in sugar until coated all over. Store in airtight container for up to a week. If freezing cookies for longer storage, freeze before dredging in sugar. Allow to thaw and dredge just before serving. Makes about 45 cookies.

Rum Bubbles

Um! Good!

2-1/4	cups sifted flour	1	egg
3/4	teaspoon baking soda	1-1/2	teaspoons rum flavoring
3/4	teaspoon cream of tartar	39	candied cherries or nutmeats
3/4	cup butter		
1-1/4	cups sifted confectioners' sugar		

Mix and sift flour, soda and cream of tartar. Cream butter well, add sugar gradually and continue creaming until light and fluffy. Add egg and rum flavoring and mix well. Add sifted dry ingredients gradually and mix. Using 1 tablespoon dough for each cookie, shape into a ball. Place balls on baking sheet and flatten with spatula. Press a candied cherry or nutmeat in center of each. Bake in a 375 degree oven for about 13 minutes. Store in airtight container. Makes about 3-1/4 dozen.

Nutmeg Butter Balls

An almond meltaway cookie.

1-1/3 cups blanched almonds	2 cups flour
1 cup butter	1/2 cup confectioners' sugar
1/2 cup confectioners' sugar	2 teaspoons nutmeg
1 teaspoon vanilla	

Chop almonds fine. Cream butter and sugar until light and fluffy. Blend in vanilla and almonds. Add flour and mix well. Chill dough. Shape into balls the size of walnuts. Place on greased cookie sheets. Bake in a 250 degree oven about 15 to 20 minutes. Combine confectioners' sugar and nutmeg and roll cookies in this mixture while hot. When cool, roll in sugar mixture again. Makes 6 dozen cookies.

Holiday Hats

A tray of these are just as pretty at Easter time - use pastel candies for decorations.

1 cup butter	1/4 teaspoon nutmeg
1/2 cup powdered sugar	1/8 teaspoon salt
1/2 teaspoon almond extract	apricot preserves
1 cup sifted flour	candied cherries
1 cup cornstarch	citron

Cream butter; add sugar gradually; blend in extract. Sift flour, cornstarch, nutmeg and salt together; blend into creamed mixture; chill. Shape 2/3 of dough into 1-inch balls. Place on ungreased cookie sheets. Flatten with bottom of glass dipped in sugar. Make slight depression in center of each cookie. Place scant 1/4 teaspoonful preserves in each depression. Shape remaining 1/3 of dough into small balls; place on top of preserves. Decorate with pieces of cherries and citron. Bake in a 375 degree oven for about 12 minutes, depending on size. Makes about 3-1/2 dozen.

Coconut Surprises

Divide dough in 3 and have 3 surprises - Nuts, Dates and Cherries.

1	cup butter	1-1/2	cups pecan halves (approximately)
1/2	cup sugar		
2	teaspoons vanilla	1	cup flaked coconut, chopped (approximately)
2	cups sifted flour		
1/4	teaspoon salt		

Cream butter; add sugar gradually; blend in vanilla and sifted dry ingredients. Wrap level teaspoonfuls of dough around pecan halves, then roll in coconut. Place on greased cookie sheets. Bake at 325 degrees about 15 minutes or until lightly browned. Makes about 7 dozen.

Note:
Whole blanched almonds, dates or candied cherries may be substituted for pecans.

Lemon Angel Halos

These halo nests taste like they really came from Heaven.

2	cups sifted flour	1	teaspoon vanilla
1	teaspoon salt	1	egg
1	teaspoon baking soda	3	egg whites
2/3	cup shortening	3/4	cup sugar
1	cup brown sugar, firmly packed	2	teaspoons lemon juice
		1/4	teaspoon lemon filling

Sift dry ingredients. Cream shortening and brown sugar well. Add vanilla and egg. Beat well. Blend in dry ingredients; mix thoroughly. Chill while preparing meringue and filling. Beat egg whites until foamy; add sugar gradually, beating thoroughly after each addition until meringue stands in heavy lustrous peaks when beater is raised. Blend in lemon juice, continue beating until meringue forms stiff peaks again. Roll chilled dough in balls, using 1 level teaspoonful of dough for each ball. Place on ungreased cookie sheets. Flatten to 1/8-inch thickness. Place 1 rounded teaspoonful of meringue on each cookie. Hollow the center of each with back of teaspoon dipped in cold water. Bake in a 300 degree oven for 10 to 12 minutes until cream colored. When cool fill each meringue "nest" with 1/4 teaspoon Lemon Filling.

Lemon Filling:

3	egg yolks	1	teaspoon grated lemon rind
1	cup sugar		
1/4	cup lemon juice	3	tablespoons butter

Mix above ingredients. Heat to boiling, stirring constantly. Remove from heat, add butter; cover and cool.

Adding a pinch of salt to chocolate frosting will enhance the flavor.

Butter Nut Drops

When you need something extra special for guests or family, these drops are just the thing.

1/2	cup shortening	1	teaspoon grated orange rind
1/4	cup sugar		
1	egg, separated	1-1/4	cups sifted flour
1/2	teaspoon vanilla	3/4	cup finely chopped nuts
2	tablespoons evaporated milk	14	candied cherries, halved
1	teaspoon grated lemon rind		

Cream shortening and sugar together. Combine egg yolk, vanilla, milk and rinds. Add to first mixture and beat well. Add flour, mix thoroughly and chill. Shape into patties with a tablespoon and dip into slightly beaten egg white. Dip 1 side into nuts, place nut-side up on greased baking sheet, place cherry on each and bake in a 325 degree oven for 20 minutes. Makes 24 drops.

Scandinavian Drops

These add color, plus good taste to your cookie tray.

1/2	cup butter	1	cup sifted flour
1/4	cup firmly packed light brown sugar	1	egg white
		3/4	cup chopped nuts
1	egg yolk		red or green jelly

Cream butter. Add sugar gradually. Add egg yolk. Beat until light. Blend in flour. Roll dough into small balls about 1-inch in diameter. Beat egg white slightly with a fork. Dip cookies in egg white. Roll in chopped nuts. Place on greased cookie sheets. Make a depression in the center of each ball. Bake at 300 degrees for about 15 minutes. Remove from oven. Press down centers again. Bake for 30 to 35 minutes longer. Cool. Fill center with jelly. Candied cherries, small pieces of candied apricot or prune may be used. Makes about 2 dozen drops.

Coconut Pennies

These are rich, crisp cookies.

2	cups sifted flour	1/2	teaspoon almond extract
3/4	teaspoon baking powder	1	cup dark brown sugar, firmly packed
1/8	teaspoon salt		
1/4	teaspoon cinnamon	1	egg
1/4	teaspoon nutmeg	2	cups shredded coconut, packed
1	cup butter		
1	teaspoon vanilla extract		

Sift together the flour, baking powder, salt, cinnamon, and nutmeg and set aside. In the large bowl of an electric mixer, cream the butter. Add the vanilla and almond extracts and the sugar and beat to mix well. Beat in the egg. On low speed, gradually add the sifted dry ingredients, scraping the bowl with a rubber spatula and beating only until incorporated. Mix in the coconut, and refrigerate for about 1-1/2 to 2 hours. Cut the dough into quarters. Work with 1 piece at a time.   On a floured board, with floured hands, form the dough into a roll 15-inches long. Cut the roll into 1-inch pieces. (Or use a slightly rounded tablespoonful of the dough for each cookie.) Keeping your hands lightly floured, roll each piece into a ball. Place the balls 2-inches apart on an ungreased cookie sheet. With the back of the tines of a floured fork, press each cookie in 1 direction only to form indentations and flatten the cookie to 1/3-inch thickness. Bake about 10 minutes at 375 degrees, until cookies are lightly colored. The cookies will be slightly darker at the edges. With a spatula, transfer cookies to racks to cool. Makes about 60 cookies.

Orange Coconut Crisps

These crisp cookies combine coconut with a subtle touch of orange for extra-tempting flavor.

1	cup butter or margarine	1-1/2	cups flour
1	cup sugar	1	cup cornstarch
1	egg	1	teaspoon baking powder
1	teaspoon grated orange peel	1/4	teaspoon salt
1	teaspoon vanilla	1-1/3	cups flaked or shredded coconut

In the large bowl of an electric mixer, beat butter and sugar until creamy; beat in egg, orange peel, and vanilla. In another bowl, stir together flour, cornstarch, baking powder, and salt. Gradually add to butter mixture, blending thoroughly. Add coconut and mix until well combined. Cover dough tightly with plastic wrap and refrigerate for about 2 hours. Roll dough into 1 to 1-1/4-inch balls and arrange about 2-inches apart on greased baking sheets. With tines of a fork, flatten each ball to a thickness of about 1/4-inch. Bake in a 375 degree oven for about 8 to 10 minutes or until lightly browned. Let cool for about a minute on baking sheets, then transfer to racks and let cool completely. Makes about 4 dozen.

Frosty Date Balls

A little confection for your cookie tray.

1/2	cup soft butter or margarine	1	teaspoon vanilla
1/3	cup confectioners' sugar	1-1/4	cups flour
1	tablespoon water	2/3	cup dates, chopped
		1/2	cup walnuts, chopped

Cream butter and sugar and stir in water and vanilla. Add flour and mix. Stir in dates and walnuts. Roll into balls or drop onto ungreased cookie sheet. Bake at 300 degrees for about 20 minutes, until set but not brown. Roll in confectioners' sugar. Makes about 2-1/2 dozen.

Crunchy Coconut Cookies

Tender little balls rolled in coconut, turn out to be beautiful toasted morsels.

3/4	cup sifted flour	3/4	cup sugar
1/2	teaspoon salt	1	egg
1-1/4	cup oatmeal	3/4	teaspoon vanilla
1/2	cup butter	3/4	cup chopped coconut

Mix and sift flour and salt; add oatmeal and mix. Cream butter well, add sugar gradually and continue creaming until light and fluffy; add well beaten egg and vanilla and mix well. Add flour mixture gradually and mix. Chill thoroughly in refrigerator. Form into small balls, using 1 tablespoon dough for each ball, and roll each in chopped coconut. Place on greased cookie sheets. Bake in a 300 degree oven for about 25 minutes. Store in covered container. Makes about 3 dozen.

Senoritas

These are crisp, crunchy, and chewy with toasted chopped almonds and a butterscotch flavor.

1	cup blanched almonds, coarsely chopped	1/2	teaspoon vanilla scant 1/2 teaspoon almond extract
3	cups sifted flour		
1	teaspoon baking soda	1	cup granulated sugar
1/2	teaspoon cream of tartar	1	cup dark brown sugar, firmly packed
1/2	teaspoon salt		
3/4	cup butter	2	eggs

Toast almonds in a preheated 400 degree oven for about 8 minutes. Sift together dry ingredients. In large bowl of electric mixer cream the butter and flavorings; gradually add both sugars and beat well. Add the eggs and beat well. Gradually add the sifted dry ingredients and beat only until thoroughly mixed. Stir in the cooled toasted almonds. Use a heaping teaspoonful of the dough for each cookie. Roll into balls and place them at least 2-inches apart on a slightly greased cookie sheet. Bake for 10 minutes. When the 10 minutes are up the cookies will still feel soft, but they harden as they cool and if are baked any longer they will become too hard. They should remain slightly soft and chewy in the centers. Transfer the cookies to racks to cool. Makes about 48 cookies.

Coconut Washboards

Make a double batch of these. The men in your life are bound to make them disappear.

2	cups sifted flour	1/2	teaspoon vanilla
3/4	teaspoon baking powder	1	cup light brown sugar
1/2	teaspoon baking soda	3-1/2	cups shredded coconut
1/8	teaspoon salt	1	egg
1/2	cup butter	2	tablespoons water

Sift dry ingredients. Cream butter, add vanilla and brown sugar and cream well. Add egg and water. Stir in dry ingredients and coconut. Mix well. Cut a piece of wax paper to fit a large cookie sheet. Use a heaping teaspoon of dough for each cookie. Place them close together on wax paper and refrigerate to chill. Cut foil to fit a large cookie sheet. Flour hands and pick up round of dough and roll into a 3-inch roll using hands. Place cookies 3-inches apart on foil. Flatten with fingers until 1/4-inch thick, 3-1/2-inches long and 2-inches wide. Dip a fork into flour and press with tines of fork to form indentations. Ridge should be parallel lengthwise of cookies. Bake in 375 degree oven for about 12 minutes. Do not under-bake. Let stand a few minutes and transfer to rack to cool. Makes about 30 cookies. Freezes well.

Gold Cookies

Cinnamon flavor makes these cookies taste real different.

1/2	cup butter	1-1/2	cups sifted flour
1-1/2	cups sugar	1/2	teaspoon baking powder
4	egg yolks	1/4	teaspoon salt
2	tablespoons milk	3/4	cup finely chopped nuts
1	teaspoon vanilla	2	teaspoons cinnamon

Cream together butter and sugar. Add egg yolks, milk and vanilla and beat well. Sift together the dry ingredients and add to creamed mixture. Chill. Roll dough into balls the size of walnuts and roll in combined sugar and cinnamon mixture. Place 3-inches apart on an ungreased cookie sheet. Bake in a 400 degree oven about 12 to 14 minutes. Makes about 60 cookies.

Princess Delights

Spicy Tender Cookies.

1	cup shortening	2-1/2	cups sifted flour
1/2	cup butter	2	teaspoons baking powder
1	cup sugar	2	teaspoons vanilla
1	cup brown sugar, packed	1	cup moist coconut, coarsely chopped
1	teaspoon salt		

Cream shortening and butter. Add sugars gradually. Blend in dry ingredients. Add vanilla and coconut and mix well. Shape level teaspoonfuls of dough into balls. Place on ungreased cookie sheet. Bake at 325 degrees 20 to 25 minutes. Roll in spiced powdered sugar. Makes about 11 dozen cookies.

Spiced Powdered Sugar:

1	cup powdered sugar	1/4	teaspoon cinnamon
1/4	teaspoon nutmeg		dash of white pepper

Combine all ingredients.

Holiday Bon Bons

How can anything this pretty taste so good?

1/2	cup finely chopped walnuts	1/8	teaspoon salt
1	cup ground dates	1/3	cup sugar
1/2	teaspoon vanilla	1/2	teaspoon vanilla
1	egg white		red and green food coloring

Combine nuts, dates and vanilla. Form into balls, using a scant 1/2 teaspoon of the mixture for each. Refrigerate mixture thoroughly. Beat egg white and salt until stiff, adding sugar gradually. Add vanilla. Divide egg white mixture in half. Tint 1 portion pink and the other green. Remove balls from refrigerator. Coat balls with meringue. Use 1 or 2 teaspoons of meringue for each ball. Swirl tops. Bake on greased cookie sheets in a 250 degree oven for about 1/2 hour. Makes about 4 to 5 dozen.

Meltaway Maple Crisps

These have a delicate maple flavor.

1/2	cup butter	2	cups sifted cake flour
1/4	cup sugar	3/4	cup chopped pecans
1	teaspoon maple flavoring		

Cream butter; add sugar gradually. Add flavoring and beat until fluffy. Stir in flour and mix until a dough forms. Fold in pecans and press into a ball. Pinch off small pieces of dough and place on ungreased cookie sheet. Flatten cookies with finger or glass dipped in sugar. Bake at 350 degrees for about 7 minutes.

Maple Rice Crisp Cookies

When you want to please your children, make these cookies flavored with maple flavoring as a special treat.

1-3/4	cups sifted flour	1	cup sugar
3/4	teaspoon baking soda	1	cup presweetened rice cereal
1	teaspoon cinnamon		
1/4	cup milk	1/2	cup chopped nuts
1	egg, beaten	1-1/2	cups presweetened rice cereal for rolling cookies
1	teaspoon maple flavoring		
1/2	cup shortening		

Combine flour, soda, salt and cinnamon. Combine milk, egg and flavoring. Cream shortening and sugar until light and fluffy. Add dry ingredients and liquids alternately 1/2 at a time. Stir only until dry ingredients are moistened. Fold in cereal and nuts carefully. Roll rounded teaspoonfuls of cookie dough in additional presweetened rice cereal. Place on greased cookie sheet and bake in 350 degree oven for about 15 minutes. Remove from cookie sheet; cool. Makes 42 cookies.

Sandies

A little ball of butter and confectioners' sugar that melts in your mouth.

1	cup butter or margarine	1	tablespoon water
1/4	cup confectioners' sugar	2	cups flour, sifted
2	teaspoons vanilla	1	cup nuts, finely chopped

Cream butter and sugar. Add vanilla and water. Mix in sifted flour and nuts. Roll dough into small balls the size of a walnut. Bake for 25 minutes at 300 degrees. Roll in confectioners' sugar while still hot. Makes about 2 dozen balls.

Parisian Orange Cookies

These are crisp like a sugar cookie, however it has a chewy like quality.

2	tablespoons coarsely grated orange rind	1	tablespoon sherry flavoring
1/2	cup water	1-1/4	cups sifted flour
1/4	cup sugar	1	tablespoon baking powder
1/2	cup butter or margarine	1/2	teaspoon salt
1	cup sugar		

Blend orange rind, water, and 1/4 cup sugar in saucepan; boil gently over medium heat for 10 to 15 minutes, until mixture is thin syrup consistency. Add enough water to make 1/4 cup syrup. Cream butter, 1 cup sugar, and flavoring until fluffy. Blend in dry ingredients. Stir syrup, then dry ingredients into creamed mixture; mix thoroughly. Roll in 1-inch balls. Place 2-inches apart on lightly greased baking sheet. Flatten with bottom of greased glass dipped in sugar. Bake in a 375 degree oven for about 8 minutes. Makes about 4-1/2 dozen cookies.

Peanut Butter Kisses

Children love to eat these easy to do cookies with a chocolate kiss hidden inside.

1-2/3	cups flour	2/3	cup powdered sugar
1/3	cup cornstarch	1/3	cup dark brown sugar
1/2	teaspoon baking powder	1	large egg
1/2	teaspoon baking soda	2	teaspoons vanilla
1/2	cup margarine	40	chocolate kisses
1/3	cup peanut butter		

Beat together butter and peanut butter until light. Add powdered sugar and brown sugar; beat well. Beat in egg and vanilla. Add dry ingredients, mix well, but do not over-mix. Roll dough into 1-1/4-inch balls. Press a chocolate kiss, flat side down, deep into center of each ball. Mold dough around kiss, leaving 1/4-inch of kiss tip showing. Place on greased baking sheet. Bake 9 to 11 minutes in a 350 degree oven. Makes about 40 cookies.

Brown Eyed Susans

Pretty as can be with the dab of chocolate frosting in center.

1	cup butter	2	cups sifted flour
3	tablespoons sugar		glossy chocolate frosting
1	teaspoon almond extract		blanched almonds
1/4	teaspoon salt		

Cream butter. Add sugar, almond extract and salt. Blend in flour. Shape level tablespoonfuls of dough into balls. Place on greased cookie sheets. Flatten to 1/4-inch thickness with bottom of glass dipped in flour. Bake at 400 degrees 10 to 12 minutes. Cool. Place 1/2 teaspoonful of frosting in center of cookies. Top with almonds. Makes about 3 dozen.

Anise Butter Cookies

These buttery cookies are extra special with the anise flavoring.

1	cup butter	1/4	teaspoon salt
1/2	cup sugar	2	cups sifted flour
1/2	teaspoon crushed anise seed		sugar for rolling red and green candied cherries
1	teaspoon vanilla		

Cream butter; add sugar gradually; mix in anise seed, vanilla and salt. Blend in flour. Shape into 1-inch balls; roll in sugar. Place on greased cookie sheets. Flatten slightly with bottom of glass dipped in sugar. Decorate with cherries. Bake at 375 degrees 12 to 14 minutes. Makes about 5 dozen.

Danish Dandies

What better way to use up all those egg yolks.

8	hard-cooked egg yolks	1	teaspoon vanilla
1	cup butter	1/2	teaspoon almond extract
3/4	cup sugar	2	cups sifted flour
1/2	teaspoon salt		granulated sugar

Press hard-cooked egg yolks through a sieve. Cream butter and sugar; beat in egg yolks. Blend in salt, extracts and flour. Shape into 1-inch balls. Place on greased cookie sheets; press with tines of fork dipped in sugar. Bake at 400 degrees about 10 minutes or until lightly browned. Makes 60 cookies.

Sesame Cookies

Try these for a different taste.

1-1/2	cups sifted flour	1	egg
1	teaspoon baking powder	3/4	teaspoon vanilla extract
1/4	teaspoon salt	3	tablespoons sesame seeds
1/2	cup butter		angelica
6	tablespoons sugar		

Mix and sift flour, baking powder and salt. Cream butter well, add sugar gradually and continue creaming until light and fluffy; add well beaten egg and extract and beat well. Add sifted dry ingredients and mix. Using about 2 teaspoons dough for each cookie, shape into a flat round and press down on sesame seeds on a plate. Then place seed-side-up on baking sheets and press a small strip of angelica on the center of each cookie. Bake in a 350 degree oven about 11 to 13 minutes. Makes about 3 dozen cookies. Store in a covered container.

Little Gems

Pretty as a picture.

3	cups flour	2	egg yolks
1	cup sugar	1	teaspoon vanilla
1/8	teaspoon salt		strawberry preserves
1-1/2	cups unsalted butter (room temperature), cut in pieces		pecan halves

Line baking sheets with parchment paper. Combine first 3 ingredients using an electrical mixer. Cut in butter until mixture resembles coarse meal. Beat yolks with vanilla and add to flour mixture. Beat until mixture is completely blended. Pinch off pieces of dough about 3/4 teaspoon each and roll into balls. Place on baking sheets. Using your finger, make a round indentation in the center of each ball. Place about 1/8 teaspoon preserves in each and top with pecan half. Bake until light brown, in a 325 degree oven for about 20 to 25 minutes.

Coconut Pompons

Hide a pecan in center of cookie for a nice surprise.

1	cup margarine	1/4	teaspoon salt
1/2	cup sugar	1/2	pound pecan halves
2	teaspoons vanilla		chopped, shredded
2	cups sifted flour		coconut

Cream together margarine, sugar and vanilla until light and fluffy. Sift together flour and salt. Add to creamed mixture and blend thoroughly. Shape dough around pecan halves to form into 1-inch balls. Roll in shredded coconut. Place on an ungreased baking sheet. Bake in a 325 degree oven for about 20 minutes. Remove to wire rack to cool. Makes about 6 dozen cookies.

Chinese Almond Cookie

Making the cookies with a combination of butter and lard brings together the best quality of each ingredient - the flavor of butter and the tender crispness that lard imparts to pastry.

2	cups flour	1	teaspoon almond extract
1/2	teaspoon baking powder	1/2	teaspoon vanilla extract
1/2	cup butter or margarine, softened	2	egg yolks
1/2	cup lard, softened	1/3	cup (approximately) blanched almonds
1	cup sugar	2	teaspoons water

In mixer bowl combine butter and lard; beat until fluffy. Add sugar and beat until well combined. Blend in almond and vanilla extracts, then 1 egg yolk. Add sifted dry ingredients. Beating until well combined. Shape dough into 1-inch balls. Place about 1-1/2-inches apart on lightly greased baking sheets. Slightly flatten each cookie with your fingertips; press an almond into center. In small bowl beat remaining egg yolk with the 2 teaspoons water until blended. Lightly brush top of each cookie with egg yolk mixture. Bake in a 350 degree oven for 10 to 12 minutes until cookies are golden brown. Let stand on baking sheets for 1 to 2 minutes, then transfer to wire racks to cool. Makes about forty-two 2-inch cookies.

Glazed Almond Cookies

Like a tender almond tasty cookie? Here's a great one.

1	cup butter	1/2	teaspoon salt
1	cup sugar	3/4	cup chopped blanched
2	egg yolks		almonds
1/2	teaspoon almond extract	2	egg whites
1/2	teaspoon vanilla		unblanched almonds
2-2/3	cups sifted cake flour		

Cream butter; add sugar gradually; beat in egg yolks and extracts. Blend in sifted dry ingredients and chopped almonds. Shape into 1-inch balls; dip into unbeaten egg whites. Place on greased cookie sheets. Press 1 almond into each ball. Bake at 350 degrees for about 12 minutes. Remove from sheets immediately. Makes about 8 dozen.

Almond Fingers

Almond paste gives these cookies their distinctive flavor.

2	cups flour	2	egg yolks
1/2	teaspoon salt	1/3	cups almond paste
1/2	teaspoon cinnamon	1	teaspoon vanilla
3/4	cup butter, softened		confectioners' sugar
1/2	cup sugar		

Combine flour, salt and cinnamon. Beat together butter and sugar until fluffy, beat in egg yolks. Stir in almond paste and vanilla. Add flour mixture; mix well. Cover; chill 2 hours. Preheat oven to 350 degrees. Roll scant tablespoonfuls of dough into 2-1/2-inch fingers. Place on greased cookie sheets. Bake at 350 degrees for about 20 minutes. Remove to wire racks; cool completely. Dip one end of cookie in Chocolate Glaze; place on waxed paper. Chill 10 to 15 minutes. Roll other end of cookies in confectioners' sugar. Makes about 3-1/2 dozen cookies.

Chocolate Glaze:

1   6-ounce package of semisweet chocolate morsels

Melt morsels over hot (not boiling) water; cool.

Mexican Wedding Cakes

In Mexico, cookies are wrapped in white tissue paper and given to guests as favors - hence the name.

2-1/2	cups flour	1/2	cup confectioners' sugar
1/4	teaspoon salt	2	teaspoons vanilla
1	cup finely chopped pecans	1-1/2	cups (approximately) confectioners' sugar
1	cup butter or margarine, softened		

In a bowl stir together flour, salt, and pecans to combine thoroughly; set aside. Preheat oven to 350 degrees. In mixer bowl combine butter and the 1/2 cup confectioners' sugar; beat until fluffy. Blend in vanilla. Gradually add flour mixture, beating just until dough clings together. Shape dough into 1-1/2-inch balls. Place about 2-inches apart on ungreased baking sheets. Bake until firm and lightly browned, about 20 to 25 minutes. Roll in powdered sugar while warm. Place on wire rack to cool. When cool re-roll again in powdered sugar.

Note:
Put cookies in tiny paper cups, makes them festive looking.

Java Sticks

Dipping the ends of these cookies in melted chocolate brings out the coffee flavor.

1	cup butter, softened	1/4	cup finely chopped pecans
3/4	cup powdered sugar		
2	teaspoons coffee powder	3	ounces semisweet chocolate, melted
2	cup flour		

Cream together butter and powdered sugar. Beat in coffee powder, flour and pecans. Roll into finger shapes and place on greased cookie sheet. Bake at 350 degrees for 8 to 10 minutes. Let the sticks cool on racks. Dip in melted chocolate. Makes 6 dozen cookies.

Russian Teacakes

Try coloring sugar to make a pretty Christmas cookie.

1	cup soft butter	2-1/4	cups sifted flour
1/2	cup sifted confectioners' sugar	1/4	teaspoon salt
		3/4	cup finely chopped nuts
1	teaspoon vanilla		

Mix thoroughly butter, confectioners' sugar and vanilla. Sift together and stir in flour and salt. Mix in nuts. Chill dough. Roll into 1-inch balls. Place on ungreased baking sheet. (Cookies do not spread.) Bake in a 400 degree oven for 10 to 12 minutes until set, but not brown. While still warm, roll in confectioners' sugar. Cool. Roll in sugar again. Makes about 4 dozen 1-inch cookies.

VI'S Pecan Fingers

A favorite recipe my dear sister loves - A good brown sugar taste.

1	cup butter	1	teaspoon vanilla
1/4	cup brown sugar, packed	2	cups finely chopped pecans
2	cups sifted flour		granulated sugar for rolling
1/2	teaspoon salt		
1	tablespoon water		

Cream butter; add brown sugar gradually. Blend in flour, salt, water, vanilla and pecans. Shape dough into date size pieces; place on greased cookie sheets. Bake at 350 degrees about 15 minutes. Roll warm cookie in sugar. Makes about 7 dozen.

Pecan Fingers

Favorite of my family.

1	cup butter	1/4	teaspoon salt
1/4	cup confectioners' sugar	2	cups finely chopped pecans
1	teaspoon vanilla		confectioners' sugar
1	tablespoon water		
2	cups flour		

Cream butter; add sugar, vanilla and water. beat well. Add flour and pecans. Chill for about 1 hour. Shape dough into small, finger-like rolls. Bake for 1 hour at 250 degrees. While cookies are still warm; roll them in confectioners' sugar. Makes about 5 dozen.

Date-Coconut Confections

Walnuts and dates ground together make these special.

2	cups walnuts	2-1/2	cups coconut
1	cup pitted dates	2	eggs, slightly beaten
1	cup brown sugar, packed		

Grind walnuts and dates in food chopper or chop very fine by hand. Add sugar, 1 cup of coconut, and eggs; mix thoroughly. Drop dough by teaspoonfuls into remaining coconut; shape into balls. Place on lightly greased baking sheet. Bake at 350 degrees for about 15 minutes. Makes 4 to 5 dozen confections.

Pecan Balls

Festive cookies that melt in your mouth.

2	tablespoons sugar	1	cup pecans, ground
1	stick butter, softened	1	cup flour
1	teaspoon vanilla		confectioners' sugar

Preheat oven to 325 degrees. Mix sugar with butter and vanilla. Add nuts and flour. Form into balls. Bake for 15 minutes. Roll in confectioners' sugar while still warm. Roll again in confectioners' sugar when cool. Makes 2-1/2 dozen.

Slice and Serve Cookies

Rolled like jellyroll with cherries inside and nuts outside, an extra special cookie you'll make over and over again.

3/4	cup dates	1/2	teaspoon vanilla
1	tablespoon flour	1/2	cup pecans, finely chopped
2/3	cup sifted flour		
1/2	teaspoon baking powder	20	maraschino cherries
1/2	teaspoon salt	1	tablespoon confectioners' sugar
3	eggs		
3/4	cup sugar	1	cup pecans, finely chopped

Prepare dates by placing in a sieve and pour boiling water over them. Cut fine with scissors which have been dipped in hot water. Coat with 1 tablespoon flour. Sift together 2/3 cup flour, baking powder and salt. Beat eggs until foamy. Gradually add sugar, beating constantly until thick and ivory colored. Blend in vanilla. Fold in the dry ingredients thoroughly. Then fold in 1/2 cup pecans and the cut-up dates. Spread in 15 by 11-inch jellyroll pan which has been lined with waxed paper, then greased generously and floured lightly. Drain cherries. Arrange 10 cherries across each end of batter about 1/2-inch in from edge of pan. Bake in a 325 degree oven for 30 to 35 minutes. Turn hot cake out onto waxed paper which has been sprinkled with 1 tablespoon confectioners' sugar. Remove paper, trim the edges and cut crosswise into two 11 by 7-1/2-inch rectangles. Roll each rectangle tightly, beginning with the cherry end. Wrap in waxed paper and chill. Spread chilled rolls thinly with butter frosting and roll in 1 cup chopped pecans. Chill. To serve, cut in 1/4 to 1/2-inch slices.

Cherry Nut Bells

Here's a cookie that really looks and tastes different.

1	cup butter	3	cups sifted flour
1-1/4	cups brown sugar	1/2	teaspoon salt
1/4	cup dark corn syrup	1/2	teaspoon soda
1	egg	1	teaspoon cinnamon
1	tablespoon cream		

Cream butter. Add sugar and syrup gradually. Beat in dry ingredients. Chill. Make Nut Filling.

Nut Filling:

1/3	cup brown sugar, packed	1-1/2	cups finely chopped pecans
3	tablespoons maraschino juice		candied cherry pieces
1	tablespoon butter		

Combine all ingredients except cherry pieces. Roll dough 1/8-inch thick. Cut with 2-inch round cutter, place on ungreased cookie sheets. Place 1/2 teaspoon of filling in center of each round. Shape into a bell by folding sides of dough to meet over the filling. Pinch edges together. Place piece of candied cherry at open end of each bell for a clapper. Bake at 350 degrees about 15 minutes, makes 8-1/2 dozen.

Spiced Cherry Bells

"Ring in the New" - with these cookies.

3	cups sifted flour	1	cup shortening
1/2	teaspoon soda	1/4	cup dark syrup
1/2	teaspoon salt	1	egg
1	teaspoon ginger	1	tablespoon cream
1/2	teaspoon instant coffee		maraschino cherries
1-1/4	cups brown sugar, packed		

Sift together, flour, soda, salt, ginger and instant coffee. Set aside. Add brown sugar gradually to shortening, creaming well. Blend in corn syrup, egg, and cream; beat well. Add dry ingredients; mix thoroughly. Roll out dough on floured surface to 1/8-inch thickness. Cut 2-1/2-inch rounds. Place on ungreased cookie sheets. Place a 1/2 teaspoonful of filling in center of each round. Shape into a "bell" by folding sides to meet over filling, making top of bell narrower than "clapper" end. Place a piece of maraschino cherry, cut in quarters or halves; at open end of each bell for clapper. Bake at 350 degrees for 12 to 15 minutes.

Nut Filling:

1/3	cup firmly packed brown sugar	3	tablespoons maraschino cherry juice
1	tablespoon butter	1-1/2	cups finely chopped pecans

Combine brown sugar, butter, cherry juice; mix well. Stir in pecans.

Oh' So Good Cookies

Our neighbor's little boy smelled cookies baking and came over for a sample - he said oh' these are so good - hence the name.

1	cup butter	1/2	cup corn flakes (measure after crushing)
1	cup brown sugar		
1	egg	1-1/4	cups oatmeal
1-1/2	cups flour	1	cup whole salted peanuts
1-1/4	teaspoons soda	1/2	cup coconut
1-1/4	teaspoons baking powder		

Cream butter and sugar. Add egg. Sift dry ingredients, add to mixture. Mix in corn flakes, oatmeal, salted nuts and coconut. Form into balls size of walnuts. Place on lightly greased cookie sheet. Bake at 350 degrees about 12 to 15 minutes. Makes about 5 dozen cookies.

Date - Nut Jumbos

A slightly different cookie full of good nutrition.

1/2	cup margarine	1/2	teaspoon soda
3/4	cup brown sugar, packed	1/2	teaspoon salt
1	egg	2	cups cornflakes
1	teaspoon vanilla	1	cup chopped pitted dates
1-1/4	cups flour	1/2	cup chopped walnuts
1/2	teaspoon baking powder		

Cream margarine and sugar; blend in egg and vanilla. Add combined dry ingredients; mix well. Stir in cornflakes, dates and nuts. Chill. Shape dough into 1-inch balls; place on ungreased cookie sheets. Bake at 375 degrees for about 12 to 15 minutes. Makes about 3-1/2 dozen.

Wheaties Cherry Blinks

These rich, Wheaties-coated, cherry-topped cookies are just the thing for parties.

1/3	cup shortening	1/4	teaspoon soda
1/2	cup sugar	1/4	teaspoon salt
1	egg	1/2	cup raisins or cut-up dates
1-1/2	tablespoons milk	1/2	cup nuts, chopped
1/2	teaspoon vanilla	1-1/2	cups Wheaties, crushed
1	cup flour		candied or maraschino cherries
1/2	teaspoon baking powder		

Mix shortening, sugar, and egg. Stir in milk and vanilla. Blend dry ingredients together; stir in. Mix in raisins and nuts. Drop dough by teaspoonfuls into Wheaties. Roll gently so balls of dough are completely coated. Place about 2-inches apart on greased baking sheet. Top with a piece of cherry. Bake in a 375 degree oven for 10 to 12 minutes, or until no imprint remains when touched lightly. Makes about 3 dozen.

Cashew Triangles

Salted cashews bring out a truly different flavor to these pretty cookies.

1/4	cup sugar	1	teaspoon water
1/4	cup brown sugar	1	cup chopped salted cashews
1/2	cup margarine		
1	large egg, separated	1	square unsweetened chocolate, melted and cooled
1/2	teaspoon vanilla		
1	cup flour		
1/8	teaspoon salt		

Beat margarine, sugar, egg yolk and vanilla until smooth. Stir in flour and salt. Refrigerate dough. With floured fingers press dough over bottom of a 13 by 9-inch ungreased pan. Beat egg white and water with a fork. Brush over dough. Sprinkle with nuts, then press them gently into dough. Bake in a 375 degree oven 25 minutes or until light brown. Cool in pan 10 minutes. Cut in 3-inch squares. Cut each square diagonally in half. Remove from pan to cool completely. Drizzle with chocolate. Makes 24 squares.

Brittle Filbert Cookies

Break cookies in as big or small pieces as desired.

3/4	cup cornflakes	1/4	teaspoon salt
1/3	cup flour	1/4	cup butter
1/3	cup sugar	2	tablespoons light corn syrup
1/2	cup toasted, coarsely chopped filberts	1/2	teaspoon vanilla
1/4	cup flaked coconut		

Crush cornflakes slightly; add flour, sugar, nuts, coconut and salt. Mix butter, syrup and vanilla and heat to boiling point. Remove from heat and add flour mixture and mix. Pat into a round about 1/4-inch thick on an ungreased cookie sheet. Bake at 400 degrees until as brown as desired, about 6 minutes. Cool and break into pieces.

Peanutty Chocolate Crinkles

Peanut butter and chocolate fans will take a shine to these crackle-top cookies.

1/2	cup butter or margarine, room temperature	1/4	teaspoon salt
1-1/2	cups granulated sugar	1/2	cup walnuts
3	eggs	1/2	cup (3 ounces) semisweet chocolate pieces, if desired
1	tablespoon vanilla extract		
3	ounces unsweetened chocolate, melted	1	cup (6 ounces) peanut butter-flavor pieces
2	cups flour		sifted powdered sugar
2	teaspoons baking powder		

In a large bowl, beat together butter or margarine, granulated sugar, eggs and vanilla until light and fluffy. Beat in melted unsweetened chocolate. Add flour, baking powder and salt, beating well. Stir in walnuts, chocolate pieces, if desired, and peanut butter pieces. Cover and refrigerate 1 hour or longer. To bake cookies, preheat oven to 350 degrees. Grease baking sheets. Shape dough into 1-inch balls; roll in powdered sugar, coating well. Place 2-inches apart on greased baking sheets. Bake 10 minutes. Cookies will be soft. Do not overbake. Remove cookies from baking sheets; cool on racks. Makes about sixty-five to seventy 1-1/2-inch cookies.

Butterscotch Melt-A-Ways

These cookies actually do melt in your mouth.

1	cup butter	1/8	teaspoon salt
3/4	cup powdered sugar	1	cup flaked coconut
1	egg yolk	3/4	cup butterscotch bits
1	teaspoon vanilla		granulated sugar
1-1/4	cups sifted flour		candied cherries, cut in halves
3/4	cup cornstarch		

Cream butter; add powdered sugar gradually; beat in egg yolk and vanilla. Sift flour, cornstarch and salt together; blend into creamed mixture. Stir in coconut and butterscotch bits. Shape rounded teaspoonfuls of dough into balls; flatten with bottom of glass dipped in granulated sugar. Place candied cherry half in center of each cookie. Place on ungreased cookie sheets. Bake at 375 degrees for 12 to 14 minutes. Makes approximately 5 dozen.

Peanutios

Let your children make these easy to do cookies.

1	cup sugar	1/4	teaspoon salt
1	cup brown sugar	1	teaspoon vanilla
3/4	cup shortening	2	eggs, beaten
1/4	cup butter	1	cup chopped peanuts
2	cups flour	1	cup coconut
1	teaspoon baking powder	1	cup oatmeal
1	teaspoon baking soda	2	cups cornflakes

Cream sugars, shortening and butter. Mix in beaten eggs and vanilla. Add sifted dry ingredients. Add nuts and cereal by hand. Form into balls. Place on lightly greased cookie sheet. Bake at 300 degrees for 15 to 20 minutes.

Peanut Butter Cookies

These often stocked the "Cookie Jar" at my home and are a favorite of all children.

1	cup shortening	1-1/2	teaspoons baking soda
1	cup sugar	1/2	teaspoon salt
1	cup brown sugar	1	teaspoon vanilla
2	eggs	1	cup peanut butter
3	cups flour		

Cream shortening. Add sugar and brown sugar and mix thoroughly with shortening. Add well beaten eggs and vanilla. Gradually add dry ingredients and mix completely. Add peanut butter. Stir in. Form into little balls about 1-inch in diameter. Press with tines of a fork to make a crisscross design. Bake at 350 degrees for about 15 minutes or until done.

Easy Peanut Butter Cookies

In a hurry? Try these delicious speedy cookies. It really works great.

1	egg, beaten	1	cup creamy peanut butter
1	cup sugar		

In a large bowl, mix all ingredients. Scoop level tablespoons and roll into balls. Place on ungreased cookie sheet and flatten with a fork. Bake at 350 degrees for about 18 minutes. Remove to wire rack to cool. Makes 2 dozen.

Peanut Butter Crisscrosses

Orange juice adds a new flavor to these and will add to the list of your favorites.

2	cups sifted flour	1/2	cup firmly packed brown sugar
3/4	teaspoon baking soda		
1/2	teaspoon baking powder	1/2	cup granulated sugar
1/4	teaspoon salt	1	egg
1/2	cup vegetable shortening	1/4	cup orange juice
1/2	cup peanut butter		

Cream shortening and peanut butter with sugars until fluffy in a large bowl; beat in egg. Stir in dry ingredients adding alternately with orange juice and blending well to make a stiff dough. Chill until firm enough to handle. Roll dough, a teaspoonful at a time, into balls. Place 3-inches apart on ungreased cookie sheets; flatten, crisscross fashion with a fork. Bake at 375 degrees for about 12 minutes, or until golden. Remove from cookie sheets; cool completely on wire racks. Makes about 5 dozen.

Choco-Peanut Butter Cookies

Speckled with grated semisweet chocolate, these peanut butter cookies give a classic recipe new flavor.

1-1/2	cups flour	1/2	cup brown sugar, firmly packed
2	teaspoons baking powder		
1/8	teaspoon salt	1	teaspoon vanilla
1/2	cup butter or margarine, softened	1	egg
		1	square semisweet baking chocolate, grated
1/2	cup peanut butter		
1/2	cup granulated sugar		

In mixer bowl combine butter and peanut butter; beat until fluffy. Add sugars and beat until well combined. Blend in vanilla, then egg, and beat until fluffy. Gradually add dry sifted ingredients beating until well blended. Stir in chocolate. Shape dough into 1-inch balls. Place about 1-1/2-inches apart on ungreased baking sheets. Flatten each cookie with a fork, pressing tines once into dough and then crisscrossing the first pattern to make a crosshatch design. Bake in a 350° oven until cookies are lightly browned and feel firm when touched gently about 10 to 12 minutes. Transfer to wire racks to cool. Makes about 42 cookies.

Chocolate Chiffon Cookies

A dainty cookie to serve at your exchange party.

1	cup butter, softened		pinch of salt
1-1/4	cups powdered sugar	1	teaspoon vanilla
6	ounces German sweet chocolate, grated	1	cup finely chopped pecans
1-1/2	cups sifted flour		pecan halves, optional

Preheat oven to 250 degrees. Combine butter and sugar, then stir in remaining ingredients (except pecan halves), blending well. Gently roll dough into 1 to 1-1/2-inch balls, placing about 2-inches apart on an ungreased cookie sheet. Press a pecan half into each one, if you wish. Bake for 45 minutes. Makes about 5 dozen.

Tiny Fudge Tarts

Almost taste like candy, with fudge filling.

1-1/2	cups sifted flour	3	tablespoons water
1/4	teaspoon salt	1	teaspoon vanilla
1/2	cup butter or margarine		Fudge Filling

Mix flour and salt; cut in butter. Sprinkle with water and vanilla; mix well with fork. Using 1/2 of dough at a time, roll out 1/16-inch thick on cloth-covered board generously sprinkled with sugar. Cut in 2-1/2-inch squares. Spread 1 teaspoonful of filling in center of each square. Bring corners to center; seal together. Place sealed side up or down on ungreased baking sheet. Bake in a 350 degree oven for 15 to 20 minutes. Makes about 2-1/2 dozen tarts.

Fudge Filling:

Mix the following ingredients thoroughly:

1/4	cup butter or margarine	1/4	cup cocoa
1	egg yolk	1/2	cup finely chopped nuts or flaked coconut
1/2	cup sugar		
1	teaspoon vanilla		

Fudge Cups

These cookies will blend in great on your holiday cookie tray.

1/2	cup butter	1/2	teaspoon vanilla
1	cup sugar	1/4	teaspoon salt
1	egg	1/4	teaspoon red food coloring
2	squares unsweetened chocolate (2 ounces)	2	to 2-1/4 cups sifted flour

Cream butter, gradually add sugar, creaming well. Blend in egg; beat well. Add chocolate, melted and cooled, vanilla, salt, and food coloring, blend well. Add flour and mix well. Chill about 1 hour. Shape into balls using a rounded tablespoonful for each. Place in greased or paper-lined muffin cups. (Small muffin cups can be used if desired.) Flatten and press dough about 1/2-inch up side of cups. Bake at 350 degrees for 8 to 10 minutes. Remove from pan and cool completely. Fill with fudge and top each with pecan half. Makes 24 tarts.

Note:
When using small muffin cups, use teaspoons.

Creamy Fudge:

1-1/2	cups sugar	3	tablespoons light corn syrup
1/3	cup milk		
1/4	cup butter	1/8	teaspoon salt
1-1/2	squares unsweetened chocolate	1	teaspoon vanilla

Combine sugar, milk, butter, chocolate, corn syrup and salt in saucepan. Cook over low heat until chocolate and butter melt. Bring to boil; then boil for 1 minute. Remove from heat and add vanilla. Beat until lukewarm; fill cups.

Chocolate Crackle Tops

Would you believe bread crumbs in a cookie? Be sure to try these.

2	eggs	3	squares unsweetened chocolate, grated
1	cup sugar		
2	cups pecans, ground	1/2	teaspoon cinnamon
1/4	cup dry bread crumbs	1/2	teaspoon cloves
2	tablespoons flour		powdered sugar for rolling

Beat egg with sugar until well blended. Stir in remaining ingredients except powdered sugar; mix well. Chill. Shape dough into 1-inch balls and roll in powdered sugar. Place on greased cookie sheets and bake at 375 degrees for 12 to 15 minutes. Makes about 5 dozen.

Chocolate Sandies

Light and delicate with the taste of pecans should be every one's favorite.

1-3/4	cups sifted flour	1/3	cup sifted confectioners' sugar
1	cup toasted pecans		
6	ounces semisweet chocolate bits	1	teaspoon vanilla
		2	teaspoons cold water
3/4	cup butter		

Mix flour, nuts and chocolate. Cream butter, add sugar gradually and cream until fluffy; add vanilla and water, mix well. Add flour mixture gradually and mix. Mold dough into ball, using 1 tablespoon dough for each ball. Bake on ungreased baking sheets in a preheated 350 degree oven about 23 minutes. While cookies are warm, sprinkle them with additional confectioners' sugar. Makes about 3-2/3 dozen.

Chocolate Aggies

These are dense, chocolatey, thick semi-soft.

2	cups sifted flour	4	extra large or jumbo eggs
2	teaspoons baking powder	2	ounces (generous 1/2 cup) walnuts, cut medium fine
1-1/4	teaspoons salt		
2	ounces (4 tablespoons) butter		about 1 cup confectioners' sugar (you might need a bit more)
4	ounces (4 squares) unsweetened chocolate		
2	cups granulated sugar		

In a heavy 3-quart saucepan, over low heat, melt the butter and the chocolate. Stir occasionally until smooth and then remove from the heat. With a heavy wooden spatula stir the granulated sugar into the warm chocolate mixture. Then stir in the eggs one at a time. Add the sifted dry ingredients and stir until smooth. Stir in the nuts. Cover and refrigerate. Sift confectioners' sugar. Sugar the palms of your hands with the sugar. Roll the dough into 1 to 1-1/4-inch balls, using a heaping teaspoonful of dough for each cookie. Roll the balls around in the confectioners' sugar and place them 2-inches apart on cookie sheet lined with foil. Bake at 350 degrees for 20 to 22 minutes. Do not overbake. These should be slightly soft in the centers. Transfer the cookies to racks to cool. Makes about 40 to 45 cookies.

Note:
Cookies will be more attractive if the confectioners' sugar coats them heavily.

Chocolate-Coconut Candies

Mashed potatoes in cookies? Yes! Do add these candies to your cookie tray.

3/4	cup mashed potatoes or instant	1	pound confectioners' sugar, sugar, sifted
1	pound flaked coconut		Chocolate Coating
1	teaspoon almond extract		

Combine ingredients. Drop by heaping teaspoonfuls on waxed paper. Roll in balls; refrigerate 1/2 to 1 hour. If mixture is too soft to form balls, refrigerate first, then shape balls. Dip balls in coating, turning to coat on all sides. Keep chocolate over hot water while dipping candy. With tongs or forks, lift balls out of chocolate on waxed paper or cake rack. Place candies in refrigerator to harden. Makes about 5 dozen candies.

Chocolate Coating:

1	package (6-ounce) semi-sweet chocolate pieces	1/3	paraffin bar (regular bar, 5 by 3-inches)
4	squares semi-sweet chocolate (4 ounces)		

Combine the ingredients in the top of a double boiler. Melt over hot water, stirring occasionally, until ingredients are blended.

Hidden Chocolate Cookies

A mint surprise inside of tender cookies.

1/2	cup butter	1-1/2	cups plus 2 tablespoons sifted flour
1/2	cup granulated sugar		
1/4	cup brown sugar, packed	1/2	teaspoon soda
1	egg	1/4	teaspoon salt
1	tablespoon water		about 3 dozen chocolate mint wafers
1/2	teaspoon vanilla		

Mix thoroughly butter, sugars, and egg. Stir in water and vanilla. Blend flour, soda, and salt; stir in. Chill dough. Heat oven to 400 degrees. Shape cookies by enclosing each chocolate mint wafer in about 1 tablespoon of dough. Place about 2-inches apart on greased baking sheet. Bake 8 to 10 minutes, or until no imprint remains when touched lightly. Makes about 3 dozen cookies.

Pecan Delights

The name is so right - these really are a delight to eat.

1-1/4	cups butter	1	teaspoon vanilla
1	cup powdered sugar	2	cups sifted flour
1/2	cup cocoa	1	cup chopped pecans
1/4	teaspoon salt		powdered sugar

Cream butter. Add sugar, cocoa, salt and vanilla. Cream well. Blend in flour and pecans. Refrigerate 1 hour if dough is soft. Pinch off pieces of dough the size of a large marble. Place on ungreased cookie sheet. Bake at 300 degrees about 20 minutes. Cool. Roll in powdered sugar. Makes about 5-1/2 dozen.

Chocolate Cookies

I bake many batches of cookies during the holidays. This is one of the favorites. The flavor can be varied with different flavors of chocolate. I use Calleblaut Bittersweet.

3	ounces semisweet chocolate	2	teaspoons vanilla
2	ounces unsweetened chocolate	3/4	cup plus 3 tablespoons flour
1/2	cup unsalted butter	1/2	teaspoon baking soda
1/2	cup sugar	1/4	teaspoon salt
1/2	cup light brown sugar, firmly packed	4	Hershey milk chocolate candy bars (1.45 ounces each), chilled
1	large egg		

Chop up semisweet and unsweetened chocolates and melt in microwave. Set aside to cool. Cream the butter. Add both sugars and beat until light and fluffy. Add the egg and vanilla and mix well. Stir in the cooled, melted chocolate. Add the dry ingredients. Cut the candy bars into small chunks and stir into the batter. Refrigerate until the dough is firm enough to roll into balls. Roll into 1-1/4-inch balls and space 2-inches apart on ungreased cookie sheets. Bake in a preheated 375 degree oven until lightly set, about 8 to 9 minutes. Remove from oven and cool on the sheets for 2 minutes, then transfer to the cooling racks. The cookies can be stored in an airtight container for a few days or frozen.

Double Chocolate Chews

A rich, chewy brownie-like cookie.

1-3/4	cups flour	4	large eggs
1-1/2	teaspoons baking powder	1-3/4	teaspoons vanilla
1/4	teaspoon salt	1/8	teaspoon almond extract
1/3	cup oil	3/4	cup semisweet chocolate chips
4	ounces unsweetened chocolate	1/4	cup powdered sugar
1-2/3	cups sugar		

Combine oil and chocolate in a saucepan and warm over lowest heat, stirring occasionally, until chocolate melts. Remove saucepan from heat and stir in sugar. Add eggs, one at a time, and stir until well blended. Stir in vanilla and almond extracts. Pour chocolate mixture into dry ingredients and stir until very thoroughly mixed. Add chocolate chips and stir until evenly distributed. Cover dough and refrigerate for at least 1-1/2 hours. Preheat oven to 350 degrees. Roll chilled dough between palms to form 1-1/4-inch balls. Place on greased cookie sheets. Space them about 2-inches apart, bake for 11 to 13 minutes or until just beginning to firm in the center. Remove from oven and let stand for 1 minute, then transfer cookies to wire racks to cool. Lightly dust cookies with powdered sugar shortly before serving. Makes thirty-five to forty 2-1/2-inch cookies.

Chocolate Dipped Creams

Be creative - do your own thing with these yummy cookies.

1	cup butter		powdered sugar for rolling
1/2	cup powdered sugar	1	cup chocolate bits, melted
1	teaspoon vanilla		chopped nuts
1	cup cornstarch		coconut
1	cup sifted flour		chocolate jimmies
1/8	teaspoon salt		

Cream butter; add sugar gradually; add vanilla. Sift flour, cornstarch and salt together; blend into creamed mixture; chill. Shape teaspoonfuls of dough into balls, triangles, crescents or bars. Place on greased cookie sheets. Bake at 375 degrees about 12 minutes. Cool; roll in powdered sugar. Dip part of each cookie in chocolate then in nuts, coconut or jimmies. Makes about 6 dozen.

Chocolate-Print Cookies

A chocolate filling tastes so good in these coconut cookies.

1/2	cup butter or margarine, softened	1	teaspoon vanilla
1/4	cup light brown sugar, firmly packed	1	cup sifted flour
		1	egg white, slightly beaten
1	egg yolk	3/4	cup flaked coconut

In medium bowl, with electric mixer at medium speed, or wooden spoon, beat butter with sugar until light and fluffy. Beat in egg yolk and vanilla. At low speed, gradually beat in flour; continue beating until smooth. Refrigerate dough, covered, about 1 hour, or until it is stiff enough to handle. Preheat oven to 350 degrees. Roll dough into balls 1-1/4-inches in diameter. Dip balls in egg white; then roll in coconut. Place, 1-1/2-inches apart, on ungreased cookie sheets. With finger, make a depression in center of each cookie. Bake 15 minutes, or until light golden. Let cool on wire rack.

Chocolate Filling:

1/2	cup semisweet chocolate pieces	1/2	teaspoon vanilla
2-1/2	tablespoons soft cream cheese	1/8	teaspoon salt

Melt chocolate with 2 tablespoons water over hot, not boiling, water. Remove from heat. Gradually stir in cheese, vanilla, and salt, mixing until smooth. Use chocolate mixture to fill depressions in center of cookies. Makes about 2 dozen.

Fudge Mallows

Old-fashioned semi-soft chocolate cookie with pecan hidden underneath and a marshmallow on top all covered with a chocolate icing.

1-3/4	cups sifted flour	1	teaspoon vanilla extract
1	teaspoon baking soda	1	cup granulated sugar
1/4	teaspoon salt	2	eggs
1/2	cup unsweetened cocoa, strained or sifted	28	large pecan halves
		14	large marshmallows
1/4	pound (1 stick) butter		

Cut aluminum foil to fit cookie sheets. Sift together the flour, baking soda, salt, and cocoa and set aside. In the large bowl of an electric mixer, cream the butter. Add the vanilla and the sugar and beat to mix well. Add the eggs one at a time and beat until smooth. On low speed, gradually add the sifted dry ingredients, scraping the bowl with a rubber spatula and beating only until thoroughly mixed. Use a heaping teaspoonful of dough for each cookie. Wet your hands under cold water, shake off excess water, your hands should be damp but not too wet. Pick up a mound of dough and roll it between your hands into a round ball. Press a pecan half into the ball of dough, placing the curved side (top) of the nut into the dough. Do not enclose it completely. Place the cookie on the foil so that the flat side of the pecan is on the bottom of the cookie. Continue to wet your hands as necessary while you shape the remaining cookies, placing them 2-inches apart on the foil. Slide cookie sheets under the foil. Bake at 350 degrees for 16 to 18 minutes or until cookies are barely done, not quite firm to the touch. Do not overbake. While cookies are baking, cut the marshmallows in half crosswise. (Easily done with scissors.) Remove the cookie sheets from the oven, quickly place a marshmallow half, cut side down on each cookie. Return to the oven for 1 to 1-1/2 minutes. Watch the clock! If the marshmallows bake any longer they will melt and run off the sides of the cookies, they should not melt and they should stay on top. These should not actually melt at all, only soften very slightly and not get soft enough to change shape. Let cookies stand for a few seconds until they are firm enough to be moved and then transfer to racks to cool. Frost with cocoa icing. Makes 28 cookies.

Marshmallow Clouds

What a surprise to find marshmallows inside a delicious chocolate cookie.

3	cups flour	2	large eggs
2/3	cup unsweetened cocoa powder	2	teaspoons vanilla
1/2	teaspoon baking soda	2	cups miniature semi-sweet chocolate chips
1	cup white sugar		
1	cup light brown sugar, firmly packed	8	ounces miniature marshmallows, frozen
1	cup butter, softened		

In medium bowl combine flour, cocoa and baking soda. Set aside. Combine sugars in a large bowl. Using an electric mixer, blend in butter. Add eggs and vanilla, and beat at medium speed until light and fluffy. Add the flour mixture and chocolate chips, and blend at low speed until combined. Batter will be very stiff. Put 4 to 5 frozen marshmallows in the palm of your hand and cover them with a heaping tablespoon of dough. Wrap the dough around the marshmallows, completely covering them and forming a 2-inch ball. Place balls on ungreased baking sheets, 2-inches apart. Bake in a 400 degree oven 8 to 10 minutes. Cool on pan 2 minutes, then transfer to a cool, flat surface. Makes 3-1/2 dozen.

Chocolate Shadows

Put these in a plastic bag and take to your "Bake Sale". A sure fast selling cookie.

1/2	cup chocolate chips, melted	1/2	teaspoon salt
		1/2	cup sugar
1/8	teaspoon peppermint extract	1/2	cup brown sugar
		1/2	cup shortening
1-1/4	cups sifted flour	1/2	cup peanut butter
3/4	teaspoon baking soda	1	egg, unbeaten

Sift dry ingredients together. Stir peppermint extract into cooled chocolate. Cream together, shortening, peanut butter and sugars. Add egg; mix well. Blend in dry ingredients. Add chocolate. Stir just until marbled; shape into balls, using a rounded teaspoon for each. Place on greased cookie sheet. Flatten with bottom of glass which has been dipped in sugar. Bake at 375 degrees for 8 to 10 minutes. Makes about 36 cookies.

Snickerdoodles

Delicately crisp outside, soft inside with the good taste of cinnamon.

1	cup butter or margarine	1	teaspoon soda
1-1/2	cups sugar	1/4	teaspoon salt
2	eggs	2	tablespoons sugar
2-3/4	cups sifted flour	2	teaspoons cinnamon
2	teaspoons cream of tartar		

Mix shortening, 1-1/2 cups sugar, and eggs thoroughly. Blend flour, cream of tartar, soda and salt; stir in. Shape dough in 1-inch balls. Roll in mixture of 2 tablespoons sugar and cinnamon. Place 2-inches apart on ungreased baking sheet. Bake at 400 degrees for about 8 to 10 minutes. These cookies puff up at first, then flatten out. Makes about 6 dozen cookies.

Chocolate Pretzels

These pretzels speckled with coarse sugar are as appropriate with strong coffee as their counterparts with a stein of beer.

1-2/3	cups flour	1	teaspoon vanilla
1/4	cup unsweetened cocoa	1	egg white, slightly beaten
3/4	cup butter or margarine, softened	2	tablespoons coarse sugar or decorating sugar
3/4	cup sugar		

Stir together flour and cocoa to combine well; set aside. Combine butter and sugar; beat until fluffy. Blend in vanilla. Add dry sifted ingredients beating until smooth. Gather dough into a ball and wrap in plastic. Refrigerate until firm enough to shape, about 45 minutes. Preheat oven to 350 degrees. Work with 1/4 of the dough at a time, keeping remainder in refrigerator. Divide each portion into 8 equal pieces, on a lightly floured pastry cloth or board, roll each piece into an 8-inch long strand, using the palms of your hands. Twist each strand into pretzel shape. Place cookies about 1-inch apart on lightly greased baking sheets. Lightly brush each cookie with egg white, then scatter coarse sugar over surface. Bake until cookies feel firm when touched lightly, about 12 to 14 minutes. Let stand on baking sheets for about 2 minutes, then transfer to wire racks to cool completely. Makes about 32 cookies.

Coconut Jam Fills

Red or green jam makes this a festive cookie.

3/4	cup soft butter	1	teaspoon soda
3/4	cup brown sugar, packed	1/2	teaspoon salt
1	egg	1-1/2	cups uncooked oatmeal
1	teaspoon vanilla	1-1/2	cups flaked coconut
1-1/2	cups sifted flour		strawberry or apple jam

Cream butter. Add sugar gradually. Beat in egg and vanilla. Blend in sifted dry ingredients and oatmeal. Chill several hours. Shape into 1-inch balls. Roll in coconut. Place on greased cookie sheets. Make depression in the center of each ball. Fill with jam. Bake at 350 degrees about 10 minutes. Makes about 6 dozen.

Chocolate Curls

A different look to these tasty morsels.

1	cup butter	2	cups sifted flour
3/4	cup confectioners' or regular sugar	1/4	cup brown sugar, firmly packed
1/2	cup chocolate chips, melted	1/8	to 1/4 teaspoon cinnamon
1/2	cup walnuts, finely chopped		

Cream butter in mixing bowl. Add sugar; continue creaming until light and fluffy. Blend in chocolate chips and 1/4 cups walnuts. Add flour; mix well, chill. Combine 1/4 cup walnuts, brown sugar and cinnamon. Shape teaspoonfuls of dough into 6-inch strips. Roll in sugar mixture. Place one end of strip on ungreased cookie sheet; coil around to make a round, flat cookie. Bake at 325 degrees for 12 to 15 minutes. Cool slightly; remove from sheet. Makes about 60 cookies.

Cocoroons

How easy to do, filling and cookie baked together.

1-1/2	cups flour	1/2	cup butter
2/3	cup Nestle's Quik mix	2	egg yolks
1-1/2	teaspoons baking powder	1	tablespoon milk
1/4	cup sugar	1/2	teaspoon vanilla

Sift dry ingredients together. Cream butter and sugar well. Add egg yolks, milk and vanilla. Beat well, blend in dry ingredients, mix well. Chill.

Filling:

2	egg whites	1/4	cup sugar
1	teaspoon almond extract	2	cups coconut
1/2	teaspoon vanilla	1	tablespoon water

Beat egg whites and flavoring until mounds form. Add sugar gradually. Beat until stiff peaks form. Fold in coconut and water.

Frosting:

1	cup Nestle's Quik mix	2-1/2	cups sifted confectioners' sugar
1/4	cup butter		
1/4	cup boiling water	1	teaspoon vanilla

Mix together Nestle's Quik mix, butter, boiling water. Beat well. Blend in confectioners' sugar and vanilla and beat well until spreading consistency. If necessary, add more milk. Roll cookie dough into balls, make thumb print in center and fill with filling. Bake in a 350 degree oven for 8 to 10 minutes. Frost while warm.

Tint coconut the easy way. Place a few drops of food coloring and water in a jar, add coconut and shake until evenly colored.

Frosted Pecan Cuplets

So pretty, it's a shame to eat them - makes a special addition for a tea.

1	cup butter	1/4	teaspoon salt
1	cup sugar	2	egg whites, slightly beaten
2	egg yolks	1-1/2	cups finely chopped pecans
1	teaspoon vanilla		
2	cups sifted flour		

Cream butter; add sugar gradually; beat in egg yolks and vanilla. Blend in flour and salt; chill. Shape level teaspoonfuls of dough into balls; dip in egg white, then into pecans. Place on greased cookie sheets. Bake at 375 degrees for about 5 minutes. Remove from oven; make a depression in center of each cookie. Return to oven, bake about 10 minutes longer. Cool. Fill centers with Tinted Butter Frosting. Makes about 7 dozen.

Tinted Butter Frosting:

3	tablespoons soft butter	1	teaspoon vanilla
1-1/2	cups powdered sugar		red, yellow and green food coloring
3	tablespoons cream		

Blend butter, sugar, cream and vanilla; beat until smooth. Divide frosting into 3 parts. Tint 1 part pink, 1 part yellow, and 1 part green.

Frosted Eggnog Logs

These cookies are special for the holidays. They have a rum and nutmeg flavor that will have the super taste of eggnog.

3	cup flour	1	egg
1	teaspoon nutmeg	2	teaspoons vanilla
1	cup butter	1	teaspoon rum flavoring
3/4	cup sugar		

Mix butter and sugar until light and fluffy. Beat in egg, vanilla, and rum flavoring. Add dry ingredients and mix well. Shape dough into 3-inch logs, about 1/2-inch wide. Arrange on ungreased cookie sheets. Bake in a 350 degree oven for 15 to 17 minutes or until golden. Cool on wire racks.

Rum Frosting:

3	tablespoons softened butter	2	cups sifted powdered sugar
1/2	teaspoon rum flavoring	2	to 3 tablespoons evaporated milk or cream
1/2	teaspoon vanilla		nutmeg
1/2	cup sifted powdered sugar		

Beat butter and flavorings. Beat in the 1/2 cup powdered sugar. Gradually add the 2 cups of powdered sugar with the milk or cream. Beat until frosting spreads easily over the cookies. Tint with food coloring, if desired. Frost tops with frosting. Mark frosting lengthwise with the tines of fork to resemble bark. Sprinkle with additional nutmeg. Makes about 56 cookies.

Gumdrop Macaroons

Let the children cut-up the gumdrops with a scissors - watch so they don't eat too many!

1/2	cup butter	1/2	teaspoon baking powder
1/2	cup brown sugar, packed	1/2	teaspoon soda
1/2	cup granulated sugar	1/2	teaspoon salt
1	egg	1/2	cup chopped nuts
1	teaspoon vanilla	1	cup uncooked oatmeal
1	cup finely cut gumdrops	1/2	cup flaked coconut
1	cup sifted flour		

Cream butter. Add sugars gradually. Beat in egg and vanilla. Separate gumdrops in sifted dry ingredients. Blend into creamed mixture. Mix in nuts, oatmeal and coconut. Shape into 1-inch balls. Place 2-inches apart on greased cookie sheets. Flatten slightly with a fork. Bake at 350 degrees 10 to 12 minutes. Cool. Makes about 4 dozen 3-inch cookies.

Chocolate Macaroons

Light cookies that are not too sweet.

1/4	cup butter	2	eggs, beaten
2	ounces unsweetened chocolate	1	teaspoon baking powder
1	cup flour	1	teaspoon vanilla
1	cup sugar		confectioners' sugar

Melt butter and chocolate in saucepan over low heat. Add remaining ingredients except confectioners' sugar; beat well. Chill overnight. Shape teaspoonfuls of dough into small balls; roll in confectioners' sugar. Place on lightly greased cookie sheets. Bake at 350 degrees for 10 to 12 minutes. Makes about 2 dozen.

Brazil Nut Shortbread

Brazil nuts really add an elegant taste to these buttery cookies.

1	cup butter	1	cup Brazil nuts, sliced
1/2	cup sugar		pieces of Brazil nuts for
2	cups bread flour		decorating
1/2	teaspoon salt		

Cream butter and sugar well. Add flour, salt and sliced nuts. Mix thoroughly. Place dough in refrigerator to chill an hour. Shape dough into little balls about the size of a small walnut. Place on cookie sheet. Flatten balls by pressing a piece of Brazil nut into top of each. Bake at 300 degrees for about 15 to 20 minutes. Makes about 6 dozen.

Grossmutter's Pfeffernuesse

An old-fashioned family favorite.

3	eggs	1	teaspoon anise extract
2	cups sugar		or crushed anise seed
2-3/4	cups flour		

In a large mixing bowl, beat eggs and sugar at medium speed for 15 minutes. Reduce speed and slowly add flour and anise. Mix until well combined. On a lightly floured board, shape dough into ropes about 1/2-inch in diameter. Chill for 1 hour. Slice ropes into 1/2-inch lengths. Place on greased cookie sheets. Bake at 350 degrees for about 6 to 8 minutes or until set. Cookies will harden upon standing.

Note:
They are best if allowed to age before serving. Makes about 30 dozen.

Cookies will stay moist if a slice of bread is placed in the cookie jar.

Nut Cluster Cookies

Tiny cookies dipped in chocolate, form candy-like clusters or serve individually for bite-size treats.

1-1/4	cups sifted flour	1	unbeaten egg
1/4	teaspoon salt	2	tablespoons milk
1/4	teaspoon cream of tartar	1	teaspoon vanilla
1/4	teaspoon baking soda	1/2	cup salted peanuts or toasted almonds
1/2	cup sugar		
1/3	cup margarine		

Sift dry ingredients. Cream margarine and sugar; blend in egg, milk and vanilla. Beat well; add nuts and dry ingredients. Mix thoroughly; chill 1 hour. Shape dough into 1/2-inch balls. Place on ungreased cookie sheets. Bake at 375 degrees for about 8 to 10 minutes. Drop cookies into glaze, covering completely. Lift out with fork, tapping lightly against side of double boiler to remove excess chocolate. Place 3 chocolate-coated cookies, sides touching, on a rack over waxed paper. Place a fourth chocolate-coated cookie on top to form a cluster. Repeat with remaining cookies. If desired, garnish with finely chopped nuts. Let stand until chocolate hardens. Makes about 2 dozen clusters.

Chocolate Glaze:

12	squares (12 ounces) semi-sweet chocolate	3	tablespoons sifted confectioners' sugar

Melt chocolate in top of double boiler over boiling water. Stir in confectioners' sugar. Remove from heat (keep chocolate mixture over hot water).

Peanut Blossoms

A chocolate star on top gives you an extra special peanut butter cookie.

1-3/4	cups sifted flour	1/2	cup sugar
1	teaspoon baking soda	1/2	cup brown sugar, firmly packed
1/2	teaspoon salt		
1/2	cup shortening	1	egg, unbeaten
1/2	cup peanut butter	1	teaspoon vanilla

Sift together flour, baking soda and salt. Cream shortening and peanut butter. Gradually add sugars, creaming well. Add egg and vanilla; beat well. Blend in dry ingredients gradually; mix thoroughly. Shape dough into balls using a rounded teaspoonful for each. Roll balls in sugar and place on greased baking sheets. Bake in a 375 degree oven for 10 minutes. Remove from oven. Top each cookie with a milk chocolate star, pressing down firmly so cookie cracks around edge. Return to oven; bake 2 to 3 minutes longer until golden brown. Makes about 3 dozen cookies.

Accordion Treats

A little time involved, but it's truly different and well worth it.

3/4	cup butter	1/4	teaspoon salt
3/4	cup sugar	1-1/4	cups flour
2	eggs	1/2	cup chopped nuts
1	teaspoon vanilla		

Cream butter; and sugar. Beat in eggs, salt and vanilla. Gradually add flour and nuts, mix thoroughly. Fold 1 yard of heavy-duty foil lengthwise. Fold the double foil crosswise into 1-inch pleats to make an "accordion pleated" pan. Place on baking sheet. Drop a rounded teaspoonful of dough into each fold of foil. (Dough spreads during baking.) Bake in a 325 degree oven for 25 to 30 minutes until golden brown. Cool 10 minutes. Remove cookies; turn foil over for second baking. (Or clean foil with damp cloth and re-use.) If desired, sprinkle cookies with confectioners' sugar or frost with an icing. Decorate with jimmies of chopped nuts. Makes about 4 dozen.

Rum Apple-Raisin Cookies

An old-fashioned spice cookie, loaded with rum soaked raisins.

1	cup seedless raisins	1-1/2	teaspoons cinnamon
2/3	cup finely chopped dried apples	1/2	teaspoon mace
		1/2	teaspoon cloves
1/3	cup rum	1	cup margarine, softened
2	teaspoons lemon juice	1-1/4	cups light brown sugar
1-1/4	cups flour	1	large egg
1	cup whole wheat flour	1	large egg yolk
1	cup oats	1-1/2	teaspoons vanilla
1	teaspoon baking soda	1/4	teaspoon lemon zest
1/2	teaspoon baking powder	1-1/4	cups walnuts, chopped
1/2	teaspoon salt		

Mix together, raisins, rum, apples and lemon juice. Let stand 20 minutes. Mix the dry ingredients together. Beat margarine in large bowl and beat with brown sugar until fluffy; add egg yolk, egg, vanilla and lemon zest. Beat in half of dry ingredients. Stir in raisin-apple mixture and then remainder of dry ingredients. Form into 1-1/4-inch balls. Dip top in chopped walnuts. Place on greased baking sheets. Flatten tops. Bake in a 350 degree oven 10 to 12 minutes. Makes about 36 cookies.

Jumbo Peanut Butter Apple Cookies

Perfect for a child's lunch box, a cookie that's good for them.

1	cup sifted flour	1/4	cup sugar
1	cup sifted whole wheat flour	1-3/4	cups brown sugar
		2	eggs
2	teaspoons baking soda	1	teaspoon vanilla
1	teaspoon cinnamon	1	cup oats
3/4	teaspoon salt	1	cup peeled, diced apple
1/3	cup butter, softened	1/2	cup raisins
2/3	cup chunk style peanut butter		

Mix and sift first 5 ingredients. Cream butter, peanut butter and sugars. Add eggs and vanilla and mix. Add sifted dry ingredients to creamed mixture and mix well. Stir in oats, apple and raisins. Using about 1/4 cup of dough for each, shape into balls. Place on ungreased cookie sheet and flatten slightly. Bake in a preheated 350 degree oven about 12 to 14 minutes. Let stand on pan for 1 minute before removing to wire cooling rack. Makes about 1-1/2 dozen.

Fruitcake Cookies

Even if you aren't a lover of fruitcake - do try this different cookie.

1/4	cup shortening	1-1/2	cups (8 ounces) golden seedless raisins
1/4	cup butter or margarine, softened	3/4	cup (4 ounces) pitted chopped dates
1/2	cup firmly packed light brown sugar	3	slices candied pineapple (1 each of red, yellow and green), chopped
2	eggs, well beaten	3	cups chopped pecans
2-1/2	cups flour	3/4	cup (4 ounces) candied cherries, halved
1/2	teaspoon baking soda		
1/2	teaspoon cinnamon		
1/2	cup dark rum		

Grease 2 large cookie sheets; set aside. In large mixer bowl with mixer at medium speed, cream shortening and butter or margarine and sugar. Mix in beaten eggs until light and fluffy. In medium bowl combine 2 cups flour, baking soda and cinnamon. Add to creamed mixture alternately with rum; mix well. Mix remaining 1/2 cup flour with fruits and nuts (except cherries). Fold into dough. Form by tablespoonful into balls; place on cookie sheet. Top each with cherry half. Bake in a 300 degree oven for about 15 minutes or until barely set. Makes about 6-1/2 dozen.

Ginger Spice Cookies

Sometimes these don't have time to cool before they're gone.

2	cups sifted flour	1/2	teaspoon cloves
1	teaspoon baking soda	3/4	cup shortening
1/2	teaspoon salt	1	cup sugar
1	teaspoon cinnamon	2	tablespoons molasses
1	teaspoon ginger	1	egg

Combine flour, baking soda, spices and salt. Mix shortening and sugar, beat until fluffy. Add molasses and egg. Beat well. Add dry ingredients and beat on low speed until well combined. Shape into 1-1/2-inch balls. Dip into a small bowl of water, then a bowl of additional sugar. (For a lighter coating, just dip in sugar.) Arrange 3-inches apart on ungreased cookie sheets. Bake in a 350 degree oven for 15 minutes or until light-brown on bottom. Cool on wire racks. Makes about 20 cookies.

Frosted Crisp Molassies

Crispy cookies with a true lemon icing.

2-1/2	cups sifted flour	3/4	cup butter
1/2	teaspoon salt	3/4	cup brown sugar
1	teaspoon baking soda	1	egg
1	cup flaked coconut	1/2	cup dark molasses

Mix and sift flour, salt and baking soda; add coconut and mix. Cream butter, add sugar gradually and cream until fluffy. Add unbeaten egg and mix well. Add molasses and mix. Add sifted ingredients and mix. Using about 1 teaspoon for each, shape into about 1/2-inch balls on ungreased cookie sheets; allow space for spreading. Bake in a preheated 350 degree oven about 10 minutes. Frost cooled cookies with Lemon Frosting.

Lemon Frosting:

2	tablespoons butter	yellow food coloring, optional
2-1/2	cups sifted confectioners' sugar	cream
2	tablespoons lemon juice	

Cream butter, and sugar and juice alternately and mix well. Add food coloring as desired. Add cream gradually to give desired consistency. Makes about 7 dozen.

Molasses Cookies

Black pepper gives these cookies an interesting "Bite", but you can't taste the pepper.

3/4	cup sugar	1/2	teaspoon salt
3/4	cup butter, softened	1	tablespoon allspice
1	large egg	1	teaspoon cinnamon
1/4	cup dark molasses	1	teaspoon black pepper
2	cups sifted flour		sugar
2	teaspoons baking soda		

Sift together dry ingredients. Cream butter and sugar until fluffy. Beat in egg, then molasses. Add sifted dry ingredients, mix well. Form into 1-inch balls and roll into additional sugar. Place 2-inches apart on ungreased cookie sheet. Bake at 400 degrees for 12 to 15 minutes. Makes 4 dozen.

Spicy Gingersnaps

These cookies disappear so fast - be sure to make enough.

3/4	cup butter	2	teaspoons soda
1	cup sugar	1	teaspoon cinnamon
1/4	cup molasses	1	teaspoon cloves
1	egg	1	teaspoon ginger
2	cups sifted flour		granulated sugar for
1/2	teaspoon salt		rolling

Cream butter. Add sugar gradually; beat in molasses and egg; mix well. Blend in sifted dry ingredients; chill. Shape into 1-inch balls. Roll in sugar. Place 2-inches apart on greased cookie sheets. Bake at 375 degrees for about 10 to 12 minutes. Cookies become crisp when cool. Makes about 6 dozen.

Swedish Gingersnaps

Crunch, zip and flavor go into these attractive tasty cookies.

2-1/3	cups flour	2	teaspoons unsweetened cocoa powder
2-3/4	teaspoons ginger		
1-1/2	teaspoons cinnamon	1/2	cup butter
1/2	teaspoon cloves	1/2	cup dark molasses
1/2	teaspoon allspice	1/2	cup light brown sugar
	pinch of salt	1	large egg
1	teaspoon baking powder	1	teaspoon vanilla
3/4	teaspoon baking soda	2-1/2	tablespoons sugar

Sift dry ingredients together, combine butter, molasses, and sugar in a large bowl and beat until light. Beat in egg and vanilla. Stir in dry ingredients until smooth. Wrap dough in waxed paper and refrigerate overnight. Shape dough into 1-inch balls and place 1-1/2-inches apart on lightly greased baking sheet. Lightly grease bottom of flat bottomed glass and dip into sugar. Flatten each ball to about 1/4-inch thick and 1-3/4-inch in diameter. Dip glass in sugar after each cookie. Bake in a 350 degree preheated oven about 10 to 11 minutes. Let stand on baking sheet about 1-1/2 minutes before removing to wire racks. Cookies firm as they cool. Makes 40 to 45 cookies.

Hermits

Traditional, spicy hermits, chock-full of raisins and nuts. Crisp on the outside and moist inside.

3-1/3	cups flour	1/2	cup brown sugar, firmly packed
1	teaspoon cinnamon		
1	teaspoon ginger	2	eggs
1/2	teaspoon salt	1/2	cup light molasses
1/2	teaspoon nutmeg	1	teaspoon baking soda, dissolved in 1/4 cup warm water
1/2	teaspoon cloves		
1/2	cup vegetable shortening		
1/2	cup butter or margarine, softened	1	cup dark raisins
		1	cup golden raisins
1/2	cup granulated sugar	1	cup chopped walnuts

Preheat oven to 375 degrees. In mixer bowl combine shortening, butter and sugars; beat until fluffy and well blended. Add eggs, one at a time, beating until fluffy after each addition. Blend in molasses. Add sifted dry ingredients alternately with baking soda mixture, blending after each addition. Stir in raisins and walnuts. Using about 1/6 of the dough for each strip, spread dough in 1-1/2-inch wide, 3/4-inch thick strips, about 2-inches apart, down the length of greased baking sheets. Bake until a toothpick inverted in center of each strip comes out barely clean, about 12 to 15 minutes. Let strips stand on baking sheets on a wire rack for about 10 minutes, then cut, slightly on the diagonal, into 1-inch wide bars. Makes about 66 bars.

Molasses Rum Balls

Flavored with rum, molasses and pecans - Tasty as can be.

1	cup butter, softened	2-1/2	teaspoons dark rum flavoring
1/4	cup dark molasses		
2	tablespoons sugar	2	cups flour
1/4	teaspoon salt		powdered sugar
1	cup finely chopped pecans		

Cream butter and sugar with molasses. Add flour and salt; stir in nuts. Blend thoroughly, add rum. Shape dough into small balls, about the size of a large grape. Place on ungreased cookie sheet and bake in preheated 350 degree oven for about 15 to 20 minutes. Roll in powdered sugar while still warm. Makes about 6 dozen.

Honeyed Apricot Biscotti

Delicious dipped in melted bittersweet chocolate when cool.

3	egg whites	1-1/4	teaspoon ground anise
1/4	cup plus 2 tablespoons honey	3/4	teaspoon baking powder
2	cups flour	1/4	teaspoon baking soda
2/3	cup light brown sugar, packed		dash salt
		2/3	cup finely chopped dried apricots

Preheat oven to 325 degrees. Lightly coat large baking sheet with non stick cooking spray; dust with flour. In small bowl whisk together egg whites and honey until well blended; set aside. In large mixing bowl combine flour, brown sugar, anise, baking powder, baking soda and salt. Make a well in center and add egg white mixture and apricots. Mix until dough is smooth and combined, about 1 minute. Transfer dough to lightly floured work surface; divide in half. Shape each portion into an approximate 12 by 2-inch log. Arrange logs on baking sheet spaced about 6-inches apart. Bake until logs are golden brown, about 40 minutes. Reduce heat to 300 degrees. Transfer logs to work surface and let cool 3 minutes. Using sharp serrated knife, slice each log diagonally into 1/2-inch thick slices. On baking sheet arrange slices upright and slightly apart. Bake until crisp, 15 to 20 minutes more. Place cookies on wire rack and cool completely. Store in airtight containers up to 3 weeks.

Greek Cookies

Flavored with anise and sesame seed, these cookies are excellent for dunking in coffee or serving with an after-dinner brandy.

1/4	cup sesame seeds	2	teaspoons baking powder
1/2	cup unsalted butter, softened	1/4	teaspoon salt
1/2	cup sugar	2	teaspoons anise seed
2	eggs	1/4	cup brandy
1	teaspoon vanilla		whipping cream, for glazing
1	teaspoon grated orange rind		confectioners' sugar, for dusting
2-1/2	cups flour		

Toast sesame seeds in a small skillet over moderately low heat, shaking skillet constantly, until seeds are lightly colored. Let cool. In large mixer bowl cream butter; gradually add sugar and beat until light. Add eggs, one at a time, beating well after each addition. Beat in vanilla and orange rind. In medium bowl stir together flour, baking powder, salt, anise seed, and toasted sesame seeds. Add to creamed mixture alternately with brandy. Beat until just blended. Gather dough into a ball and enclose in plastic wrap or waxed paper; refrigerate. Preheat oven to 400 degrees. Work with a third of the dough at a time, keeping remainder in refrigerator. Divide un-refrigerated dough into 12 pieces. On a lightly floured board, roll each piece into a rope about 1/4-inch in diameter. Bring 2 ends of rope together. Hold 1 end of doubled rope in each hand and twist in opposite directions to form a spiral. Repeat with rest of dough. Arrange spirals about 1-1/2-inches apart on ungreased baking sheets. Brush lightly with cream. Bake until lightly browned, about 10 to 12 minutes. Transfer to wire racks. While cookies are still hot, sift confectioners' sugar over them. Leave on wire racks to cool completely. Makes about 3 dozen cookies.

Orange Tuiles

Tuiles make a dramatic appearance as part of dessert. Lovely with a rich espresso.

1/3	cup flour	2	egg whites, lightly beaten
2/3	confectioners' sugar		finely grated zest of 2 oranges
	pinch of salt		
2	teaspoons Grand Marnier liqueur	1	cup sliced blanched almonds
1	teaspoon orange flower water	1/2	cup butter, softened

Preheat oven to 400 degrees. Lightly butter a heavy baking sheet. Sift flour, confectioners' sugar, and salt together in a large bowl. Make a well in the center, and add the Grand Marnier, orange flower water, egg whites, orange zest, and almonds. Mix thoroughly. Then add the butter and stir until smooth. Drop the batter by teaspoonfuls, at least 3-inches apart, onto the prepared baking sheet. Using a fork dipped in cold water, spread the batter out slightly. Only 3 or 4 will fit on the baking sheet. Bake until cookies are golden brown, 6 to 8 minutes. Remove them immediately and drape them over a rolling pin. Allow them to cool on the pin. Remove the cooled, shaped cookies very carefully. Repeat with the remaining batter. Store the cookies in a large plastic container with a tight seal. Makes about 12 cookies.

Note:
Cookies must be shaped while still hot.

In a hurry? Roll out cookie dough and cut with a pastry wheel or pizza cutter.

Sugar-and-Spice Madeleines

An easy dessert for a Christmas party, served with a dish of cherry ice cream.

1/4	teaspoon salt	1/4	teaspoon cloves
2	eggs	1/4	cup margarine, melted
1/2	cup sugar	1	teaspoon vanilla
2/3	cup flour		vegetable cooking spray
1	teaspoon cinnamon	1	tablespoon powdered sugar
1/2	teaspoon nutmeg		

Combine the salt and eggs in a medium bowl, and beat at high speed of mixer until foamy. Gradually add sugar beating constantly until eggs are thick and pale (about 5 minutes). Combine flour and spices. Gradually fold into egg mixture. Gradually fold margarine and vanilla into egg mixture. Spoon about 1 tablespoon of batter into each madeleine pan coated with cooking spray. Bake at 400 degrees for 8 minutes or until lightly browned. Loosen madeleines from pans, using the tip of a knife. Remove from pans, and let cool completely on wire racks. Sprinkle with powdered sugar. Makes about 2 dozen.

Ladyfingers

Dainty double ladyfingers are intriguing on the tea table or when they are served with a frozen dessert.

2	egg yolks	1/8	teaspoon salt
1/2	cup sifted confectioners' sugar	2	egg whites
1/3	cup sifted cake flour	1/2	teaspoon vanilla

Line cookie sheets with unglazed paper. Beat confectioners' sugar and egg yolks until thick and lemon colored. Fold in flour and salt. Beat egg whites until rounded peaks are formed and egg whites do not slide when bowl is partially inverted. Fold into egg yolk flour mixture with vanilla. Force mixture through pastry bag onto prepared cookie sheets, using guide lines to shape ladyfingers. Use decorating tube number 10 for small ladyfingers and pastry bag coupling for large ladyfingers. Sprinkle lightly with confectioners' sugar. Bake at 325 degrees for 12 to 18 minutes, or until delicately browned. With spatula, remove at once to wire rack. Makes about 2 dozen large fingers or 3 dozen small fingers.

Note:
For double ladyfingers, brush bottom sides of baked fingers with slightly beaten egg white and press together in pairs.

Orange Madeleines

Adding an orange tang to Madeleines is a taste that is sure to please.

3	large eggs	1/4	teaspoon salt
2	large egg yolks	1	cup sifted flour
2/3	cup sugar	1/4	cup butter, melted, cooled
1	tablespoon orange zest		to lukewarm
1	teaspoon vanilla		powdered sugar
1/2	teaspoon orange extract		

Preheat oven to 375 degrees. Butter and flour madeleine pans. Using electric mixer, beat first 7 ingredients in large bowl until pale yellow about 6 minutes. Sift flour over; fold in gently but thoroughly; do not overwork or batter will deflate. Pour butter into small bowl. Fold in 1/4 cup batter. Quickly fold butter mixture back into remaining batter. Spoon batter into prepared pans, filling almost to top. bake until golden, about 10 minutes. Cool 1 minute in pans. Using small sharp knife, gently remove madeleines from pans. Cool. Sift powdered sugar over and serve. Makes 24.

Springerle

These are easy, pretty and fun to make.

1	egg	1/8	teaspoon salt
1/2	cup sugar	1/2	teaspoon baking powder
1	cup sifted flour	1/2	teaspoon anise extract

Beat eggs at high speed in small bowl of electric mixer until thick and light colored. Add sugar very gradually. Turn mixer to low speed; beat until sugar is dissolved. (This takes about 10 minutes.) Fold in sifted dry ingredients and anise extract. Place a small portion of dough at a time on well floured canvas; coat dough with flour. Pat with hands to 1/3-inch thickness. Dust springerle rolling pin with flour; press on dough to emboss the designs and get a clear imprint. Work quickly. Cut out the squares; place on greased cookie sheets; allow to dry at room temperature 4 to 6 hours. Bake at 350 degrees 10 to 12 minutes. Cool; store in covered container to mellow and soften. Makes about 1-1/2 dozen.

Pecan Nut Puffs

Bake these in Christmas cupcake liners and put in a pretty Christmas basket.

2/3	cup sifted flour	1/2	teaspoon vanilla
1/2	teaspoon baking powder	1	cup moist shredded coconut
1/4	teaspoon salt		
2	eggs	1	cup chopped pecans
1	cup brown sugar, sifted and packed		confectioners' sugar

Mix and sift flour, baking powder and salt. Beat eggs slightly, add sugar and vanilla and beat until thick. Add sifted dry ingredients, coconut and nutmeats and mix. Bake in greased muffin pans (bottom diameter, 1-1/3-inches) in a 350 degree oven for about 15 minutes. Remove from pans immediately and sprinkle with additional confectioners' sugar. Store in airtight container. Makes about 2 dozen.

Popcorn Macaroons

If your looking for an altogether different tasting cookie, try these, actually using popcorn for flavor.

2	cups popped popcorn	2	teaspoons vanilla
6	egg whites	2	cups pecan halves, finely chopped
1/4	teaspoon salt		
1	teaspoon cream of tartar	30	cherries, well drained
2	cups sifted confectioners' sugar		

Put popcorn in blender and chop fine. Beat egg whites at high speed until foamy. Add salt and cream of tartar and beat until egg whites form soft peaks. With mixer on low speed, gradually beat in confectioners' sugar. Fold in vanilla, pecans and popcorn. Turn oven on 275 degrees. Using a small ice cream scoop or a large serving spoon of 2 tablespoon size, drop cookies, 1-inch apart on lightly greased paper covered cookie sheet. Refrigerate rest of batter. Top each with a cherry; bake 1 hour, they will be soft. Remove from cookie sheet. Cool cookies on paper while baking rest of batter, then remove cooled ones; store, covered until time to serve. Makes about 30 macaroons.

Surprise Teacakes

To make these even tastier, use Hershey almond kisses.

1	cup butter	1	cup finely chopped nuts
1/2	cup powdered sugar	60	milk chocolate kisses
1	teaspoon vanilla		powdered sugar
2	cups sifted flour		

Cream butter; add sugar gradually; blend in vanilla. Mix in flour and nuts. Shape rounded teaspoonfuls of dough around each kiss, making sure candy is completely covered. Place on ungreased cookie sheets. Bake in oven at 375 degrees for about 12 minutes. Cool. Roll in powdered sugar. Makes about 5 dozen.

Graham Cracker Marguerites

Happy faces when children see you making these.

1-1/2	cups sugar	1/4	teaspoon vanilla
1/2	cup water	1	cup pecans, chopped
5	marshmallows	1/8	teaspoon salt
2	egg whites, well beaten	16	graham crackers
2	tablespoons shredded coconut		

Boil sugar and water together to the soft ball stage (236 to 238 degrees). Add the marshmallows which have been cut in pieces and stir until dissolved. Pour over the well beaten egg whites and beat until stiff enough to hold its shape. Add the vanilla, coconut, salt and pecans. Spread on graham crackers and bake in a 350 degree oven for about 15 minutes or until light brown.

Nut Toasties

It's a clever cook who can turn bread into cookies - serve with afternoon tea.

4	slices bread, 1-inch thick	1	teaspoon sugar
1	egg	1	cup finely chopped nutmeats
1/4	cup milk		
1/2	teaspoon salt		

Remove crusts from bread and cut each slice into strips 1-inch wide. Beat egg, add milk, salt, and sugar and dip bread in batter. Roll in nutmeats and fry in hot deep fat (385 degrees) until brown or bake in a 450 degree oven for 15 minutes. Makes 1 dozen.

Note:
Shredded coconut may be used in place of nutmeats.

Totcicles

Tots and grownups will love these chewy date cookies.

1-1/2	cups sifted flour	1/3	cup butter, melted
1	teaspoon baking powder	1	egg
1/2	teaspoon salt	1	teaspoon vanilla
1-1/4	cups dates, ground		wooden skewers or popsicle sticks
3/4	cup firmly packed brown sugar		

Combine dates, brown sugar and melted butter. Blend in egg and vanilla. Add dry ingredients; blend thoroughly. Refrigerate overnight. Shape well-rounded teaspoon of dough around end of skewers. Form into oblongs 2-inches long. Place on greased cookie sheets. Bake in a 350° oven for 12 to 15 minutes until golden brown. Cool. Dip each cookie into icing. Roll in 2 cups flaked coconut. Coconut may be tinted for a pretty holiday tray.

Coconut Grove Cookies

These are chocolate cookies with hidden chunks of chocolate and a baked-on coconut meringue.

2-1/2	cups sifted cake flour	1/2	cup sugar
1-1/2	teaspoons baking powder	1/4	cup dark brown sugar, firmly packed
1/4	teaspoon salt		
8	ounces sweet, bittersweet, or semi-sweet chocolate	2	egg yolks (reserve the whites for the meringue topping)
1/4	pound butter		
1	teaspoon vanilla	1/3	cup milk
2	teaspoons instant coffee		

Melt 4 ounces of chocolate. Cool. Cut the remaining chocolate into pieces measuring 1/4 to 1/2-inch across. Set aside. In a large bowl of an electric mixer, cream the butter. Add the vanilla and the instant coffee and then both sugars, and beat well. Beat in the egg yolks. Beat in the melted chocolate. On low speed gradually add half of the sifted dry ingredients. Now gradually add the milk and then the remaining dry ingredients and beat only until smooth. Stir in the cut chocolate pieces. Set the chocolate dough aside at room temperature and prepare the topping.

Meringue Topping:

2	egg whites pinch of salt	2	tablespoons sifted cake flour
1/2	cup sugar scant 1/4 teaspoon almond extract	2	cups, packed, finely shredded coconut

Beat the egg whites together with the salt until the whites hold soft peaks. Gradually add the sugar, 1 to 2 spoonfuls at a time, and then beat at high speed for 3 to 5 minutes until the meringue is very stiff. Toward the end of the beating, beat in the almond extract. Remove the bowl from the mixer and fold in the flour and then the coconut. Use a rounded teaspoonful of the chocolate dough for each cookie and place them 2-inches apart on ungreased cookie sheets. Then top each cookie with a slightly rounded teaspoonful of the meringue topping. Try to place the topping carefully so that it won't all run off the chocolate cookie while it is baking. A little of it will probably run down the side of the cookie, no matter what, but it's okay; it looks nice anyhow. Bake in a 325° oven for 12 to 13 minutes, until topping is lightly browned. With a wide metal spatula transfer the cookies to racks to cool. Makes about 44 cookies.

Apple Cobbler Cookies

An old-fashioned goodness in every bite.

3	cups flour	2	teaspoons vanilla
1	teaspoon baking powder	1/4	cup apple juice
1	teaspoon cinnamon	1/2	cup apple butter
1/2	cup white sugar	1	cup tart apples, peeled and chopped
1/2	cup light brown sugar, firmly packed	1	cup raisins
1	cup butter, softened	1	cup pecans, finely chopped
2	large eggs		

Mix flour, baking powder and cinnamon. Set aside. Mix sugars in a large bowl. Add butter and mix using an electric mixer at medium speed. Add eggs and vanilla, and blend until smooth. Thoroughly mix the apple juice and apple butter. Add the flour mixture, chopped apples, raisins and pecans, and blend at low speed until just combined. Do not over-mix. Roll dough into 1-inch balls. Roll each ball into crumb mixture until well coated. Place cookies on ungreased cookie sheets 2-inches apart. Bake in a 300 degree oven 24 to 26 minutes, or until cookie is firm to the touch and crumb mixture begins to brown. Makes 4 dozen cookies.

Crumb Coating:

1-1/4	cups light brown sugar, firmly packed	1-1/4	teaspoons cinnamon
1-1/2	cups quick oats (not instant)	9	tablespoons butter, melted

Combine sugar, oats and cinnamon in medium bowl. Mix well. Add melted butter and mix until dry ingredients are well moistened.

For ease in cutting candied fruit or dates dip scissors into cup of warm water. Also useful for cutting marshmallows.

Candied Apple Cookies

These intriguing butter cookies are pierced with a toothpick while hot, dipped in caramel and nuts when cool, then nestled in miniature paper muffin cups.

1/2	cup unsalted butter, softened	1-1/3	cups flour
1/3	cup firmly packed brown sugar	30	light caramels
		1	can (5-ounce) evaporated milk
	pinch of salt	1	cup finely chopped toasted walnuts
1/2	teaspoon vanilla		

In large mixer bowl cream butter; gradually add brown sugar and beat until light. Add salt and vanilla and beat until thoroughly blended. Gradually add flour, stirring until well mixed. Divide dough into 32 pieces, and roll each piece to form a ball. Place about 2-inches apart on ungreased baking sheets. Chill for 30 minutes. Preheat oven to 350 degrees. Bake cookies until lightly browned, about 12 to 15 minutes. Remove from oven and, while cookies are still hot, insert a toothpick in the top of each. Transfer to wire rack to cool. In top of double boiler over simmering water, combine caramels and evaporated milk. Cook, stirring, until mixture is smooth. Place walnuts in a shallow bowl. Dip cooled cookies into caramel mixture, letting excess drip off. Roll cookies in walnuts and set in miniature paper muffin cups. Makes about thirty-two 1-1/4-inch diameter cookies.

Fortune Cookies

Good luck! Put only happy fortunes inside.

2	eggs	1/4	teaspoon ginger
3/4	cup powdered sugar	1/4	cup melted butter
1/2	cup sifted flour	48	paper fortunes
1/4	teaspoon salt		

Beat eggs in small bowl of electric mixer; add sugar gradually; beat well. Blend in dry ingredients and butter. Drop rounded teaspoonfuls, 3-inches apart, onto greased and floured cookie sheets. Bake only 6 cookies at a time. Bake at 300 degrees about 10 minutes. Remove 1 cookie at a time; leave others in oven. (Cookies are difficult to shape when cool.) Fold each hot cookie in half slowly and carefully. Keep top of cookie on outside. Press edges together until cookie holds shape. Repeat with each remaining cookie. Cool. Slip fortunes into side openings of cookies. Makes about 4 dozen.

Rosettes

Perfect rosettes are crisp and yet tender.

1/2	cup sifted flour	1	egg, slightly beaten
1	tablespoon sugar	1	tablespoon vegetable oil
1/2	teaspoon salt		confectioners' sugar
1/2	cup milk		

Blend dry ingredients together. Mix remaining ingredients; stir in. Strain mixture. Heat rosette iron in hot fat (400 degrees) 2-inches deep in small saucepan. Tap off excess fat on absorbent paper. Dip into batter until 2/3 covered. Immerse in hot fat. Fry until delicately browned. Remove; tip upside-down to drain. Push off rosette. Heat iron in fat again; repeat process. If iron is too cool, batter will slip off into fat; if iron is too hot, batter will stick. Stir batter each time before dipping in iron. Sprinkle rosettes with confectioners' sugar. Store rosettes in single layers in waxed paper-lined boxes. Makes about 18 rosettes.

Vanilla Krumkake
(Fancy Norwegian Cookie)

One of our favorite cookies.

3	eggs	1	teaspoon vanilla
1/2	cup sugar	1/2	cup sifted flour
1/2	cup melted butter, cooled slightly		

Beat eggs until light. Add sugar gradually. Add butter and vanilla. Mix. Blend in flour. Preheat krumkake iron about 5 minutes at a medium high heat. Place 2 level teaspoonfuls of batter in center of iron. Lower the lid. Press lightly. Bake 1 to 2 minutes or until krumkake is delicately browned. Turn 3 or 4 times. Watch carefully. Remove from iron. Roll immediately on krumkake cone. Makes 4 dozen.

Note:
Excellent dessert when filled with cream.

Grybai

A spiced cookie that resembles mushrooms. Easy to make but takes a little time to frost. Results are worth it.

3	tablespoons butter	3/4	teaspoon baking soda
1/4	cup sugar	1/2	teaspoon cinnamon
1	egg	1/4	teaspoon cloves
1/2	cup honey, heated and cooled to lukewarm	1/4	teaspoon ginger
2	cups flour	1/4	teaspoon nutmeg
2	tablespoons lemon-flavored instant tea		White Icing
			Chocolate Icing

Blend butter and sugar; beat in honey and egg. Stir together the dry ingredients and add to butter mixture, blending well. Wrap dough in waxed paper and refrigerate for several hours. Shape 1/3 of dough into mushroom-like stems 1/4-inch in diameter and 1/2-inch long. Shape remainder of dough into an equal number of balls 1-inch in diameter. Indent 1 side of each ball with thumb to form a mushroom-like cap. Place balls rounded side up, laying stems separately on sides, on greased cookie sheets. Bake 10 minutes in a 350 degree oven. Cool on wire racks. Makes about 3 dozen cookies.

Assemble: Dip end of stem into White Icing and fit into indentation of cap; allow icing to set. Coat stem and underside of cap with White Icing, then top cap with Chocolate Icing.

White Icing:

In small bowl, blend 2-1/2 cups confectioners' sugar with 2 to 3 tablespoons milk.

Chocolate Frosting:

In small bowl, blend 2 cups confectioners' sugar, 1 tablespoons cocoa and 2 to 3 tablespoons milk.

Note:
Package in pretty flowerpots or little colored straw baskets for gifts. Look like plump mushrooms. Make some fat and sassy, and some tiny buttons.

Salt Dough Decorations

One of my favorite fun recipes. It has nothing to do with food, so don't try eating it. They keep forever, and make special holiday gifts. Try braided breads, cookies, ornaments or anything that strikes your fancy. Children love to help. Dough wrapped in foil will keep up to 2 weeks.

2	cups flour	1/2	teaspoon powdered alum
1	cup salt	3/4	cup water

Mix all ingredients completely with hands. (If dough is too dry, work in 1 to 1-1/2 teaspoons water.) Form shapes as desired. Mark all details (facial features, clothing and the like) on surface of dough with wooden pick or sharp knife before baking.

<u>To roll</u>: Roll dough 1/8-inch thick on lightly floured board. Cut with cookie cutters or cut around paper patterns with sharp knife.

<u>To mold by hand</u>: Form dough into shapes (flowers, fruits, animals, storybook characters) no more than 1/2-inch thick.

<u>To hang ornaments</u>: Cut fine craft wire 1-1/2 to 2-inches long and twist several times to form loop; spread ends apart slightly and insert into unbaked ornament so that only loop shows. Or make a hole 1/4-inch from top of ornament with end of plastic straw.

Heat oven to 250 degrees. Place ornaments on ungreased cookie sheet. Bake until completely hard and dry, about 2 hours. Remove from cookie sheet; cool. When cool, rub any rough edges with fine sandpaper until smooth. If desired, outline designs or other details to be painted with pencil. Paint with plastic-based poster or acrylic paint. Allow paint to dry. Place ornaments on waxed paper and seal by spraying with clear plastic (polyurethane) or brushing with clear shellac. Makes about 5 dozen 2-1/2-inch ornaments.

<u>Techniques and tips</u>: Complete ornaments one at a time, don't use the assembly-line principle. If the surface of the basic shape dries out, it will be difficult to work with. If desired, dough can be tinted by dividing into several parts and kneading a different food color into each part. (Past food color is more vivid.) After baking, seal as directed for painted ornaments. Indications for clothing, features and texture can be marked with a sharp knife or wooden pick. The wooden pick is best for small details. When adding small pieces (arms, legs, hats) to a 3 dimensional ornament, always put a dab of water in the spot where the piece is going to be added. As with appliqués, baking will "cement" the piece in place. Remember to paint the sides and backs of ornaments.

Bar Cookies

*Half the fun of baking
is baking things to share;
is sending messages of love
to those for whom we care.*

Macaroon Polka Dots

A sweet candy like topping makes the taste unique.

1/3	cup butter	1/4	teaspoon baking soda
1/2	cup brown sugar	1/4	teaspoon salt
2	egg yolks	1	cup flour
1	teaspoon vanilla		

Cream butter and brown sugar well. Add egg yolks, vanilla, soda, and salt, mix well. Blend in flour, mix thoroughly. Spread in 11 by 7 or 9 by 10-inch pan, greased on bottom only. Bake in a 325 degree oven for 15 minutes. Do not brown.

Topping:

2	egg whites	1/2	cup chocolate chips
1	tablespoon sugar	2	cups grated coconut
3/4	cup sweetened condensed milk		

Beat egg whites until soft peaks form. Add sugar and continue beating until stiff peaks form. Fold in milk, chips and coconut. Spread over base of baked cookies. Bake at 325 degrees for 25 to 30 minutes. Cool. Cut into 36 bars.

Rocky-Road Oaties

Good cookies for children's lunches.

4	cups rolled regular oats	2	cups semisweet chocolate pieces
1	cup packed light brown sugar	1/2	cup crunchy peanut butter
1/2	cup light corn syrup		
6	tablespoons butter or margarine, melted	2	cups miniature marshmallows

Preheat oven to 375 degrees. Line a 15x10-inch jellyroll pan with foil; grease foil generously. In a large bowl combine oats, brown sugar, corn syrup and melted butter or margarine, blending well. Press mixture evenly in greased, foil-lined pan. Bake 8 to 10 minutes or until light golden. Cool completely in pan. Meanwhile, in top of a double boiler, combine chocolate pieces and peanut butter. Heat over hot but not boiling water until melted, stirring occasionally. Remove pan from water. Stir in marshmallows. Immediately spread chocolate mixture evenly over cooled crust. Refrigerate. Cut chilled cookies into bars. Store in refrigerator if desired. Makes about fifty 2 by 1-1/2-inch cookies.

Milk Chocolate Caramel Bars

Ice cream topping adds rich caramel flavoring to this chewy, moist bar cookie.

1-1/4	cups flour	1/2	cup butter or margarine, softened
1/2	cup firmly packed brown sugar		

Bar:

11	ounce jar (3/4 cup) caramel ice cream topping	1	egg
		1	cup chopped nuts
3	ounce package cream cheese, softened	5-3/4	ounce package (1 cup) milk chocolate pieces or 2 milk chocolate bars (1-3/8 ounce each)
1	teaspoon vanilla		

In large bowl, mix first 3 ingredients until crumbly. Reserve 2/3 cup; press remainder in ungreased 9-inch square or 11 by 7-inch pan. In same bowl, combine 2/3 cup reserved flour mixture and first 4 bar ingredients. Mix at low speed until blended. Stir in nuts. Pour over crust. Bake in a 375 degree oven for about 30 to 35 minutes or until firm. Immediately sprinkle with chocolate pieces; spread when softened. Cool before cutting. Makes about 3 dozen small bars.

Caramelitas

Made with caramel topping in batter.

1	cup plus 3 tablespoons flour	1	jar (12-1/4-ounce) caramel topping
1	cup quick oats, uncooked	1	package (6-ounce) semisweet chocolate pieces
3/4	cup firmly packed light brown sugar		
1/2	teaspoon baking soda	1/2	cup walnuts, chopped
1/4	teaspoon salt		
3/4	cup butter or margarine, melted		

In large mixer bowl combine 1 cup flour and next 5 ingredients; beat at low speed until well mixed. Evenly pat into an ungreased 13 by 9-inch baking pan. Bake in a 350 degree oven for about 10 minutes. Meanwhile, stir caramel topping and remaining 3 tablespoons flour until well mixed. Remove pan from oven; sprinkle on chocolate pieces and walnuts. Drizzle on caramel mixture. Return pan to oven, continue baking 20 to 25 minutes more or until browned. Cool before cutting into 36 bars (2-3/4 by 1-inch).

Caramel Candy-Bar Cookies

My husband's top choice each year.

1	cup flour	1	14-ounce package caramels
1	cup quick-cooking oats	1/3	cup evaporated milk
1/2	teaspoon baking soda	1/2	cup chopped nuts
1/4	teaspoon salt	1	cup butterscotch chips or semi-sweet chocolate pieces
3/4	cup butter or margarine		
3/4	cup sugar		

Combine flour, oats, baking soda and salt. In a mixer bowl, beat the butter or margarine for 30 seconds. Add sugar and beat until fluffy. Beat in oat mixture until crumbly. Do not over-mix. Reserve 1 cup of this crust mixture, then press the remainder of the mixture onto the bottom of a 13 by 9 by 2-inch baking pan. Bake the crust layer in a 350 degree oven for 10 minutes. Cool in the pan for 10 minutes. Meanwhile, in a saucepan, cook the unwrapped caramels and evaporated milk over low heat until caramels melt and mixture is smooth. Spread over the pre-baked cookie crust. Sprinkle the nuts over the top, then the reserved crumbs and butterscotch chips or chocolate. Bake in a 350 degree oven for 15 to 20 minutes or until the top crumbs turn golden. Cool in a pan on a wire rack. Cut into bars. Makes 32 cookies.

Candy Bar Squares

These are so popular, it's sure to be a winner in your circle.

3/4	cup powdered sugar	1	teaspoon vanilla
3/4	cup butter or margarine, softened	1-3/4	cups flour
2	tablespoons milk or light cream	1/4	teaspoon salt

Preheat oven to 325 degrees. In large bowl, blend first 4 ingredients until smooth. Stir in flour and salt. Press into ungreased 15 by 10-inch jellyroll pan. Bake 20 to 25 minutes until light golden brown. Cool.

Filling:

2	tablespoons firmly packed brown sugar	2	tablespoons butter or margarine
1/2	cup caramel ice cream topping	1-1/4	cups powdered sugar
		1/2	to 1 cup chopped nuts

In small saucepan, heat brown sugar, topping and butter until butter melts. Stir in powdered sugar until smooth; stir in nuts. Spread filling over crust.

Frosting:

1	square unsweetened chocolate	1	to 2 tablespoons milk or light cream
1	tablespoon butter or margarine	1/2	teaspoon vanilla

In saucepan, heat chocolate, butter and 1 tablespoon milk until chocolate melts, stirring constantly. Remove from heat; stir in remaining frosting ingredients until smooth. If necessary, thin with additional milk to drizzling consistency. Drizzle frosting over filling. Cool completely; cut into bars. (May be refrigerated to cool.) Makes 3 to 4 dozen bars.

Jeweled Bars

A chewy, moist bar with the added fun of candied orange slices. It contains no shortening.

4	eggs, separated	1	teaspoon baking powder
2-1/4	cups brown sugar, packed	1/2	teaspoon salt
1	tablespoon water	1	cup candied orange slices (about 18), finely cut
1	teaspoon vanilla	3/4	cup chopped walnuts
2	cups flour		

Beat egg yolks; add sugar, water, and vanilla. Blend dry ingredients; stir in. Mix in orange pieces and walnuts. Beat egg whites until stiff but not dry; stir in. Spread in well-greased oblong pan, 13 by 9-1/2 by 2-inches. Bake in a 350 degree oven for 30 to 35 minutes. Cut in bars while warm. Makes about 3 dozen bars.

Orange Gumdrop Slice Bar

A pretty cookie to add to your Christmas gift box.

1/3	cup flour	1/2	cup orange slices, cut-up
1/8	teaspoon baking powder	1/2	cup chopped nuts
1/8	teaspoon salt	2	eggs, well beaten
1	cup brown sugar	1	teaspoon vanilla

Mix flour, soda, salt and sugar in sifter. Sift in bowl. Add gumdrops and nuts. Blend in eggs and vanilla. Pour into a greased pan, 9 by 9 by 2-inches, lined with greased waxed paper. Bake in a 350 degree oven for 25 minutes. Remove cookies from pan immediately. Peel off paper carefully. Cool. Sprinkle with confectioners' sugar. Cut into bars. Decorate with orange slices. Makes 24 bars.

Sugar Plum Squares

A chewy, flavorful bar cookie. Excellent anytime, especially during the holidays.

1/2	cup butter	3/4	cup flaked coconut
1/4	cup brown sugar, packed	3/4	cup chopped pecans
1/4	teaspoon salt	2	tablespoons flour
1	cup sifted flour	2	tablespoons crystallized ginger
2	eggs		
1	cup brown sugar, packed	1	teaspoon baking powder
1	teaspoon vanilla	1/4	teaspoon salt
1	cup raisins		confectioners' sugar

Cream butter, 1/4 cup brown sugar and 1/4 teaspoon salt until light and fluffy. Blend in flour; mix well. Spread on bottom of 8-inch square pan. Bake at 325 degrees for 15 minutes. Beat eggs until thick and lemon colored. Beat in 1 cup brown sugar and vanilla. Add remaining ingredients except confectioners' sugar; mix well. Spoon mixture over crust. Continue baking 30 to 35 minutes until filling is set. Cool; dust with confectioners' sugar. Cut into squares. Makes about 2 dozen.

Strawberry-Filled Butter Slices

As festive in looks as they are in flavor, these tender butter cookies are good to serve as a sweet with tea.

1-2/3	cups flour	1	teaspoon vanilla extract
1/2	teaspoon baking soda	1/2	cup finely chopped unblanched hazelnuts or walnuts
1/4	teaspoon salt		
1/2	cup butter or margarine, softened		
3/4	cup confectioners' sugar	1/2	cup strawberry preserves
1	egg		confectioners' sugar, optional

Preheat oven to 350 degrees. In mixer bowl combine butter and the 3/4 cup confectioners' sugar; beat until fluffy and well combined. Beat in egg until fluffy. Blend in vanilla. Gradually add flour mixture, then hazelnuts, blending until well combined. Using 1/3 of the dough for each strip, spread dough in 1-1/2-inch wide, 1/2-inch thick strips, about 2-inches apart, down the length of greased baking sheets. With your floured finger or teaspoon, make a 1/2-inch wide depression down the entire length of the center of each strip. Bake for about 5 minutes, then remove from oven and press depressions down again. Return cookies to oven and bake until golden brown, about 10 to 12 minutes. Fill depressions in warm cookie strips with preserves. Let cool on baking sheets for about 15 minutes, then cut, slightly on the diagonal, into 1-inch wide bars. Sift lightly with confectioners' sugar, if desired. Makes about 42 cookies.

Swedish Butter Slices

A rich golden butter cookie with a bright red jelly filling. Sliced after baking.

2	cups sifted flour	1	egg
2/3	cup sugar	2	teaspoons vanilla
1/2	teaspoon baking powder	1/3	cup red jelly or jam
3/4	cup soft butter		

Sift flour, sugar and baking powder in a bowl. Blend in butter, egg and vanilla to form a dough. Place on floured canvas. Divide in 4 parts. Roll each part 13-inches long and 3/4-inch thick. Place on ungreased cookie sheets 4-inches apart and 2-inches from edge of sheet. Make a depression 1/3-inch deep lengthwise down center of each with a knife handle. Fill depressions with jelly or jam. Bake in a 350 degree oven about 15 to 20 minutes. While warm, cut diagonally into bars. Makes about 4 dozen bars.

Banana Oat Bars

Just another good healthy breakfast bar.

1-1/3	cups flour	1/2	cup raisins
1	cup quick-cooking oats	2	medium sized ripe bananas, mashed
1/2	cup sugar		
2	teaspoons baking powder	1/4	cup nonfat milk
1	teaspoon cinnamon	2	large egg whites
1/2	teaspoon baking soda	1	teaspoon vanilla

In large bowl, stir together flour, oats, sugar, baking powder, cinnamon, soda, and raisins. Add bananas, milk, egg whites, and vanilla; beat until smoothly mixed. Spread batter evenly in a non stick (or lightly oiled regular) 9 by 13-inch pan. Bake in a 350 degree oven until golden brown, just begins to pull from pan sides, and springs back when lightly touched in center, 35 to 40 minutes. Serve warm or cool, cut into about 2-inch squares. Wrap bars individually and freeze.

Tangy Banana Bars

These moist, cake-like bar cookies with a mild banana flavor can double as a dessert.

1	cup firmly packed brown sugar	1-3/4	cups flour
		1/2	teaspoon baking powder
1	cup apricot preserves	1/2	teaspoon baking soda
1/2	cup butter or margarine	1	cup mashed bananas
1	teaspoon vanilla	1/2	to 1 cup chopped nuts
2	eggs		powdered sugar

Preheat oven to 350 degrees. Grease a 13 by 9-inch pan. In large bowl, combine first 5 ingredients; blend well. By hand, stir in next 5 ingredients just until moistened. Pour into prepared pan. Bake 30 to 40 minutes until toothpick inserted in center comes out clean. Cool; sprinkle with powdered sugar. Makes 3 dozen bars.

Cranberry Crunch Bars

A tart unusual cranberry taste.

1-3/4	cups sifted flour	3/4	cup sugar
3/4	teaspoon salt	2-1/2	tablespoons cornstarch
1	teaspoon cinnamon	2	14-ounce jars cranberry orange relish
1-1/4	cups brown sugar, packed	1	egg
2	cups uncooked oatmeal	1	tablespoon water
1	cup butter		powdered sugar
1	cup finely chopped walnuts		

Sift flour, salt and cinnamon into a large mixing bowl; add brown sugar and oatmeal. Cut in butter with pastry blender until mixture resembles coarse crumbs; mix in walnuts. Press half of mixture into greased 13 by 9 by 2-inch pan. Bake at 375 degrees about 8 minutes. Cool slightly. Mix granulated sugar and cornstarch in saucepan. Add cranberry relish. Cook and stir until mixture thickens and boils about 3 minutes. Spread evenly over baked crust; sprinkle with remaining crumb mixture; pat down firmly. Beat egg well; add water; brush lightly over crumb mixture. Bake at 375 degrees for 35 to 40 minutes. Cool. Cut into bars. Sprinkle with powdered sugar. Makes about 48.

Apricot Shortbread

Cut these luscious bars small and serve with ice cream.

Shortbread:

1/3	cup soft butter or margarine	1	cup sifted flour
		1/2	cup light brown sugar, firmly packed

Preheat oven to 350 degrees. Make shortbread. In medium bowl, with portable electric mixer, beat butter with sugar until light and fluffy. At low speed, beat in flour. Pat mixture evenly into bottom of an 8 by 8 by 2-inch baking pan. Bake about 12 minutes, or until light-golden in color. Let cool completely in pan on wire rack.

Filling:

3/4	cup dried apricots	2/3	cup sugar
1	teaspoon grated lemon peel	2	teaspoons cornstarch
		1/3	cup chopped walnuts

Place apricots in small saucepan. Add just enough water to cover; bring to boiling. Reduce heat, and simmer, covered, for about 15 minutes. Drain apricots, reserving 3 tablespoons cooking liquid. Chop apricots fine. Combine in small saucepan with reserved liquid, lemon peel, sugar, cornstarch. Bring to boiling, stirring; boil 1 minute. Let filling cool 10 minutes. Spread evenly over shortbread crust. Sprinkle with walnuts. Bake about 20 minutes. Let cool completely in pan on wire rack. Cut into bars. Makes about 20.

Need crushed candy bars for a recipe? Freeze bars; leave in wrappers and pound gently with hammer.

Luscious Apricot Bars

A fruity bar that freezes well.

2/3	cup dried apricots	1	cup brown sugar, packed
1/2	cup butter	2	eggs, well beaten
1/4	cup sugar	1/2	teaspoon vanilla
1-1/3	cups sifted flour	1/2	cup chopped nuts
1/2	teaspoon baking powder		confectioners' sugar
1/4	teaspoon salt		

Cover apricots with water; bring to a boil. Boil for 10 minutes; drain. Cool and chop apricots. Combine butter, sugar and 1 cup flour; mix with a fork until crumbly. Press lightly into greased 8-inch pan. Bake at 350 degrees for about 25 minutes or until lightly browned. Sift together 1/3 cup flour, baking powder and salt; reserve. Gradually beat brown sugar into eggs; add dry ingredients; mix well. Stir in vanilla, nuts and apricots. Spread over crust. Bake at 350 degrees for about 30 minutes or until done. Cool; cut into bars. Roll bars in confectioners' sugar. Makes about 2 dozen.

Lemon Creme Bars

A combination of condensed milk and lemon juice make the filling easy to prepare in this oatmeal bar cookie.

14	ounce can sweetened condensed milk (not evaporated)	1	cup quick cooking oats
		1	cup firmly packed brown sugar
1/2	cup lemon juice	1	teaspoon baking powder
1-1/2	cups flour	2/3	cup butter or margarine

Preheat oven to 350 degrees. Grease 13 by 9-inch pan. Combine first 2 ingredients; set aside. In large bowl, combine all remaining ingredients; mix at low speed until crumbly. Press half of crumb mixture into prepared pan. Spread with lemon mixture. Crumble remaining mixture over all. Bake 25 to 30 minutes until light golden brown. (Bars will be soft.) Chill. Cut into bars. Refrigerate any leftovers. Makes 2 to 3 dozen bars.

Fresh Lemon Bars

These fresh lemon bars have a special appeal to lovers of lemon meringue.

1	cup butter or margarine, softened	2	cups sugar
1/2	cup confectioners' sugar	1	lemon rind, grated
1	teaspoon vanilla	6	tablespoons lemon juice
2	cups flour	1/4	cup (approximately) confectioners' sugar for topping
4	eggs		

Preheat oven to 350 degrees. Generously grease a 9x13-inch pan. Cream butter, 1/2 cup confectioners' sugar, and vanilla; beat until fluffy. Gradually add flour, mixing until well combined. Spread evenly in prepared pan. Bake for 20 minutes. In a bowl combine eggs, granulated sugar, lemon rind, and lemon juice; stir to blend all ingredients (do not beat). Pour lemon mixture over baked layer. Return to oven and bake until topping is set and lightly browned, about 18 to 20 minutes. Sift additional sugar over warm cookies to cover top generously. Cut into bars. Remove from pan when cool. Makes about 3 dozen bars.

Lemon Filbert Tea Bars

A favorite way to use filberts.

1/2	cup butter or margarine	2	tablespoons lemon juice
1	cup plus 2 tablespoons flour	1/2	teaspoon baking powder
1/4	cup confectioners' sugar	1/2	cup ground toasted filberts
2	eggs		additional confectioners' sugar
1	cup sugar		
1	teaspoon grated lemon peel		

In a mixing bowl, combine butter, 1 cup flour and confectioners' sugar. Press into the bottom of an 11-1/2 by 7-1/2-inch baking pan. Bake at 350 degrees for 10 minutes. Combine the remaining ingredients except additional confectioners' sugar. Pour over the crust; bake for 20 minutes. Cool. Cut into squares and sprinkle with confectioners' sugar. Makes about 15 bars.

Rickety Uncle

Almost a shortbread taste to these crunchy bars.

1/2	cup soft butter	1/2	cup chopped walnuts
1	cup light brown sugar, firmly packed	2	cups quick cooking oatmeal
1	teaspoon vanilla		

Cream butter. Add brown sugar and vanilla. Blend well. Add walnuts and oatmeal. (Mixture appears very dry.) Pat into a greased 7 by 11 by 1-1/2-inch pan. Bake at 350 degrees for about 30 minutes. Cut in squares while warm. Makes about 24 squares.

Oriental Crunch

These cookies may be broken-up to any desired size.

1	cup butter, very soft	1	cup sugar
3	tablespoons instant coffee	2	cups flour
1/2	teaspoon salt	1	cup chocolate chips
1/2	teaspoon almond extract	1	cup almonds, broken and coarsely chopped
1	teaspoon vanilla		

In large bowl, cream together butter, coffee, salt and flavorings until smooth; gradually add sugar, beating mixture until light and fluffy. Blend in flour, chocolate chips and nuts. Press mixture into a 15 by 10-inch jellyroll pan, greased lightly. (Don't press down too hard.) Bake 20 minutes in a 375 degree oven. Cool pan on wire rack about 5 minutes. Break cooled cookies into pieces. These cookies freeze well. Makes about 48 cookies.

Peanut Brittle Cookies

A fun looking cookie that tastes as good as it looks.

1	cup sifted flour	1	teaspoon vanilla
1/4	teaspoon baking soda	1/2	cup salted peanuts, finely chopped
1/2	teaspoon cinnamon	1	tablespoon egg
1/2	cup butter or other shortening		additional 1/2 cup salted peanuts or other nuts
1/2	cup firmly packed brown sugar		
2	tablespoons beaten egg (reserve remainder)		

Sift together flour, soda, and cinnamon. Cream butter or other shortening; gradually add sugar, creaming well. Add 2 tablespoons beaten egg and vanilla; beat well. Blend in dry ingredients and 1/2 cup chopped peanuts. Mix thoroughly. Spread or pat dough on greased baking sheet to a 14 by 10-inch rectangle. Brush with remaining 1 tablespoon egg. Sprinkle with 1/2 cup salted peanuts or other nuts. Bake in 325 degree oven for 20 to 25 minutes. Do not overbake. Cut or break into pieces while warm. Makes about 2 dozen.

Happy the individual who gets a beautiful glass bowl filled with dainty "Holiday Cookies".

Peanut Brittle Bars

These are hard, chewy, and crunchy like brittle candy.

1/2	pound butter	1	cup salted peanuts,
1	cup sugar		chopped into
2	cups sifted flour		medium-sized pieces

Preheat oven to 375 degrees. Cream the butter. Add the sugar and beat to mix well. On low speed, gradually add the flour, beating only until the dough holds together. Mix in 1/2 of the nuts (reserve the remaining nuts for topping). Turn the dough into an unbuttered 15-1/2 by 10-1/2-inch jellyroll pan. Dip your fingertips in flour and use them to press the dough into a thin layer. Don't worry about smoothing the layer now, that will come soon. Sprinkle the reserved nuts evenly over the dough. Place a large piece of wax paper over the nuts. With a small rolling pin or a straight-sided glass, roll over the paper to press the nuts firmly into the top of the dough and to smooth the dough at the same time. Bake for 23 to 25 minutes until golden brown. Reverse the pan once during baking to insure even browning. The cake will puff up during baking and then sink, leaving the edges higher and the surface slightly wrinkled. Cool in the pan for about 5 minutes and then, while the cake is still warm, cut into bars. (When cool, it will become too hard and brittle to cut.) With a metal spatula remove the bars from the pan and finish cooling them on racks.

Peanut Streusel Banana Bars

People have known for a long time that peanut butter and bananas are a great combination. We now bring them together in this easy to make bar.

1	cup flour	1/4	cup peanut butter
3/4	cup firmly packed brown sugar	2	tablespoons milk
		2	tablespoons cooking oil
1	teaspoon baking powder	1/2	teaspoon vanilla
1/4	teaspoon salt	1	egg
1/2	cup thinly sliced, ripe banana		

Preheat oven to 350 degrees. Grease a 13 by 9-inch pan. In large bowl, combine ingredients. Beat 1 minute at medium speed. Pour batter into greased pan.

Topping:

1/2	cup flour	1/4	cup butter or margarine, softened
1/2	cup firmly packed brown sugar	1/2	cup chopped peanuts

Blend first 3 ingredients at low speed until crumbly. Stir in peanuts. Sprinkle over batter. Bake 20 to 30 minutes until toothpick inserted in center comes out clean. Cool. Cut into bars. Makes 2 to 3 dozen bars.

Peanut Toffee Diamonds

Boys and girls love eating their favorite food in these cookies.

1/2	cup butter	2	cups sifted flour
1/2	cup chunk-style peanut	1	cup chocolate bits, melted
1	cup brown sugar, packed		
1	egg	1/2	cup chunk-style peanut butter
1	teaspoon vanilla		
1/4	teaspoon salt		whole salted peanuts

Cream butter and 1/2 cup peanut butter; add sugar gradually; beat in egg and vanilla. Blend in salt and flour. Pat into greased 15 by 10 by 1-inch pan. Bake at 325 degrees for about 25 minutes. Combine chocolate and 1/2 cup peanut butter; spread over hot baked surface. Cut into diamonds while warm; place a peanut in center of each diamond. Makes about 4 dozen.

Chocolate Oatmeal Peanut Bars

Chocolate and peanuts are a tempting combination.

2/3	cup butter	16	ounces chocolate chips
1/2	cup brown sugar	2/3	cup creamy peanut butter
1/2	cup light corn syrup	1/3	cup chopped dry roasted peanuts
2	teaspoons vanilla		
4	cups quick cooking oats		

Beat sugar and butter until creamy; stir in corn syrup and vanilla and oats, blending thoroughly. Pat dough evenly over bottom of a greased 9 by 13-inch baking pan. Bake in a 350 degree oven for about 20 minutes. Cool in pan, then cover and refrigerate until cold. Meanwhile, place chips and peanut butter in a pan and stir over low heat until melted and smooth. Spread mixture evenly over baked crust; sprinkle with peanuts. Refrigerate until topping firms slightly. Then cut into bars about 1 by 2-inches. Store, uncovered, in refrigerator. Makes about 4-1/2 dozen.

Peanut Butter Crunchies

Chow mein noodles add an extra crunch to these cookies.

1/2	cup butter	1	cup sifted flour
1/2	cup brown sugar, packed		

Cream butter; add sugar gradually; blend in flour. Spread into a greased 9 by 9 by 2-inch pan. Bake at 350 degrees for about 15 minutes or until golden brown; cool. Make Crunchy Noodle Topping.

Crunchy Noodle Topping:

1	cup chunk style peanut butter	1/4	cup diced maraschino cherries, drained
1/2	cup brown sugar, packed		
1/4	cup half and half cream	1/2	cup semi-sweet chocolate bits
5	cups miniature marshmallows		
1	5-1/2-ounce can chow mein noodles, slightly crushed		

Combine peanut butter, sugar, cream and marshmallows in a saucepan. Cook at a low heat until marshmallows are melted. Stir constantly. Mix in noodles and cherries. Sprinkle chocolate bits over crust; spread marshmallow mixture evenly over chocolate bits; cool. Cut into squares. Makes about 3 dozen.

Peanut Strips

So easy to do - it's bound to be one of your favorites.

1/2	cup margarine	1	teaspoon baking powder
1	cup brown sugar	1/4	cup milk
2	beaten eggs	3/4	cup peanuts, chopped
1	cup sifted flour	1	teaspoon vanilla
1/4	teaspoon salt		

Cream margarine and sugar, add eggs, beat well. Sift flour with salt and baking powder. Add alternately to the creamed mixture with the milk. Add nuts and vanilla. Pour into well-greased 10 by 14-inch pan. Bake at 350 degrees for 30 minutes. Cut into strips and roll in powdered sugar. Makes 36 strips.

Choco Peanut Pan Cookie

What a nice treat for after school appetites, kids love M & M's.

1	cup butter	1-1/4	cups flour
1	cup peanut butter	1	teaspoon baking soda
1	cup sugar	1/2	teaspoon salt
1	cup firmly packed brown sugar	2-1/4	cups quick oats
2	eggs	1	cup M & M's candy

Beat together the butter, peanut butter and sugars until light and fluffy. Blend in eggs. Combine flour, soda and salt and add to butter mixture. Mix well. Stir in oats and 1/3 cup M & M's. Pour onto a greased, foil lined cookie sheet with sides. Sprinkle remaining M & M's on top. Bake at 325 degrees for 25 to 30 minutes or until done. Makes about 24 cookies.

Rinse measuring cup or spoons with warm water before measuring honey or molasses. It will slide right out.

Congo Squares

These cookies can double as a dessert for dinner served with a big scoop of vanilla ice cream.

2/3	cup margarine	3	eggs, beaten
2-1/4	cups brown sugar, packed	1	tablespoon vanilla
2-3/4	cups flour	2	cups chocolate chips
2-1/2	teaspoons baking powder	1	cup chopped walnuts
1/2	teaspoon salt		

Melt margarine over medium heat. Stir in brown sugar. Cool slightly. Combine flour, baking powder and salt; add gradually with eggs to mixture. Stir in vanilla, nuts, and chocolate chips. Spread into a greased and floured 9 by 12-inch baking pan. Bake at 350 degrees for 25 to 30 minutes. Cut into squares while warm. Makes 48 squares.

Chocolate Peanut Bars

Try putting these peanut butter, chocolate, and peanut cookies in your mouth without grabbing another right away.

1/3	cup butter	1-1/3	cups flour
1	cup brown sugar	1	teaspoon baking powder
1	teaspoon vanilla	1/2	teaspoon salt
2	eggs		

Melt butter in top of double boiler. Remove from heat. Blend in brown sugar. Let cool slightly. Add vanilla. Blend in eggs 1 at a time, beating well after each. Sift together flour, baking powder and salt, add to egg mixture. Blend well. Spread into a well-greased 9 by 9 by 2-inch pan. Bake at 375 degrees for 15 to 18 minutes. Let cool slightly. Spread lightly with Peanut Butter Topping, then carefully spread with the Chocolate Topping. If desired, sprinkle 1/2 cup peanuts, chopped fine, over the chocolate. When cold, cut in bars. Makes about 21 bars.

Peanut Butter Topping:

1/2	cup peanut butter	1	tablespoon cream

Heat in top of double boiler over hot water, stirring to blend well. Do not boil. Remove from hot water.

Chocolate Topping:

1	cup semi-sweet chocolate chips	1	tablespoon shortening

Melt chocolate chips over hot water, add shortening and blend well. Do not boil. Remove from hot water.

Chocodiles

Crunchy peanut butter in cookie and topping.

2-1/2	cups flour	1/2	teaspoon salt
1-1/4	cups firmly packed brown sugar	1/3	cup crunchy peanut butter
1/2	cup butter, softened	1	egg
1/2	cup shortening	1	teaspoon vanilla

Preheat oven to 350 degrees. In a large mixer bowl combine flour, brown sugar, butter, shortening, salt, peanut butter, egg and vanilla. Blend with mixer to form a dough. Press in ungreased 15 by 10 by 1-inch jellyroll pan. Bake for 20 to 25 minutes. Cool slightly.

Topping:

1	cup semi-sweet chocolate pieces	1-1/2	cups slightly crushed cornflakes
1/2	cup crunchy peanut butter		

Melt chocolate pieces in medium saucepan. Stir in peanut butter and cornflakes. Spread on top of baked dough. While warm cut into bars.

Kentucky Cheese Cake

Easy to make, and no one suspects a cake mix.

1	18-ounce package yellow cake mix	1	8-ounce package cream cheese
1/2	cup butter	1	pound package confectioners' sugar
3	eggs		

Combine cake mix, butter and 1 egg; mix together to make a stiff dough. Press onto bottom and halfway up sides of ungreased 13 by 9-inch baking pan. Combine softened cream cheese, 2 eggs and sugar; mix until well blended. Spoon over dough. Bake at 350 degrees for about 35 to 40 minutes. Cool thoroughly before cutting. Chill, if desired. Makes about 4 dozen squares.

Toffee Squares

A rich cookie that looks and tastes like toffee candy. A sure hit at holiday time.

1	cup butter or margarine	1/4	teaspoon salt
1	cup brown sugar, packed	3	to 4 milk chocolate bars
1	egg yolk		(7/8-ounce each)
1	teaspoon vanilla	1/2	cup chopped nuts
2	cups sifted flour		

Mix butter, sugar, egg yolk, and vanilla. Stir in flour and salt until dough is well blended. Spread in a rectangle about 13 by 10-inch on greased cookie sheet, leaving about 1-inch all around edge of cookie sheet. Bake in a 350 degree oven for 20 to 25 minutes, or until nicely browned. Crust will still be soft. Remove from oven. Immediately place separated squares of chocolate on top. Let stand until soft; spread evenly over entire surface. Sprinkle with nuts. Cut into small squares while warm. Makes 6 to 7 dozen.

Heavenly Honey Bars

These bars are for those who have a sweet tooth.

2/3	cup butter	1	teaspoon vanilla
1/2	cup honey	2	cups flour
2	cups (7-ounce) jar marshmallow creme	2	teaspoons baking powder
		1	teaspoon salt
2	eggs, slightly beaten	1	cup chopped nuts

Combine butter and honey in saucepan. Cook over low heat, stirring constantly, until well blended. Remove from heat; cool slightly. Add marshmallows creme, eggs and vanilla; beat until well blended. Stir in remaining ingredients, pour into greased 13 by 9-inch pan. Bake at 350 degrees for 25 to 30 minutes. Cool; cut into bars. Makes about 36 bars.

Blitz Kuchen

No frosting needed on these. Almond meringue is baked on top.

1	cup butter	4	egg yolks, beaten
1	cup sugar	2	egg whites, beaten
3	cups cake flour	1/2	teaspoon salt

Cream the butter and sugar together until light. Add the 4 egg yolks which have been beaten until thick and lemon colored. Add salt and flour. Fold in the beaten egg whites. Spread thin on a buttered baking sheet and spread with the topping. Spread the sliced almonds over the topping and sprinkle the remaining sugar and cinnamon over all. Bake in a 350 degree oven for 8 to 10 minutes. Cool slightly, cut in bars and remove to wire rack.

Topping:

2	egg whites	1/2	cup blanched almonds, chopped
1/4	cup sugar		
3/4	teaspoon cinnamon		

Beat 2 egg whites until stiff but not dry. Add 1/2 the sugar to which the cinnamon has been added.

Crisscross Jelly Squares

Everyone will think you spent hours making this pretty sparkling cookie.

3/4	cup butter	3/4	cup red jelly or jam
3/4	cup powdered sugar		small pieces, red and
1	egg yolk		green candied pineapple
1	teaspoon vanilla		or candied cherries
2	cups sifted flour		

Cream butter. Add sugar. Blend in egg yolk, vanilla and flour. Divide dough in half. Press 1/2 onto bottom of ungreased 9 by 9-inch pan. Spread with jelly. Shape small pieces of remaining dough into thin pencil-like strips. Place strips, crisscross fashion 1/2-inch apart on jelly. Sprinkle with pieces of candied fruit. Bake at 350 degrees for about 35 minutes. Cool. Makes about 16 squares.

Scottish Yule Bannock

These butter rich bite-size Scottish cookies literally melt in your mouth.

1-1/2 cups flour	1/4 cup finely minced, toasted almonds
1/4 teaspoon salt	
3/8 cup confectioners' sugar	3/4 cup unsalted butter, cut into pieces and slightly softened
1/3 cup finely minced, candied citron or mixed candied fruit	
	1-1/2 tablespoons sugar

In bowl of food processor, combine flour, salt, and confectioners' sugar. Pulse briefly until just blended. Add citron, almonds, and butter. Pulse several times until mixture resembles fine crumbs. Lightly press dough into an 8-inch square baking pan, then sprinkle with sugar. Bake in a 325 degree oven for about 30 minutes or until lightly browned. Immediately cut into 64 squares. Let cool in pan for 10 minutes, then transfer to a wire rack to finish cooling.

Marzipan Bars

Jelly, almond filling and chocolate icing - what a great combination.

1/2 cup butter	2 cups sifted flour
1/2 cup brown sugar, packed	1/4 teaspoon salt
1 egg yolk	1/4 cup milk
1 teaspoon vanilla	1 cup red raspberry jelly
1/2 teaspoon soda	

Cream butter and sugar; beat in egg yolk and vanilla. Blend in sifted dry ingredients and milk. Spread onto bottom of a greased 10 by 15 by 1-inch pan; cover with jelly.

Almond Paste Filling:

8 ounces almond paste, cut in small pieces	1 teaspoon vanilla
	3 tablespoons soft butter
1 egg white	3 eggs
1/2 cup sugar	green food coloring

Blend almond paste, egg white, sugar, vanilla and butter until smooth. Add eggs one at a time and beat well. Tint mixture a delicate green; pour over jelly layer. Bake at 350 degrees for 35 to 40 minutes. Cool. Frost with chocolate icing.

Calypso Bars

A cookie everyone will love, filled with a date and chocolate filling.

Oatmeal Mixture:

3/4	cup butter	1/2	teaspoon baking soda
1-1/4	cups brown sugar, packed	1	cup chopped nuts
1-1/2	cups sifted flour	1-1/2	cups uncooked oatmeal
1/2	teaspoon salt		

Cream butter. Add sugar gradually. Cream well. Blend in sifted dry ingredients. Add nuts and oatmeal. Mix until crumbly. Divide mixture in half. Press 1/2 firmly into greased 9 by 13 by 2-inch pan. Spread filling on top. Sprinkle remaining mixture over filling. Press down lightly. Bake at 350 degrees about 30 minutes. Cool, cut into bars. Makes about 3 dozen.

Chocolate Date Filling:

2-1/2	squares unsweetened chocolate	1-1/3	cups finely cut dates
2/3	cup hot water	1/4	cup butter
1-1/3	cups sugar	1	teaspoon vanilla

Combine chocolate and water in saucepan. Add sugar and dates. Cook at a low heat until thickened. Stir occasionally. Add butter and vanilla. Blend. Cool.

Sesame Seed Bars

Not the ordinary taste to these bars. Cut into small squares.

1/2	cup sesame seeds	1	cup packed light brown sugar
1/2	cup butter		
1-1/4	cups sifted flour	2	eggs
1	teaspoon baking powder	1	teaspoon vanilla
1/2	teaspoon salt		

Preheat oven to 375 degrees. Toast seeds in medium size saucepan, over low heat stirring frequently, until light brown, about 10 minutes; remove from heat. Add butter to seeds and stir to melt. Cool slightly. Sift flour, baking powder and salt onto waxed paper. Beat sugar, eggs and vanilla into butter mixture with wooden spoon until smooth. Stir in flour mixture, beat until combined. Pour into greased 9 by 9-inch pan. Bake at 375 degrees for 25 minutes until top springs back when lightly touched with fingertips. Frost with butter cream frosting.

Jan Hagel

These are crisp, buttery-rich strips with baked-on nut glaze.

1	cup butter or margarine	1/2	teaspoon cinnamon
1	cup sugar	1	tablespoon water
1	egg, separated	1/2	cup very finely chopped walnuts
2	cups sifted flour		

Heat oven to 350 degrees. Lightly grease a jellyroll pan, 15-1/2 by 10-1/2 by 1-inch. Mix butter, sugar, and egg yolk. Blend flour and cinnamon; stir into butter mixture. Pat into pan. Beat water and egg white until frothy; brush over dough; sprinkle with nuts. Bake 20 to 25 minutes or until very lightly browned. Cut immediately into finger-like strips. Makes fifty 3 by 1-inch strips.

Brown Sugar Jan Hagel

A thin buttery cookie that resembles peanut brittle in appearance.

3/4	cup butter or margarine	1/4	cup almonds, slivered
3/4	cup brown sugar	1	egg, beaten and divided
1-1/4	cups flour		in half
1	teaspoon cinnamon		

Cream butter and sugar together. Add flour and cinnamon and 1/2 of egg mixture. Grease a cookie sheet. Press dough in an 11 by 13 by 2-inch pan to all edges. Pat down thin, like pizza dough. Brush rest of egg on top and sprinkle with almonds. Bake at 275 degrees for about 20 minutes. Cut into wedges while still warm.

Butterscotch Chewy Logs

Wonderful butterscotch flavor and real chewy, with lots of nuts.

3/4	cup eggs	1-1/2	teaspoons baking powder
2	cups brown sugar, firmly packed	1-1/2	cups pecans, chopped
1	tablespoon butter	1	teaspoon vanilla
1-1/2	cups sifted flour		confectioners' sugar

Beat eggs in top of double boiler until blended. Blend in brown sugar and butter. Place over rapidly boiling water, about 5 minutes. Remove from heat. Add sifted dry ingredients, mix until blended. Stir in nuts and vanilla. Put in well-greased and floured 13 by 9-inch pan. Bake in a 350 degree oven about 30 minutes. Sprinkle with confectioners' sugar, cut into strips.

Delta Bars

Nutty brown sugar meringue bakes into cookie base to make chewy butterscotch bar.

1/2	cup shortening	1-1/4	cups sifted flour
1	cup granulated sugar	1	teaspoon baking powder
1	whole egg	1/2	teaspoon salt
1	egg, separated	1	cup brown sugar, packed
1	teaspoon vanilla	1/2	cup chopped nuts

Mix shortening, granulated sugar, egg, egg yolk, and vanilla well. Stir dry ingredients together; blend into shortening mixture. Mix thoroughly. Spread in greased oblong pan, 13 by 9-1/2 by 2-inch. Beat egg white until foamy. Gradually beat in brown sugar. Continue beating until mixture is stiff and glossy. Fold in nuts. Spread meringue over dough in pan. Bake in a 375 degree oven for about 25 minutes. Cut while warm in 2-inch squares. Makes about 2 dozen cookies.

Norwegian Almond Bars

These cookies are a tradition of our Norwegian heritage.

1-1/2	cups sifted flour	1	cup ground, blanched almonds
1/4	cup sugar		
1/4	teaspoon salt	1	cup sifted confectioners' sugar
3/4	cup butter		
1	egg, separated	1	tablespoon water

Combine flour, granulated sugar and salt; cut in butter until the particles are about the size of large peas. Add slightly beaten egg yolk and mix (mixture should be crumbly). Reserve 1/2 cup crumbs for topping. Firmly press remainder on bottom of an ungreased pan, 9 by 9 by 2-inch. Combine almonds, confectioners' sugar, egg white and water. Spread carefully over layer in pan. Sprinkle with reserved crumbs. Bake at 350 degrees for about 30 to 35 minutes. Cool and cut into squares. Makes about 3 dozen.

Note:
One can (12-ounce) of almond cake and pastry filling may be substituted for the almond confectioners' sugar mixture.

Almond Toffee Bars

A yummy bar, just right for a rainy day pickup.

Cookie:

1 cup butter, softened	1 6-ounce package semi-sweet chocolate morsels
1 cup sifted confectioners' sugar	1-1/2 cups sliced almonds, toasted
2 cups flour	

Beat together butter and confectioners' sugar until fluffy. Gradually beat in flour. Pat into ungreased 15 by 10 by 1-inch baking pan. Sprinkle with morsels. Bake in a 350 degree oven about 15 minutes. Remove from the oven and sprinkle with almonds; drizzle evenly with hot syrup, bake an additional 15 minutes. Cool slightly. Cut into bars. Makes about 48 bars.

Brown Sugar Syrup:

1/3 cup butter	2 tablespoon water
1 cup firmly packed brown sugar	1-1/2 teaspoons lemon juice
	1-1/2 teaspoons vanilla

In saucepan, melt butter; add brown sugar, water and lemon juice. Bring to a boil, stirring constantly. Remove from heat; stir in vanilla. Keep hot.

Two-Way Almond Bars

Two different-looking almond cookies from a single pan.

1	cup butter or margarine, room temperature	2	cups flour
2/3	cup sugar	32	pecan halves
2	eggs	2	tablespoons apricot jam or preserves, heated, strained
1	tablespoon vanilla		
1	7-ounce package almond paste, room temperature, cut into pieces	1/3	cup semi-sweet chocolate pieces, melted

In a large bowl, beat together butter or margarine and sugar until light and fluffy. Add eggs, vanilla and almond paste, beating until well blended. Beat in flour until well blended. Spread mixture evenly in 15 by 10-inch jellyroll pan lined with foil. Lightly score surface of dough in half so you have 2 rectangles, each measuring 10 by 7-1/2-inches. Score surface of 1 dough rectangle into 4 rows of 8, pressing a pecan half in center of each scored bar. Leave other half of dough as is. Bake in a 325 degree oven for 25 to 30 minutes or until edges are lightly browned. Cool in pan. Brush pecan-topped cookies with warm jam or preserves. When glaze has set, cut through score lines making 32 pieces with pecan half in center of each. Cut remaining rectangle in 32 pieces. Top center of each plain piece with a dollop of melted chocolate. Let stand until set. Makes 64 cookies.

Toffee-Nut Bars

Almond-coconut topping on melt-in-the-mouth crust.

Bottom Layer:

1/2	cup soft butter	1	cup sifted flour
1/2	cup brown sugar, packed		

Mix thoroughly, shortening, brown sugar, stir in flour. Press and flatten with hand to cover bottom of ungreased 13 by 9-inch oblong pan. Bake for 10 minutes in a 350 degree oven. Then spread with topping.

Almond-Coconut Topping:

2	eggs	1/2	teaspoon salt
1	cup brown sugar, packed	1	cup moist shredded coconut
1	teaspoon vanilla		
2	tablespoons flour	1	cup cut-up almonds (or other nuts)
1	teaspoon baking powder		

Beat eggs well. Stir in brown sugar and vanilla. Mix and stir in flour, baking powder and salt. Add coconut and almonds. Return to oven and bake 25 minutes more until topping is golden brown. Cool slightly, then cut into bars. Makes about 2-1/2 dozen bars.

Butter Pecan Turtle Bars

The heavenly combination of pecans, chocolate and caramel makes these bars irresistible.

2	cups flour	1/2	cup light brown sugar, packed
3/4	cup light brown sugar, packed	2/3	cup butter
1/2	cup butter, softened	1-1/2	cups milk chocolate chips
1-1/2	cups pecan halves		

Combine flour, 3/4 cup brown sugar and 1/2 cup butter. Blend until crumbly. Pat firmly onto bottom of ungreased 9 by 13-inch pan. Sprinkle pecan halves over unbaked crust. Set aside. In small saucepan, combine 1/2 cup brown sugar and 2/3 cup butter. Cook over medium heat, stirring constantly, until mixture begins to boil. Boil for 1 minute, stirring constantly. Drizzle caramel over pecans and crust. Bake at 350 degrees for 18 to 20 minutes. Remove from oven and immediately sprinkle with chocolate chips. Spread chips evenly as they melt. Cool completely before cutting. Makes 48 bars.

Pecan Pie Surprise Bars

A rich bar cookie for coffees, meetings and desserts.

1	18-1/2-ounce package butter or yellow cake mix, divided	1-1/2	cups dark corn syrup
		1/2	cup brown sugar, packed
		1	teaspoon vanilla
1/2	cup margarine, melted	1	cup chopped pecans
4	eggs		

Reserve 2/3 cup dry cake mix for filling. Combine remaining dry cake mix, margarine and 1 egg in large bowl; mix until crumbly. Press into greased 13 by 9-inch baking pan. Bake at 350 degrees for about 15 to 20 minutes until light golden brown. Combine reserved cake mix, corn syrup, sugar, 3 eggs and vanilla. Beat at medium speed 1 to 2 minutes. Pour over crust; sprinkle with pecans. Continue baking 30 to 35 minutes until filling is set. Cool; cut into squares. Makes about 3 dozen.

Graham Pecan Treats

Graham cracker crust gives an excellent taste to these easy-do cookies.

1-1/2	cups graham cracker crumbs	3/4	cup light corn syrup
1/2	cup sifted flour	3	tablespoons flour
1/4	cup brown sugar, packed	1	teaspoon vanilla
1/2	cup melted butter	1/2	teaspoon salt
2	eggs	1-1/4	cups coarsely chopped pecans
1/4	cup brown sugar, packed		

Combine first 4 ingredients; mix well. Press evenly into a greased 9 by 9 by 2-inch pan. Bake at 350 degrees for 10 minutes. Beat eggs slightly; blend in 1/4 cup brown sugar, syrup, 3 tablespoons flour, vanilla and salt. Pour over hot crust; sprinkle with pecans. Bake about 20 minutes longer. Cool; cut into bars. Makes about 2-1/2 dozen.

Chocolate-Almond Cookie Bark

Baked in a large pan, then broken into irregular pieces, these rich, buttery chocolate-chip cookies are as delicious as they are easy to make.

3/4	cup butter or margarine, softened	1-1/2	cups flour
1/3	cup sugar	1	package (6-ounce) semisweet chocolate chips
1/3	cup light brown sugar, firmly packed	1/2	cup slivered almonds
2	tablespoons coffee-flavored liqueur		

Preheat oven to 375 degrees. In large mixer bowl combine butter and sugars; beat until light and fluffy. Gradually blend in coffee liqueur. Gradually add flour, mixing until blended. Stir in chocolate chips. Spread mixture evenly in an ungreased, shallow, 10 by 15-inch pan. Sprinkle evenly with almonds, pressing them lightly into dough. Bake until cookies are well browned about 18 to 20 minutes. Cool completely in pan on a wire rack, then turn out and break into irregular shaped pieces. Makes about 4 dozen cookies.

Almond Fudge Topped Shortbread

Extra tasty with an extra special unbaked topping.

1	cup butter or margarine, softened	1	can (14-ounce) sweetened condensed milk (not evaporated milk)
1/2	cup powdered sugar		
1/4	teaspoon salt	1/2	teaspoon almond extract
1-1/4	cups flour		sliced almonds, toasted
2	cups semi-sweet chocolate chips		

Heat oven to 350 degrees. Grease a 13 by 9-inch baking pan. In mixer bowl, beat butter, sugar and salt until fluffy. Mix in flour. With floured hands, press into prepared pan. Bake 20 minutes or until lightly browned. In heavy saucepan over low heat, melt chocolate chips with sweetened condensed milk, stirring constantly until chips are melted. Stir in almond extract. Spread evenly over shortbread. Sprinkle with almonds; press down firmly. Refrigerate 3 hours or until firm. Cut into bars. Store covered at room temperature. Makes 24 to 36 bars.

Maple Walnut Bars

A taste from Vermont - what a great idea.

2	cups flour	1	cup pure maple syrup
1/2	teaspoon baking soda	1	large egg
1/2	cup light brown sugar, packed	2	teaspoons vanilla
1/2	butter, softened	1	cup walnuts, chopped

Cream together sugar and butter in an electric mixer. Add syrup, egg and vanilla. Beat at medium speed until smooth. Add sifted dry ingredients and walnuts, and blend at low speed just until combined. Pour batter into baking pan and smooth top with a spatula. Bake in a 325 degree oven 40 to 45 minutes or until toothpick inserted in center, comes out clean. Cool in pan 15 minutes, then invert onto cooling rack. Cool completely before icing. Makes 12 to 16 bars.

Maple Frosting:

1/2	cup butter, softened	3	tablespoons pure maple syrup
2	ounces cream cheese, softened	1/4	cup plus 2 tablespoons confectioners' sugar
1	tablespoon light brown sugar, packed		walnut halves

In a medium bowl cream butter and cream cheese with an electric mixer at high speed. Add brown sugar and maple syrup, and beat until smooth. Reduce mixer speed to medium, and slowly add confectioners' sugar. Increase speed to high, and mix until smooth. If frosting appears thin, gradually add confectioners' sugar until frosting thickens. Spread frosting on top and sides of maple bars. Make designs on frosting and decorate with walnut halves. May be cut into diamond shapes.

Walnut Bars

Another good bar that should be on your cookie list.

Bottom Layer:

1/2	cup soft butter	1	cup sifted flour

Blend butter and flour thoroughly. Press firmly into a greased 9 by 9 by 2-inch pan. Bake at 350 degrees for about 15 minutes.

Top Layer:

1-1/2	cups firmly packed light brown sugar	2	eggs, slightly beaten
2	tablespoons flour	1-1/2	teaspoons vanilla
1/4	teaspoon baking powder	1	cup broken walnuts
1/2	teaspoon salt	1/2	cup coconut

Combine brown sugar, flour, baking powder and salt. Add remaining ingredients. Stir to blend. Spread evenly over baked bottom layer. Bake at 350 degrees about 25 minutes. Cool. Spread with Orange Frosting.

Orange Frosting:

1-1/2	cups powdered sugar	2	tablespoons orange juice
2	tablespoons melted butter	2	teaspoons lemon juice

Combine all ingredients. Blend until smooth. Spread evenly over top layer. Cut into bars. Makes 32 bars.

Coconut Crunch Bar

A favorite of coconut lovers.

Bottom Layer:

1	cup flour	1/4	cup shortening
1/3	cup brown sugar		

Sift together flour and brown sugar until blended. Cut shortening into flour until mixture is in small crumbs, pat firmly into an 8-inch square pan. Bake in a 350 degree oven for 12 minutes.

Top Layer:

2	eggs	1/2	teaspoon vanilla
1-1/4	cups brown sugar	2	cups finely chopped or shredded coconut
1/4	cup flour		

Beat eggs until light. Gradually add brown sugar, beat well. Fold in the flour, vanilla and coconut. Spread on top of warm baked bottom layer. Return pan to oven. Bake in a 350 degree oven about 20 to 25 minutes. Cut into bars while warm. Makes 32 narrow bars.

Glazed Lebkuchen

It's not Christmas without these cookies to give as gifts.

3/4	cup honey	1/2	cup finely chopped candied lemon peel
1/2	cup sugar		
1/4	cup brown sugar, packed	3/4	cup chopped blanched almonds
2	eggs, beaten		
2-1/2	cups sifted flour	1	cup powdered sugar
1	teaspoon baking soda	3	tablespoons hot milk
1/4	teaspoon cloves	1/4	teaspoon vanilla
1-1/4	teaspoons cinnamon		candied cherries, citron, Christmas seals
1/8	teaspoon allspice		
1/2	cup finely chopped citron		

Bring honey to a boil; cool. Mix in sugars. Add eggs; beat well. Blend in sifted dry ingredients, citron, lemon peel and almonds. Spread batter into greased 15 by 10 by 1-inch pan. Bake at 350 degrees about 25 minutes. Blend powdered sugar, hot milk and vanilla. Spread over top of warm lebkuchen. Cut into 3 by 2-inch bars while warm. Decorate with candied cherries and citron. Wrap with transparent material and decorate with Christmas seals. Makes about 2 dozen.

White Fruit Bars

This is an elegant addition to your holiday cookie selection.

2/3	cup shortening	2	teaspoons baking powder
1/2	cup sugar	1	teaspoon salt
2	eggs, separated	1	cup cream
1	tablespoon sherry flavoring	1/2	cup flaked coconut
		1/4	cup chopped citron
1/4	teaspoon almond flavoring	1/2	cup chopped blanched almonds
1-3/4	cups sifted flour	1/4	cup broken pecans

Mix together shortening, sugar, egg yolks, and flavorings until fluffy. Blend dry ingredients with cream to the shortening mixture, starting and ending with dry ingredients. Mix only enough to blend after each addition. Stir in coconut, citron, and nuts. Beat egg whites until stiff; fold into dough. Spread in greased oblong pan, 13 by 9-1/2 by 2-inch. Bake in a 400 degree oven for about 30 minutes. Spread with butter icing while still warm. When cool, cut into squares or bars. Cookies improve with mellowing; so bake at least 24 hours before serving. Makes about 3 dozen bars.

Baseler Leckerle

Wonderful Christmas cookies with a delicate rose water icing.

4	eggs	1	teaspoon cinnamon
2-1/2	cups sugar	1	teaspoon cloves
1/3	cup ground citron	1/2	teaspoon salt
1	cup ground unblanched almonds	1/2	teaspoon nutmeg
		2-1/2	cups flour
	grated rind of 1 lemon	1/4	teaspoon baking soda

Beat eggs and sugar until thick. Mix in rest of ingredients, except baking soda. Moisten baking soda and stir in. Spread in greased 17 by 14 by 1/2-inch pan. Pat dough flat with floured hands. Bake at 350 degrees for 15 to 20 minutes, or until slightly browned at edges. Cool. Spread with icing. Cut into 2-1/2 by 1-inch pieces. Makes about 9 dozen.

Rose Icing:

Mix 1-1/2 cups confectioners' sugar with 1-1/2 ounces of rose water (purchased from a pharmacy).

Merry Mincemeaters

Don't like mincemeat? Awe C'mon, try these anyway, you'll love them.

3/4	cup butter	2-1/2	cups sifted flour
2/3	cup sugar	1/2	teaspoon cinnamon
1	egg, reserve 1 tablespoon egg white	1/4	teaspoon salt
		1-1/2	cups mincemeat
1	teaspoon vanilla	1/3	cup blanched, chopped almonds

Cream butter and sugar well. Add egg and vanilla and beat well. Stir in sifted dry ingredients; mix thoroughly. Roll 1/2 of dough on greased baking sheet to a 10 by 8-inch rectangle. (Baking sheet will not slip if placed on damp cloth.) Spread with 1-1/2 cups of mincemeat. Roll out remaining dough between sheets of wax paper to a 10 by 8-inch rectangle. Remove top sheet; invert dough over mincemeat. Remove paper. Brush with reserved egg white, slightly beaten. Sprinkle with 1/3 cup blanched almonds, chopped. Bake in a 350 degree oven for about 25 to 30 minutes until light golden brown. Cool and cut into bars.

Plantation Fruit Bars

These raisins, nuts and molasses tasting cookies are a must for all bakers.

1/4	cup shortening	1/2	teaspoon salt
1/2	cup sugar	1/4	teaspoon soda
1	egg	1-1/2	cups raisins or cut-up dates
1/2	cup molasses		
1/2	cup milk	1	cup chopped nuts
2	cups sifted flour		Lemon Glaze
1-1/2	teaspoons baking powder		

Heat oven to 350 degrees. Mix shortening, sugar, egg, and molasses thoroughly. Stir in milk. Blend in dry ingredients; add to milk mixture. Stir in raisins and nuts. Spread in greased oblong pan, 13 by 9-1/2 by 2-inches. Bake about 25 to 30 minutes, or until toothpick stuck in center comes out clean. When cool, spread with glaze. Cut in bars. Makes about 4 dozen 2 by 1-inch bars.

Lemon Glaze:

Gradually beat 1/2 cup confectioners' sugar into 1 egg white, stiffly beaten. Add 1/4 teaspoon salt and 1/2 teaspoon grated lemon rind. Blend until smooth.

Spice Bars

The bar with a soft, chewy texture and an old-fashioned spice cake flavor.

1	cup flour	2/3	cup sugar
1/2	teaspoon baking soda	1	egg, lightly beaten
1/4	teaspoon salt	1/4	cup molasses
1-1/2	teaspoons cinnamon	1/2	teaspoon vanilla
1/2	teaspoon allspice	2	tablespoons white Crystal sugar
1/4	teaspoon ginger		
1/2	cup butter		

Cream together the butter and sugar. Stir in the beaten egg, vanilla, and molasses; blend well. Stir in sifted dry ingredients. Mix thoroughly. Put mixture into a greased and floured 9-inch square pan. Sprinkle a layer of Crystal sugar over top of batter. Bake in a 325 degree oven 20 to 25 minutes. Do not overbake. Cool on a rack. Cut into bars when cool. They will sink slightly while cooling. Makes about 15 cookies.

Iced-Spiced Ginger Bars

Moist and flavorful describes these tasty and easy bars.

2	cups flour	1	cup hot coffee
1	cup sugar	1/2	cup margarine, softened
1	teaspoon soda	1/2	cup shortening
1	teaspoon cinnamon	1/2	cup molasses
1	teaspoon ginger	1	teaspoon lemon extract
1	teaspoon cloves	2	eggs
1/8	teaspoon salt		

Preheat oven to 350 degrees. Grease a 15 by 10-inch jellyroll or 13 by 9-inch pan. In large bowl, combine all ingredients. Beat 2 minutes at medium speed. Pour into greased pan. Bake 25 to 30 minutes until top springs back when touched lightly in the center. Cool.

Frosting:

1/4	cup butter	1/2	teaspoon vanilla
1-1/2	cups powdered sugar	2	to 3 tablespoons water

In small saucepan over low heat, cook butter until light golden brown, stirring constantly. Add remaining frosting ingredients; blend until smooth. Spread over bars. Makes 2 to 3 dozen bars.

Old-Fashioned Raisin Bars

A raisin lover's dream come true.

2	cups sifted flour	2/3	cup butter
1/4	teaspoon soda	2/3	cup sugar
1/2	teaspoon salt	1/4	cup molasses
1	teaspoon cinnamon	1	egg
1/2	teaspoon nutmeg	2	tablespoons water
1/2	teaspoon allspice	1	tablespoon vinegar
1/2	teaspoon ginger	1-1/2	cups seedless raisins
1/4	teaspoon cloves	3/4	cup chopped nuts

Sift flour, soda, salt and spices together. Cream butter; add sugar gradually; beat in molasses and egg. Stir in water and vinegar. Blend in dry ingredients, raisins and nuts. Spread into greased 15 by 10 by 1-inch pan. Bake at 375 degrees for about 20 minutes. Cool slightly; spread with thin powdered sugar frosting. Cut into bars. Makes about 3 dozen.

Jiffy Jimmy Bars

Kids really go for these buttery crisp bars.

1	cup butter or margarine	2	cups flour, sifted
1	cup sugar	3/4	cup nuts, ground or chopped very fine
2	eggs, separated and beaten separately	3/4	cup chocolate jimmies
1	teaspoon cinnamon		

Preheat oven to 325 degrees. Grease and flour a 15 by 10 by 3/4-inch baking pan. Cream butter or margarine with sugar. Add beaten egg yolks, cinnamon and flour. Stir well. Mixture will be heavy. Spread on pan, evenly distributing mixture with fingers and fork. Press down lightly after it is evened out. Paint mixture with beaten egg whites. Egg whites should be beaten until stiff. Sprinkle with nuts. Sprinkle jimmies over nuts. Bake for 25 minutes. Cut into squares and run spatula under squares while still warm.

Spiced Prune Bars

Moist and chewy with prunes, these lemon-glazed cookie strips are encrusted with crisp, chopped walnuts.

2	cups flour	1/2	cup butter or margarine, softened
1	teaspoon ground cinnamon	1	cup firmly packed dark brown sugar
1/2	teaspoon baking soda	1	egg
1/4	teaspoon salt	1	cup finely chopped walnuts
1/4	teaspoon ground nutmeg		
1/8	teaspoon ground cloves		
1	cup chopped large pitted prunes		

Preheat oven to 375 degrees. Place butter and brown sugar in a mixer bowl and beat until well combined. Beat in egg until mixture is fluffy. Add dry sifted ingredients then divide dough into 4 equal portions. Spread walnuts on a large piece of waxed paper. Shape each portion of dough into a long roll and turn in nuts to coat well on all sides. Transfer nut-encrusted rolls to greased baking sheets. Flatten rolls into strips with your fingertips until they are about 1-1/2-inches wide and 3/4-inch thick. Sprinkle strips with any remaining nuts. Bake until a toothpick inserted in center of each strip comes out clean and nuts are toasted, about 15 to 20 minutes. Let cool on baking sheets for 10 minutes. Drizzle strips with Lemon Glaze. Then cut, slightly on the diagonal, into 1-inch wide bars. Transfer bars to wire racks to cool completely. Makes about 4 dozen cookies.

Lemon Glaze:

2/3	cup confectioners' sugar	1	to 1-1/2 tablespoons lemon juice
1/4	teaspoon grated lemon rind		

In a small bowl combine confectioners' sugar and lemon rind. Gradually add lemon juice, stirring until glaze is smooth and of good drizzling consistency.

Colonial Pumpkin Bars

A good cookie for a fall "bake sale".

3/4	cup margarine	1	teaspoon cinnamon
2	cups sugar	1/2	teaspoon soda
16	ounce can pumpkin	1/2	teaspoon salt
4	eggs	1/4	teaspoon nutmeg
2	cups flour	1	cup chopped walnuts
2	teaspoons baking powder		Vanilla Frosting

Cream margarine and sugar until light and fluffy. Blend in pumpkin and eggs. Add dry ingredients; mix well. Stir in nuts. Spread mixture into greased and floured 15-1/2 by 10-1/2-inch jellyroll pan. Bake at 350 degrees, 30 to 35 minutes or until wooden pick inserted in center comes out clean. Cool. Frost with Vanilla Frosting.

Vanilla Frosting:

3	ounce package cream cheese	1	teaspoon vanilla
1/3	cup margarine	3	cups sifted confectioners' sugar

Combine softened cream cheese, margarine and vanilla, mixing until well blended. Gradually add sugar, mixing well after each addition. Makes 24 servings.

Note:
Bars can be frozen.

Zucchini Bars

A bar cookie that is a sell-out at a Christmas bazaar.

3/4	cup butter or margarine	1-3/4	cups flour
1/2	cup brown sugar	1-1/2	teaspoons baking powder
1/2	cup sugar	1	cup shredded coconut
2	eggs	2	cups shredded zucchini
1	teaspoon vanilla	1/2	cup nuts, chopped

Beat butter until light and fluffy. Gradually beat in sugar. Add eggs and beat well. Add vanilla. Sift together flour and baking powder. Stir into egg mixture. Stir in zucchini, coconut, and nuts. Spread evenly in well-greased 10 by 15 by 1-1/2-inch pan. Bake at 350 degrees for 40 minutes. Cool. Cut in bars. Frost with butter cream frosting flavored with a bit of cinnamon and vanilla. Makes about 2 dozen bars.

Winter Squash Squares

So nice to have on hand for that neighbor who drops in for a chat.

2	cup flour	1/8	teaspoon salt
2	cups sugar	4	eggs, beaten
2	teaspoons baking powder	2	cups, mashed cooked winter squash
1	teaspoon baking soda		
1/2	teaspoon cinnamon	1	cup oil

In a mixing bowl, combine flour, sugar, baking powder, baking soda, cinnamon and salt. Stir in eggs, squash and oil; mix well. Spread into a greased 15 by 10 by 1-inch baking pan. Bake at 350 degrees for 25 to 30 minutes or until bars test done. Cool on a wire rack.

Cream Cheese Frosting:

1	3-ounce package cream cheese, softened	6	tablespoons butter or margarine, softened
2	cups confectioners' sugar	1	tablespoon milk
1	teaspoon vanilla		

Beat together cream cheese, confectioners' sugar, vanilla and butter. Add milk; stir until smooth. Frost cooled cake. Cut into squares. Makes about 4 dozen squares.

Buttermilk Cinnamon Bars

The delicious crumb crust becomes the base for the cake-like bar. Topped with an almond flavored frosting, it's great.

2	cups flour	1	teaspoon soda
1-1/4	cups sugar	1	teaspoon cinnamon
1/4	cup firmly packed brown sugar	3/4	teaspoon salt
		1	cup buttermilk
1/2	cup butter or margarine, softened	1	teaspoon vanilla
		1	egg
1/2	cup chopped nuts		

Preheat oven to 350 degrees. (Lightly spoon flour into measuring cup; level off.) In large bowl, combine first 4 ingredients; blend at low speed until crumbly. Press 2 cups crumb mixture into ungreased 13 by 9-inch pan. To remaining crumb mixture, add nuts, soda, cinnamon, salt, buttermilk, vanilla and egg; blend well. Pour evenly over crumb mixture. Bake 20 to 25 minutes until toothpick inserted in center comes out clean. Cool 20 minutes. Then frost with almond confectioners' frosting, cut into bars. Makes about 3 dozen bars.

Mother's Chinese Chews

So easy to do, great when in a hurry.

1	cup dates, cut-up	2	eggs
1	cup pecans, chopped	1	teaspoon baking powder
1	cup sugar	1/4	teaspoon salt
3/4	cup flour		

Beat eggs and add to sugar, mix well. Sift flour over dates and nuts. Add sugar and eggs to flour and nuts. Spread mixture in buttered 8 by 8-inch pans and bake 30 to 35 minutes at 325 degrees. Cut into squares.

Crispy Date Bars

A different taste to these date, cereal and nut bars.

Base:

1	cup flour	1/2	cup butter, softened
1/2	cup brown sugar		

In small bowl, mix base ingredients; mix until crumbly. Press into ungreased 11 by 7-inch pan. Bake at 375 degrees for 10 to 12 minutes.

Filling:

1	cup chopped dates	2	cups crisp rice cereal
1/2	cup sugar	1	cup chopped nuts
1/2	cup butter	1	teaspoon vanilla
1	egg, well beaten		

In medium saucepan, combine dates, sugar and butter, cook over medium heat to boiling, stirring constantly. Simmer 3 minutes. Blend about 1/4 cup hot mixture into beaten egg; return to saucepan. Cook until mixture bubbles, stirring constantly. Remove from heat; stir in cereal, nuts and vanilla. Spread over baked base. Cool.

Frosting:

2	cups powdered sugar	1	3-ounce package cream cheese, softened
1/2	teaspoon vanilla		

In small bowl, combine frosting ingredients; beat at low speed of mixer until smooth. Spread over filling. Cut into bars. Makes about 24 bars.

Chow Mein Date Bars

Chow mein noodles, dates and pecans - a tasty combination.

1/2	cup soft butter	1/4	teaspoon salt
1/4	cup brown sugar, packed	1	teaspoon baking powder
1	cup sifted flour	1	cup chopped pecans
3	eggs, slightly beaten	1	cup cut dates
1-1/2	cups brown sugar, packed	1	cup chow mein noodles
2	tablespoons flour		

Mix butter, 1/4 cup brown sugar and 1 cup flour together; press into greased 13 by 9 by 2-inch pan. Bake at 375 degrees for 10 minutes. Beat eggs slightly; blend in remaining ingredients. Spread over warm crust. Reduce temperature to 350 degrees. Bake about 20 minutes longer. Cut into small bars while warm. Makes about 5-1/2 dozen.

Maple Date Bars

Maple syrup and dates make this a great pick me up.

3/4	cup whole wheat flour	1/2	cup maple syrup
1/2	teaspoon baking powder	2	large egg whites
1/2	teaspoon baking soda	1/2	teaspoon vanilla
1/2	cup chopped dates		

In large bowl, stir together flour, baking powder, soda and dates. Add syrup, egg whites, and vanilla; beat until smoothly mixed. Spread batter evenly in a non stick (or lightly oiled regular) 8-inch square pan. Bake in a 350 degree oven until golden brown, just begins to pull from pan sides, and springs back when lightly touched in the center, about 20 minutes. Serve warm or cool, cut into about 2-inch squares. Wrap individually and freeze. Makes 16 bars.

Sherry Date Strips

Sherry gives these a little Christmas lift.

Sherry Date Filling:

1	pound pitted dates, ground	1/4	teaspoon salt
1	cup firmly packed light brown sugar	1/16	teaspoon black pepper
1	cup sherry wine	1	cup toasted blanched almonds, chopped
1/4	teaspoon nutmeg		

Cook dates, sugar, wine, nutmeg, salt and black pepper at a medium heat until slightly thickened. Stir frequently. Cool. Add almonds. Blend well. Prepare pastry.

Pastry:

2	cups flour	2	cups firmly packed light brown sugar
1/2	teaspoon baking soda	1	cup soft butter
1/2	teaspoon salt		
2	cups quick cooking oatmeal		

Sift flour, soda and salt together. Add oatmeal and brown sugar. Mix well. Cut butter into flour mixture with pastry blended until mixture resembles coarse meal. Divide mixture in half. Press 1/2 firmly into greased 9 by 13 by 2-inch pan. Spread Sherry Date Filling over oatmeal mixture. Sprinkle remaining mixture over filling. Press down lightly. Bake at 350 degrees for about 30 minutes. Cool. Cut into strips. Makes about 5 dozen.

Merry Christmas Bars

It won't be Christmas without a plate of these cookies filled with cream cheese, nuts, and cherries.

1	cup flour	2	tablespoons lemon juice
1/2	cup packed brown sugar	1/2	teaspoon vanilla
1/3	cup margarine or butter, softened	1/4	teaspoon almond extract
1/2	cup chopped pecans	1/4	cup red maraschino cherries, finely chopped and well drained
1	8-ounce package cream cheese, softened	1/4	cup green maraschino cherries, finely chopped and well drained
1	egg		
1/4	cup sugar		
2	tablespoons milk		

In a large mixing bowl combine flour, brown sugar, and margarine or butter; beat with an electric mixer on low speed until mixture resembles fine crumbs. Stir in nuts. Reserve 1 cup of the nut mixture for topping. Press remaining nut mixture into an ungreased 8 by 8 by 2-inch baking pan. Bake in a 350 degree oven for 8 to 10 minutes or until light brown. For filling combine cream cheese, egg, sugar, milk, lemon juice, vanilla, and almond extract; beat until smooth. Stir in red and green cherries. Spread filling over partially baked crust. Sprinkle with reserved nut mixture. Bake in a 350 degree oven for 25 to 30 minutes or until light brown and set. Cool in pan on a wire rack. Cut into bars. Store in refrigerator. Makes 24 bars.

Fig Bars

Just like "Newton's" only better.

1/4	cup margarine	1/2	teaspoon baking soda
1/2	cup brown sugar	1/2	teaspoon baking powder
1	teaspoon vanilla	1/4	teaspoon salt
1/4	teaspoon lemon juice	1	egg
1-1/2	cups flour		Filling

Cream margarine and sugar; add vanilla, lemon, flour, baking powder, baking soda, salt and eggs. Mix into a dough ball. Chill 2 hours. Roll very thin between 2 sheets of waxed paper. Cut into 3-inch strips. Put filling down center of each and fold each over to meet. Put on cookie sheet and bake at 350 degrees until brown about 18 to 20 minutes. Cut into bars.

Filling:

1/2	cup figs	1/4	cup sugar
1	cup water	1-1/2	teaspoons orange juice
1/2	cup nuts	1/2	tablespoon flour

Cook figs until soft with water until water is gone. Add chopped nuts to figs with remaining ingredients. Cook until thick. Put on cookies. Turn seam side down in pan.

A thoughtful giver always attaches a copy of her recipe.

Frosted Fig Bars

A cookie so tasty, guests will forget it's filled with healthy figs.

1	cup flour	1/4	teaspoon baking soda
1	cup rolled oats	1/2	cup margarine or butter
2/3	cup packed brown sugar		

In a mixing bowl combine flour, oats, brown sugar, and baking soda. Cut in margarine or butter until mixture resembles coarse crumbs. Reserve 1/2 cup of the flour mixture. Press remaining flour mixture in bottom of an ungreased 9 by 9 by 2-inch baking pan. Spread with Fig Filling. Sprinkle with reserved flour mixture. Bake in a 350 degree oven about 30 minutes or until golden. Cool in the pan on a wire rack.

Filling:

1-1/2	cups finely chopped dried figs	3	tablespoons sugar
1/3	cup water	1	teaspoon finely shredded orange peel
1/4	cup orange juice		

Combine ingredients in a medium saucepan, bring to boiling. Reduce heat and simmer, uncovered, 5 to 10 minutes or until thick.

Glaze:

1/2	cup sifted powdered sugar	1	to 2 teaspoons orange juice
1/4	teaspoon vanilla		

Mix powdered sugar, vanilla, and enough orange juice to make of drizzling consistency. Drizzle over top. Cut into bars. Makes 20 to 24 bars.

Heavenly Hash

These must be served in heaven, they are out of this world.

1/2	cup margarine	1	cup flour
1	cup sugar	1	teaspoon baking powder
4	eggs	10-1/2	ounce bag miniature marshmallows
1	pound can, chocolate syrup	1	cup chopped pecans
1	teaspoon vanilla		

Preheat oven to 350 degrees. Cream butter and sugar. Add eggs, one at a time, beating well after each addition. Add chocolate syrup and vanilla. Sift together flour and baking powder. Add to mixture, beating well. Line a 9 by 13 by 2-inch pan with aluminum foil. Pour batter into the pan and bake for 30 minutes. Remove from oven and immediately cover with marshmallows and pecans; set aside for about 1 hour. Spoon topping onto cake. Set in freezer about 20 minutes, then refrigerate until serving time. Cut into 48 bars.

Topping:

3	squares unsweetened chocolate	1	teaspoon vanilla
		2	eggs
1	cup margarine	3	cups confectioners' sugar

Melt chocolate and butter. Let cool. Add vanilla, eggs and confectioners' sugar, beating until smooth.

Bringing a treat to school for the children? Surprise them by making brownies into cupcakes. Fill Christmas paper-lined muffin tins half full. Bake 20 minutes in a 325° oven. Frost and decorate with Christmas candies.

Frango Mint Bars

An elegant cookie you have been searching for, plus the taste you've dreamed of.

Layer - 1:

4	eggs, beaten	4	squares unsweetened chocolate, melted
1-3/4	cups sugar		
1	cup melted butter	1/2	cup chopped nuts, optional
1	teaspoon vanilla		
1	cup flour		

Melt butter and chocolate. Set aside. Combine beaten eggs and sugar. Beat 5 minutes. Add butter, chocolate, vanilla, flour and nuts. Pour into greased 13 by 9-inch pan. Bake at 350 degrees for about 18 to 20 minutes.

Layer - 2:

4	tablespoons melted butter	green food coloring (a few drops)
2	tablespoons milk	
2	cups confectioners' sugar	
1/4	teaspoon peppermint extract	

Mix together to spreadable consistency. Spread on pan of warm bars. Put in refrigerator until hardened.

Layer - 3:

3	squares or ounces semi-sweet chocolate	3	tablespoons melted butter

Melt chocolate and butter together. Cool slightly. Spread lightly and thickly on top of green layer. Chill before cutting. Cut in small squares, diamonds or rectangles.

Cherry-Coconut Bars

A rich cookie, pretty and loaded with goodies.

1	cup sifted flour	1/2	teaspoon baking powder
1/2	cup butter or margarine	1/4	teaspoon salt
3	tablespoons confectioners' sugar	1	teaspoon vanilla
		3/4	cup chopped nuts
2	eggs, slightly beaten	1/2	cup coconut
1	cup sugar	1/2	cup quartered maraschino cherries
1/4	cup sifted flour		

With hand, mix 1 cup flour, butter, and confectioners' sugar until smooth. Spread thin with fingers in ungreased square pan, 8 by 8 by 2-inch. Bake in a 350 degree oven for about 25 minutes. Stir rest of ingredients into eggs. Spread over top of baked pastry (no need to cool). Bake about 25 minutes. Cool. Cut into bars. Makes 18.

Butter Chews

A delicious cookie with a chewy coconut and nut topping.

3/4	cup butter	1	cup nuts, chopped
3	tablespoons sugar	3/4	cup shredded coconut
1-1/2	cups flour	3	egg whites, stiffly beaten
3	egg yolks, beaten		confectioners' sugar
2-1/4	cups brown sugar		

Cream butter, add sugar, and beat well. Blend thoroughly with flour. Pat mixture into a greased 9 by 12-inch cake pan and bake in a 375 degree oven for 15 minutes or until a delicate brown. Add brown sugar to beaten egg yolks and blend well. Add chopped nuts and coconut, then fold in beaten egg whites. Pour over the baked mixture and return to oven for 25 to 30 minutes. Cut into 1-inch squares and dust with confectioners' sugar. Makes 35 cookies.

V. J.'s Cookie Surprise

A graham cracker layer makes this an unusual treat.

1-3/4	cups flour	1	envelope (1-ounce) pre-melted unsweetened chocolate
1/2	teaspoon salt		
1/4	teaspoon soda		
3/4	cup butter, softened	3/4	cup chopped walnuts
1	cup sugar	15	single graham crackers
1/3	cup milk	1	cup semisweet chocolate pieces
2	eggs		
1	teaspoon vanilla		

In large mixer bowl, combine all ingredients except chocolate, walnuts, crackers and chocolate pieces. Blend well. To half of dough, in another bowl, add envelope of chocolate and nuts. Spread in greased 13 by 9-inch pan. Arrange crackers over dough. Add chocolate pieces to remaining dough. Drop by tablespoon over crackers and spread carefully to cover. Bake at 375 degrees for 25 to 30 minutes. Cool; cut into bars.

Checker Bars

Fudge filled shortbread cookies make an attractive and unusual display on your holiday tray.

Fudge Bar:

1	cup Nestle's semisweet chocolate morsels	1/2	cup sifted powdered sugar
1	tablespoon shortening	3/4	cup walnuts or pecans, chopped

Melt morsels and shortening over hot water; remove from heat and add powdered sugar, walnuts or pecans; mix well. Spread on wax paper or aluminum foil to a 12 by 3-inch rectangle. Chill for 30 minutes. Meanwhile prepare vanilla bars. Cut fudge bar lengthwise into 8 strips. Chill until firm.

Vanilla Bar:

1	cup butter	2-1/2	teaspoons vanilla
1	cup sifted powdered sugar	2-1/4	cups sifted flour

Cream butter. Gradually add powdered sugar, creaming well. Blend in vanilla and flour, mix well. Shape into a 12 by 6-inch rectangle on wax paper or aluminum foil. Wrap; chill until firm. Cut lengthwise into twelve 1/2-inch strips. Place 3 strips of the vanilla bar alternately with 2 strips of the fudge bar on ungreased cookie sheet. Press strips together. Cut crosswise in 1/2-inch bars. Do not separate. Repeat with remaining dough. Bake at 350 degrees for 20 to 25 minutes until lightly browned. Cool 5 minutes. Re-cut bars; transfer carefully to cooling rack. Store in flat container, do not stack.

Note:
For tiny party cookies, combine 1 strip of the fudge bar with 2 strips of vanilla bar. The vanilla bar will have to be cut into 16 strips.

Sunshine Dream Bars

Make a pretty tray of assorted bar cookies, always a hit with men.

1	cup sifted flour	1	8-ounce package cream cheese
2/3	cup sugar		
1	tablespoon grated lemon rind	2	eggs
		2	tablespoons lemon juice
1/4	cup butter		

Sift the flour with 1/3 cup sugar into a bowl and stir in 2 teaspoons lemon rind. Cut in the butter and 1/4 cup cream cheese until particles are fine. Press into well-greased 9 by 13-inch shallow baking pan. Bake at 350 degrees for 12 to 15 minutes or until golden brown. Cream remaining cream cheese with remaining sugar, lemon rind and lemon juice and spread over baked mixture.

Golden Nut Topping:

2	eggs	2	tablespoons flour
1	teaspoon vanilla	1	teaspoon baking powder
1	cup firmly packed brown sugar	1/2	teaspoon salt
		1	cup chopped walnuts

Beat the eggs with vanilla in a bowl until foamy. Add brown sugar gradually and beat well. Sift the flour with baking powder and salt and stir into egg mixture. Stir in 3/4 cups walnuts and spoon over cream cheese mixture. Sprinkle with remaining walnuts. Bake at 350 degrees for 25 to 30 minutes. Cool and cut into bars with a damp knife. Sprinkle with powdered sugar before serving, if desired. Makes about 3 dozen.

Chocolate-Chip Cheesecake Fantasies

These cookies are irresistible.

1-1/2	cups graham cracker crumbs	1	teaspoon vanilla extract
2	tablespoons sugar	1	tablespoon grated orange peel
1/3	cup butter or margarine, melted	1	cup chopped walnuts or almonds
1	8-ounce package cream cheese, room temperature	1	cup (6 ounces) semisweet chocolate pieces
1/3	cup sugar	2/3	cup flaked or shredded coconut
1	egg		

Preheat oven to 350 degrees. In a medium bowl, combine graham cracker crumbs, 2 tablespoons sugar and melted butter or margarine. Press mixture evenly in bottom of an ungreased 13 by 9-inch baking pan. Bake 7 to 8 minutes. In a medium bowl, beat together cream cheese, 1/3 cup sugar, egg, vanilla and orange peel until well blended. Spread evenly over baked crust. In a small bowl, combine nuts, chocolate pieces and coconut. Sprinkle evenly over cream cheese mixture, pressing in lightly. Bake 25 to 30 minutes or until brown. Cool in pan. Cut cooled cookies into squares. Store in refrigerator. Makes forty-eight 1-1/2-inch cookies.

Chocolate-Cherry Cookie Pizza

Use a pizza pan to bake this giant sugar-dusted cookie. Then cut it into pizza-shaped wedges.

1/2	cup butter or margarine, softened	1/2	cup coarsely chopped pecans
1/2	cup firmly packed brown sugar	1/3	cup red candied cherries, halved
1	teaspoon vanilla extract		confectioners' sugar
1	cup flour		
1	cup coarsely chopped semisweet chocolate		

Preheat oven to 375 degrees. In large mixer bowl beat butter and brown sugar until light and fluffy; blend in vanilla. Gradually add flour, mixing until blended. Stir in chocolate, pecans, and cherries. Pat mixture evenly over surface of a lightly greased, flat, 11 to 12-inch diameter pizza pan (dough will be thick; use your fingers if necessary), spreading nearly to outer edge of pan. Bake until well browned, about 14 to 16 minutes. Cool for 10 minutes in pan on wire rack, then use a pizza cutter or knife to cut into wedges. Sprinkle lightly with confectioners' sugar. Remove from pan when cool. Makes about 18 wedge-shaped cookies.

Chocolate Covered Cherry Squares

Cherries covered with chocolate - who could ask for more?

1	cup sifted flour	36	maraschino cherries, well drained
1/4	teaspoon salt		
1/3	cup brown sugar, packed	2	tablespoons chopped nuts
1/2	cup butter		
1	cup semi-sweet chocolate bits, melted		

Combine flour, salt and sugar; cut in butter. Form dough into a ball. Press into ungreased 8 by 8 by 2-inch pan. Bake at 350 degree oven for about 20 minutes. Cut into 36 squares while warm. Place a small amount of melted chocolate on a square; top with cherry; cover cherry with melted chocolate; swirl top; sprinkle with nuts. Makes about 3 dozen.

Chocolate-Cherry Squares

No one will refuse these pretty squares - served on a silver tray.

1	cup flour	1/2	cup chopped nuts
1/3	cup butter or margarine		Filling
1/2	cup packed light brown sugar		red candied cherry halves

Combine flour, butter and brown sugar in large mixer bowl. Blend on low speed to form fine crumbs, about 2 to 3 minutes. Stir in nuts. Reserve 3/4 cup crumb mixture for topping; pat remaining crumbs into ungreased 9-inch square pan. Bake at 350 degrees for 10 minutes or until lightly browned. Prepare Filling; spread over warm crust. Sprinkle with reserved crumb mixture and garnish with cherry halves. Bake at 350 degrees for 25 minutes or until lightly browned. Cool; cut into squares. Store in refrigerator. Makes 3 dozen squares.

Filling:

1	8-ounce package cream cheese, softened	1	egg
1/2	cup sugar	1/2	teaspoon vanilla
1/3	cup cocoa	1/2	cup chopped red candied cherries
1/4	cup milk		

Combine cream cheese, sugar, cocoa, milk, egg and vanilla in small mixer bowl; beat until smooth. Fold in cherries.

Chewy Chocolate Brownies

My mother made these brownies regularly for us when we were youngsters. They are extra rich in eggs.

4	eggs	2	teaspoons vanilla
2	cups sugar	1/4	teaspoon salt
1	cup butter or margarine, melted	1	cup cake flour
3	squares unsweetened chocolate	1	cup nutmeats, ground

Beat eggs until foamy; add sugar and beat. Melt butter and chocolate together and then add slowly to eggs and sugar. Beat well. Add vanilla and salt and mix. Add sifted flour and mix until smooth. Add nuts. Pour batter into a greased and floured 9 by 13-inch cake pan. Bake at 350 degrees for 30 to 40 minutes.

Double-Frosted Brownies

The double frosting of creamy peppermint and melted chocolate make them as rich and good as candy.

3/4	cup sifted flour	2	eggs
1/2	teaspoon baking powder	2-1/2	squares chocolate
1/2	teaspoon salt	1	teaspoon vanilla
1/2	cup shortening	1/2	cup chopped nuts
1	cup sugar		

Sift together dry ingredients. Add shortening and sugar; cream well. Add eggs, melted and cooled chocolate and vanilla. Blend in dry ingredients and nuts, mix well. Pour into well-greased and floured 9 by 9 by 2-inch pan. Bake in moderate 350 degree oven for 25 to 35 minutes. Cool and frost. Cut into bars or squares. Makes about 1-1/2 dozen brownies.

Mint Cream Frosting:

1-1/2	cups sifted confectioners' sugar	1/4	teaspoon peppermint flavoring
1/2	cup light cream or evaporated milk	1	drop green food coloring
1	tablespoon butter	2	squares chocolate (semisweet)

Put sugar and cream in saucepan. Cook over direct heat until a little syrup dropped in cold water forms a soft ball (232 degrees). Remove from heat. Add butter and cool to lukewarm (110 degrees). Add peppermint flavoring and green food coloring and beat until thick and creamy. Frost cooled brownies. Spread melted chocolate over frosting. Cut into bars or squares when thoroughly cool.

Caramel Brownies

In a hurry? Try these tasty cookies.

1	cup flour	2	cups brown sugar
2	teaspoons baking powder	2	eggs
1	teaspoon salt	2	teaspoons vanilla
1/2	cup butter	1	cup chopped nuts

Melt butter; add eggs, sugar and vanilla. Combine dry ingredients; stir into egg mixture. Add nuts. Spread in a 10 by 15-inch pan. Bake at 350 degrees for about 1/2 hour.

Snowcap Brownies

Swirled meringue give these brownies a unique appearance.

1/2	cup margarine	2	eggs
2-1/2	squares unsweetened chocolate	1	egg yolk
		3/4	cup flour
1-1/4	cups sugar	1	teaspoon baking powder
1/2	teaspoon red food coloring	1/2	teaspoon salt
		1	cup nuts, chopped

Melt margarine and chocolate. Blend in sugar, vanilla and food coloring. Add eggs and yolk and beat well. Blend in dry ingredients and nuts. Spread batter in a well-greased jellyroll pan. Drop meringue by teaspoonfuls over batter; draw tip of knife through batter lengthwise, then crosswise, to give meringue a design. Bake in a 325 degree oven 25 to 30 minutes. When cool, cut into squares. Makes 24 brownies.

Meringue:

1	egg white	1/2	teaspoon vanilla
1/2	cup sugar		

Beat egg white until stiff peaks form. Blend in sugar and vanilla.

Swedish Almond Brownies

Almonds and a hint of bitter-almond flavor are the Scandinavian touches in these delicately thin brownies.

1-1/2	squares unsweetened chocolate	1/4	teaspoon almond extract
1/2	cup butter	1/3	cup flour
2	eggs, room temperature	1/2	cup sliced almonds
1	cup sugar		confectioners' sugar

Preheat oven to 400 degrees. Combine chocolate and butter in a small heavy saucepan over low heat. Let stand until melted, then stir well to blend. Let chocolate mixture cool. Grease a 9 by 13-inch pan; dust with flour. In mixer bowl, beat eggs at high speed until thick and light colored. Gradually add granulated sugar, beating until well combined. Stir in cooled chocolate mixture and almond extract until blended. Mix in flour, then almonds. Spread batter in prepared pan. Bake until top springs back when touched lightly, about 15 to 18 minutes. Let cool in pan on a wire rack for about 5 minutes, then cut into bars. Sift lightly with confectioners' sugar. Remove from pan when cool. Makes about 30 bars.

Cheesecake Cookies

Nothing better for a pick-me-up than these cheesy cookies.

1/3	cup butter	8	ounce package cream cheese
1/3	cup brown sugar, firmly packed	1	egg
1	cup flour	2	tablespoons milk
1/2	cup walnuts, finely chopped	1	tablespoon lemon juice
1/4	cup sugar	1/2	teaspoon vanilla

Cream butter with brown sugar in small mixing bowl. Add flour and walnuts; mix to make a crumb mixture. Reserve 1 cup for topping. Press remainder into bottom of 8-inch square pan. Bake at 350 degrees for 12 to 15 minutes until lightly browned. Blend sugar with cream cheese in small mixing bowl until smooth. Add egg, milk, lemon juice and vanilla; beat well. Spread over baked crust. Sprinkle with reserved crumb mixture. Bake at 350 degrees for 25 minutes. Cool; cut into 2-inch squares. Makes 16 squares.

Cream Cheese Brownies

Cream cheese filling is a great addition to brownies.

Chocolate Batter:

4	ounces German sweet chocolate	1/2	teaspoon baking powder
3	tablespoons margarine or butter	1/4	teaspoon salt
		1/2	cup flour
2	eggs, beaten	1/2	cup nuts, chopped
3/4	cup sugar	1	teaspoon vanilla

Cheese Batter:

2	tablespoons butter	1	egg
1	3-ounce package cream cheese	1	tablespoon flour
		1/2	teaspoon vanilla
1/4	cup sugar		

Melt chocolate with 3 tablespoons margarine, stirring constantly. Set aside to cool. Meanwhile, in a medium bowl, beat 2 eggs until thick and lemon colored, gradually add 3/4 cup sugar, beating until thickened. Add baking powder, salt and 1/2 cup flour. When chocolate is cool, blend it into batter, adding nuts and vanilla. Set aside. In small bowl, cream 2 tablespoons butter with the cream cheese. Gradually add 1/4 cup sugar, cream well. Blend in 1 egg, 1 tablespoon flour and 1/2 teaspoon vanilla. Spread 1/2 of chocolate mixture in a greased 8- or 9-inch pan. Then layer on all of cheese mixture. Spoon the remaining chocolate mixture on top in various spots. Zigzag through batter with a rubber spatula in order to create a marbling effect. Bake for 35 to 40 minutes in a 350 degree oven. Cool on wire rack before cutting into squares. Freezes beautifully. Be sure to put waxed paper or plastic between layers. Makes about 48 brownies.

Candy Bar Brownies

The super flavor of chocolate and coconut comes from melted candy bars. Moist and chewy.

1-1/8	cups sifted flour	1/2	cup shortening
1/2	teaspoon salt	1	cup sugar
2	double chocolate-covered coconut candy bars (2-1/4-ounce each)	1	teaspoon vanilla
		2	eggs
		1/2	cup chopped nuts

Melt candy bars and shortening. Blend in sugar and vanilla; add eggs. Beat well, blend in flour and salt. Stir in nuts. Pour into a 9 by 9 by 2-inch well-greased pan. Bake at 350 degrees for 25 to 30 minutes. Cut into bars. Makes about 3 dozen cookies.

Toffee Filled Brownies

Toasted coconut filling gives a different taste to these tempting brownies.

1/2	cup butter	1/2	teaspoon salt
1-1/4	cups sugar	1	teaspoon vanilla
3	eggs	1	cup finely chopped walnuts
1	cup flour, sifted		confectioners' sugar
1/3	cup cocoa		
1/2	teaspoon baking powder		

Grease and line bottom of 9-inch square pan with waxed paper, then grease again. Sift flour with cocoa, baking powder and salt. Melt butter; stir in sugar. Cool to lukewarm. Blend in eggs, one at a time, beating well after each. Add dry ingredients; mix well. Stir in vanilla and walnuts. Spread in pan. Bake at 350 degrees for 30 to 35 minutes until brownie springs back when touched lightly in center. Cool 10 minutes; remove from pan. Cool completely. Cut into 16 squares. Split each square and fill. Cover; store in the refrigerator. Before serving sprinkle confectioners' sugar on top. Makes about 16 brownies.

Toasted Coconut Filling:

1	cup coconut, flaked	1	tablespoon flour
1	egg	1/8	teaspoon salt
1/2	cup evaporated milk	1	teaspoon vanilla
1/4	cup butter		
1	cup brown sugar, firmly packed		

Toast coconut at 350 degrees for 10 to 12 minutes, stirring occasionally, until golden brown. Beat egg. Add milk, butter, brown sugar, flour and salt. Bring to a boil; cook until thick, stirring constantly. Stir in vanilla and coconut. Cool.

Brownie Petit Fours

An elegant accompaniment to coffee.

Petit Fours:

1	6-ounce package of semisweet chocolate morsels	1	teaspoon vanilla
		4	eggs, separated
		2/3	cup finely ground pecans
2	teaspoons instant coffee	2	tablespoons flour
1/3	cup butter, softened	1/4	teaspoon cream of tartar
1	tablespoon coffee-flavored liqueur		

Combine over hot (not boiling) water, morsels and instant coffee; stir until smooth. Remove from heat. In large bowl, combine butter, liqueur, vanilla and morsel mixture; mix well. Beat in egg yolks just until combined; do not over-beat. Add pecans and flour. In small bowl, beat egg whites and cream of tartar until soft peaks form. Fold 1/4 cup of beaten whites into chocolate mixture. Gently fold into remaining egg white mixture. Spread in greased and floured (bottom only) 8 by 8 by 2-inch baking pan. Bake at 350 degrees for about 30 minutes. Cool 1 hour; remove from pan. Cool. Cut cake into 36 squares. Using a fork, hold squares over glaze; spoon over to coat squares. Dry on wire racks. Chill until set. Decorate as desired. Makes about 3 dozen Petit Fours.

Coffee Glaze:

1/2	cup butter	2	teaspoons vanilla
3	tablespoons water	3	cups sifted confectioners' sugar
1	tablespoon instant coffee		

In saucepan, combine butter, water and instant coffee. Heat until coffee dissolves and butter melts; remove from heat. Stir in vanilla. Gradually stir in confectioners' sugar; mix well.

Frosted Fudge Bars

These really are one of the best bars you will ever make.

1/2	cup butter or margarine	2	eggs
2	ounces unsweetened chocolate	1	cup sugar
		1/2	teaspoon vanilla
1	cup sifted cake flour	1	cup broken walnuts
1/4	teaspoon salt		Bittersweet Frosting
1/4	teaspoon baking powder		chopped walnuts

Preheat oven to 350 degrees. Grease sides and bottom of 8-inch square cake pan. Melt butter and chocolate. Sift dry ingredients together. Put eggs into mixing bowl and beat thoroughly. Gradually add sugar, and beat well, stir in chocolate mixture and vanilla beating well for 1 minute. Add broken walnuts and stir well. Add the dry ingredients in thirds, stirring well after each addition. Turn the mixture into prepared pan. Bake 35 minutes or until a slight imprint remains when the top is lightly touched with the fingertip. Place pan on wire rack. While still warm, spread the frosting over the cake and sprinkle with chopped nuts. When the frosting is set, cut into bars, about 4 by 1-inches. Makes about 16 bars.

Bittersweet Frosting:

2	ounces unsweetened chocolate	1/4	cup sugar
		1/2	teaspoon vanilla
3	tablespoons water		

Melt chocolate. Put water and sugar in small pan. Cook and stir over low heat until sugar is dissolved, then boil 1 minute. Slowly stir the syrup into the chocolate, then beat until thick. Stir in vanilla. Makes about 1/2 cup.

Fudge Four O'Clocks

Watch men drool when they taste these cookies. Spread with fluffy frosting and crowned with pecan halves.

1/4	cup butter	1	cup cake flour
2	ounces chocolate	1/2	teaspoon salt
3	eggs	1	teaspoon baking powder
1	cup sugar	1	cup toasted nuts
1/2	cup milk		

Toast the nuts by spreading in a pan and placing in a hot oven for a few minutes. Melt chocolate and pour over butter. Mix well together. Beat whole eggs until thick and lemon colored. Add sugar gradually, beating well with each addition. Combine mixtures. Add a little of the flour which has been sifted with the salt and baking powder, then alternate the remaining flour with the milk. Add the nuts. Spread in two 8 by 8-inch pans which have been buttered and lined with waxed paper. Bake in a 325 degree oven for 25 to 30 minutes until firm. When cool, frost with vanilla confectioners' icing, cut into bars 1-inch wide.

Chocolate Coconut Slices

This is a moist bar, thick with chewy coconut.

6	ounces semi-sweet chocolate	1/2	teaspoon almond extract
1	ounce plus 4 ounces butter	1/2	cup Dutch-process cocoa powder
2	cups shredded coconut	1-1/2	cups flour
1-1/2	cups sugar	1/2	teaspoon salt
2	eggs		

Melt the chocolate. Remove the chocolate from the heat and swirl in 1 ounce of the butter. After the butter is blended in, add the coconut. Cool to room temperature. Cream the remaining 4 ounces butter and the sugar until light and fluffy. Beat in the eggs until just blended; stir in the almond extract. Sift the cocoa, flour and salt together; stir into the creamed mixture until thoroughly combined. Blend in the cooled chocolate mixture. Pour the mixture into a buttered jellyroll pan and smooth with a spatula. Bake in a 325 degree oven about 18 to 20 minutes. Cool on a rack before cutting into slices. Makes 45 to 50 cookies.

Chocolate Nut Squares

Delicious candy bar cookie.

1	cup butter or margarine	2	cups flour
1	cup brown sugar	1/4	teaspoon salt
1	egg yolk	2	thin milk chocolate bars
1	teaspoon vanilla	3/4	cup chopped walnuts

Cream together butter, brown sugar, egg yolk and vanilla. Mix flour and salt together and blend into butter mixture. Pat dough into a rectangle, 12-1/2 by 10-1/2-inches, on a greased cookie sheet, leaving 1-inch around edge of cookie sheet. Bake in a 350 degree oven about 20 to 25 minutes or until nicely browned. Remove from oven. Immediately place separated squares of chocolate on top. Let stand until chocolate is soft. Spread evenly over surface and sprinkle with nuts. Cut into small squares while still warm. Makes about 80 small squares.

Kahlua Chocolate Squares

A new taste to a brownie like bar.

1-1/4	cups flour		
3/4	teaspoon baking powder	1/4	cup Kahlua
1/2	teaspoon salt	1	cup semi-sweet chocolate chips
1/2	cup butter		
3/4	cup brown sugar, packed	1/3	cup chopped walnuts
1	large egg		walnut pieces

Cream butter and brown sugar, beat in egg. Stir in Kahlua alternately with dry ingredients. Blend well. Fold in chocolate chips and nuts. Spread evenly in a greased 7 by 11-inch pan. Bake 30 minutes in a 350 degree oven. Cool 15 minutes. Frost with Brown Sugar Icing. Put walnut pieces on top.

Brown Sugar Icing:

2	tablespoons butter	2	teaspoons cream
1	tablespoon Kahlua	1-1/3	cups confectioners' sugar

Heat butter until lightly brown. Remove from heat, add Kahlua, cream and confectioners' sugar. Beat until soft.

Chocolate Meltaways

Just try keeping a man away from these scrumptious cookies.

1/2	cup butter or margarine	1	teaspoon sugar
1	egg yolk	1	teaspoon baking powder
2	tablespoons water	1	cup semisweet chocolate pieces
1-1/2	cups flour		

In a medium bowl, beat together the butter, egg yolk, and water. Stir in flour, 1 teaspoon sugar and baking powder. Mix together, pat into a greased 9 by 13-inch greased pan. Bake for 10 minutes in a 350 degree oven. Remove and sprinkle with chocolate pieces. Return to oven for 1 minute to melt. Remove from oven and spread chocolate as you would a frosting. Set aside.

Topping:

2	eggs	2	teaspoons vanilla
3/4	cup sugar	2	cups nuts, coarsely chopped
6	tablespoons margarine or butter, melted		

In a small bowl, beat the eggs and sugar together. Stir in the melted butter and vanilla. When well blended, fold in the chopped nuts. Spread topping over chocolate layer. Bake in a 350 degree oven for 30 to 35 minutes. Remove to wire rack to cool. Cut into squares, but leave in pan until ready to use or freeze.

Marbled Cookie Squares

A bar with a different look.

1	cup plus 2 tablespoons sifted flour	1/2	teaspoon vanilla
1/2	teaspoon baking soda	1/4	teaspoon water
1/2	teaspoon salt	1	egg
1/2	cup butter	1/2	cup chopped nuts
1/4	cup plus 2 tablespoons sugar	6	ounces semiswseet chocolate bits

Mix and sift flour, soda and salt. Cream butter, add sugar gradually and cream until fluffy. Add vanilla, water, egg and nuts and mix. Add sifted ingredients gradually and mix. Spread in greased pan, 9 by 13-inch. Sprinkle chocolate bits evenly over top. Bake in a preheated 375 degree oven 3 minutes. Remove from oven and run knife through dough to marbleize; return to oven and bake 13 to 15 minutes longer. Cool. Cut into squares. Makes about 2 dozen.

Chocolate Buttermilk Squares

Here's a new taste to an old favorite.

1	cup butter or margarine	1/2	cup buttermilk
1/4	cup unsweetened cocoa	1	teaspoon baking soda
1	cup water	2	eggs, beaten
2	cups sugar	1	teaspoon vanilla
2	cups flour	3	to 4 drops red food coloring, optional
1/2	teaspoon salt		

In a saucepan, bring butter, cocoa and water to a boil. Cool. Meanwhile, in a large mixing bowl, combine the sugar, flour and salt. Pour cocoa mixture over dry ingredients. Mix well. Combine buttermilk and baking soda; add to cocoa mixture along with eggs, vanilla and food coloring, if desired. Mix until well combined. Pour into a greased and floured 15 by 10 by 1-inch baking pan. Bake at 350 degrees for about 20 minutes.

Frosting:

1/2	cup butter	1	teaspoon vanilla
1/4	cup unsweetened cocoa		dash salt
1/4	cup buttermilk	3/4	cup chopped almonds, optional
1	pound confectioners' sugar		

Melt butter, cocoa and buttermilk. Stir in sugar, vanilla and salt. Spread over warm cake and top with nuts, if desired. Makes about 15 servings.

Rocky Road Fudge Bars

Here is a taste treat that's sure to please.

1/2	cup butter or margarine	1	cup flour
1	square unsweetened chocolate or 1 envelope Pre-melted chocolate	1	cup chopped nuts
		1	teaspoon baking powder
		1	teaspoon vanilla
1	cup sugar	2	eggs

Preheat oven to 350 degrees. Grease and flour 13 by 9-inch pan. In large saucepan over low heat; melt 1/2 cup butter and 1 ounce chocolate. Add remaining bar ingredients; mix well. Spread in prepared pan.

Filling:

8	ounce package cream cheese, softened (reserve 2 ounces for frosting)	1	egg
		1/2	teaspoon vanilla
		1/4	cup chopped nuts
1/2	cup sugar	6	ounce package semisweet chocolate pieces, if desired
2	tablespoons flour		
1/4	cup butter or margarine, softened	2	cups miniature marshmallows

In small bowl, combine 6 ounces cream cheese with next 5 filling ingredients. Beat 1 minute at medium speed until smooth and fluffy; stir in nuts. Spread over chocolate mixture. Sprinkle with chocolate pieces. Bake 25 to 35 minutes until toothpick inserted in center comes out clean. Remove from oven; sprinkle with marshmallows. Bake about 2 minutes longer.

Frosting:

1/4	cup butter or margarine		remaining 2 ounces cream cheese
1	square unsweetened chocolate	1/4	cup milk
		3	cups powdered sugar
		1	teaspoon vanilla

Meanwhile in a small saucepan, over low heat, melt 1/4 cup butter, 1 square chocolate, remaining 2 ounces cream cheese and milk. Stir in powdered sugar and vanilla until smooth. Immediately pour over marshmallows and swirl together. Cool; cut into bars. Store in refrigerator. Makes about 3 to 4 dozen bars.

Date Brownies

Adding dates to brownies gives them an entirely different taste.

1/3	cup butter, softened	1/2	teaspoon salt
3	eggs, well beaten	3/4	cup sifted flour
1	cup sugar	1	teaspoon vanilla
2	squares unsweetened chocolate, melted	1/2	cup finely chopped dates
1	teaspoon baking powder		

Cream the butter and sugar together and add the eggs. Beat until very well blended. Add the melted chocolate and sifted dry ingredients; add the vanilla and chopped dates and when thoroughly mixed, turn into a shallow greased pan about 8-inches square. Bake in a 350 degree oven for about 40 minutes. Cut in the pan while still hot into squares or bars. Makes 1-1/2 to 2 dozen brownies.

Chocolate Cake Brownies

These rich brownies are made on a cookie sheet. It's a big enough batch to feed a crowd.

2	cups sugar	1	cup boiling water
2	cups flour	1/2	cup buttermilk
1	teaspoon soda	2	beaten eggs
1	cup butter or margarine	1	teaspoon vanilla
3	tablespoons cocoa		pinch of salt

Mix in a large bowl sugar, flour and baking soda. Over low heat, in a saucepan, melt butter and cocoa. Add boiling water and stir well. Add to dry ingredients and mix. Add buttermilk, beaten eggs, vanilla and salt. Mix thoroughly. Pour into a greased 11 by 16-inch cookie sheet with sides. Bake for 15 minutes in a 400 degree oven. Frost with chocolate icing while still hot.

Mississippi Mud

Marshmallow filling makes these taste outstanding.

4	eggs	1/4	cup cocoa
1	cup margarine		dash of salt
2	cups sugar	1	cup chopped pecans
1	teaspoon vanilla	1	jar (7-ounce) marshmallow creme
1-1/2	cups flour		

Beat eggs, sugar, margarine and vanilla until light and fluffy. Add flour, cocoa and salt, beat just until blended. Fold in pecans. Spread evenly in a greased 13 by 9-inch pan. Bake 40 to 45 minutes in a 375 degree oven. Immediately place dollops of marshmallow creme on cake; spread until smooth. Let cool on wire rack for at least 1 hour before frosting.

Frosting:

1/2	cup butter or margarine	1	teaspoon vanilla
1/2	cup cocoa	2-1/2	cups confectioners' sugar
1/3	cup milk		

Melt butter in a saucepan, stir in cocoa and cook 1 minute. Remove from heat and stir in remaining frosting ingredients. Stir until smooth. Spread on top of marshmallow creme. When frosting has cooled, cut into 1-inch squares. Makes 7 dozen.

Oatmeal-Fudge Bars

A really different bar cookie that tastes as good as it looks.

Oatmeal Layer:

1/2	cup soft shortening	3/4	cup sifted flour
1	cup light brown sugar, firmly packed	1/2	teaspoon baking soda
		1/2	teaspoon salt
1	egg	2	cups quick-cooking oats
1/2	teaspoon vanilla	1/2	cup chopped walnuts

Grease a 9 by 9 by 3/4-inch baking pan. In medium bowl, with wooden spoon, beat shortening with sugar until fluffy. Beat in egg and vanilla. Sift flour with baking soda and salt into sugar mixture; mix well. Stir in oats and nuts. Remove 1 cup mixture for topping. Press rest of mixture into bottom of prepared pan.

Fudge Layer:

1	package (6-ounce) semisweet chocolate pieces	1/3	cup sweetened condensed milk
		1/4	teaspoon salt
1	tablespoon butter or margarine	1/2	cup chopped walnuts
		1	teaspoon vanilla

Preheat oven to 350 degrees. In small saucepan, combine chocolate pieces, butter, milk, and salt. Cook, stirring, over low heat until chocolate and butter are melted. Remove from heat; stir in nuts and vanilla. Spread chocolate mixture over oatmeal layer. Sprinkle top with reserved oat mixture. Bake for about 25 minutes, or until surface is lightly browned. Let cool completely in pan on wire rack. Cut into bars. Makes about 2 dozen.

Dutch Chocolate Bars

Green frosting makes these very festive looking. Add a few sprinkles for variety.

1	cup sifted flour	3	eggs, slightly beaten
1-1/2	cups sugar	3	squares unsweetened chocolate, melted
1/2	teaspoon salt		
1/2	teaspoon baking powder	1	teaspoon vanilla
1	cup soft butter	2	cups uncooked oatmeal

Sift flour, sugar, salt and baking powder into mixing bowl. Add butter, eggs, cooled chocolate and vanilla; mix until smooth. Stir in oatmeal. Spread into greased 13 by 9 by 2-inch pan. Bake at 350 degrees about 25 minutes. Cool; frost with Peppermint Butter Frosting. Cut into bars. Makes about 5 dozen.

Peppermint Butter Frosting:

1/4	cup soft butter		few drops green food coloring
2	cups powdered sugar	3	tablespoons cream (approximately)
1	teaspoon peppermint extract		

Blend butter, sugar, extract and food coloring; add enough cream to make frosting of spreading consistency; beat well.

Press Cookies

*A warm and sparkling season
a lovely time of year
a special time to wish the best
to those who we hold dear.*

Lemon-Cheese Dips

If you like lemon these are for you.

1	cup butter	1	tablespoon lemon juice
3	ounce package cream cheese	1	teaspoon finely chopped lemon rind
1	cup sugar	1	teaspoon baking powder
1	egg	2-1/2	cups flour

Blend together butter and cream cheese. Add sugar and mix well. Beat egg, add to mixture, add juice and rind mixing well. Add sifted dry ingredients and blend thoroughly. Press dough through cookie press into 2-1/2-inch long strips on lightly greased cookie sheets. Bake at 375 degrees for 8 to 10 minutes. Makes about 30 cookies.

Note:
When baked, dip ends in Lemon Icing.

Lemon Icing:

1	cup sifted confectioners' sugar	1/3	cup walnuts, finely chopped
2	tablespoons lemon juice		

Mix together confectioners' sugar and lemon juice until smooth. Dip both ends in this icing about 1/4-inch and then dip icing-covered ends into the chopped or ground walnuts. Let dry on waxed paper. Makes about 1 cup of icing.

Butter Gems

The old standby to sprinkle colored sugar on at Christmas time.

1/2	cup butter	2-1/4	cups flour
1/2	cup shortening	1/2	teaspoon baking powder
3/4	cup sugar		dash of salt
1	egg	1	teaspoon almond flavoring

Cream together the butter and sugar. Add egg and beat well. Add sifted dry ingredients and flavoring and blend well. Form cookie with a cookie press on ungreased cookie sheets, bake in a 400 degree oven 10 to 12 minutes. Makes about 60 cookies.

A story goes that "Saint Nickalus" many years ago, heard of three sisters who were to be sold into slavery because they had no dowry that was necessary for a marriage. "Saint Nickalus" threw three bags of Gold down the chimney and they landed in stockings that were hung by the fire to dry, thus the start of the Christmas stocking hung by the fire.

Fruit Filled Spritz

Nothing but praise coming your way when you serve these good tasting cookies.

Date Nut Filling:

3/4	cup dates, cut in small pieces	1/4	cup finely chopped candied cherries
1/2	cup water	1/4	cup chopped coconut
1/4	cup sugar	1/2	cup finely chopped nuts
1	teaspoon grated orange rind	1	teaspoon vanilla

Cook dates, water and sugar until dates are soft. Add remaining ingredients. Stir to blend. Cool. Prepare cookie dough.

Cookie Dough:

2	cups sifted flour	1	egg
1/4	teaspoon soda	1/2	teaspoon vanilla
1/2	teaspoon salt	1/2	teaspoon almond flavoring
1/2	cup butter	1/3	cup finely chopped nuts for topping
1/2	cup sugar		
1/4	cup firmly packed light brown sugar		

Sift flour, soda and salt together. Cream butter. Add sugars. Cream well. Add egg, vanilla and almond flavoring. Add dry ingredients. Blend. Knead with hands until dough is soft and pliable. Use saw-toothed cutter in cookie press. Press half of the dough through cookie press directly onto ungreased cookie sheets. Make strips about 12-inches long. Spread filling about 1/2-inch thick on each strip. Fill cookie press with remaining dough. Hold press above filling. Place a second strip over filling to form a long bar. Sprinkle with chopped nuts. Bake at 375 degrees 12 to 15 minutes or until delicately browned. Cut strips diagonally into 1-inch pieces while warm. Makes nine 12-inch bars or 12 dozen cookies.

Wreaths

A different kind of spritz cookie.

1	cup butter or margarine	1-1/3	cups finely chopped walnuts
1/2	cup sugar		
1	egg	1/4	cup maple syrup
1	teaspoon vanilla		red and green candied cherries
2-1/2	cups sifted flour		

Beat butter or margarine with sugar until fluffy-light in a large bowl. Beat in egg and vanilla. Stir in flour, a third at a time, blending well to make a soft dough. Measure out 1/3 cup of the dough and mix with walnuts and maple syrup in a small bowl; reserve for cookie centers. Fit a pastry bag with a small star tip; fill bag with remaining dough. Press out into 1-1/2-inch rings on ungreased large cookie sheets; fill center of each cookie with about a teaspoonful of nut mixture; decorate wreaths with slivers of red and green candied cherries. Bake at 350 degrees for about 12 minutes or until lightly golden at edges. Remove carefully from cookie sheets to wire racks; cool completely. Makes about 6 dozen.

Coconut Wreaths

Extra pretty when drizzled with colored frosting.

2-1/3	cups sifted flour	1/2	teaspoon vanilla
2	teaspoons baking powder	1/2	cup grated coconut
1	cup butter	1/2	cup unblanched almond nutmeats, grated
1	cup sugar		
2	eggs		

Mix and sift flour and baking powder. Cream butter well, add sugar gradually and continue creaming until light and fluffy; add well beaten eggs and vanilla and mix well. Add sifted dry ingredients, coconut and nutmeats gradually and mix. Using a cookie press, form into wreaths on baking sheets. Bake in a 375 degree oven for about 13 minutes. Makes 4-1/2 dozen.

Noel Wreaths

These are almost to pretty to eat.

1	cup butter	1	teaspoon vanilla
1/2	cup sugar	2-1/2	cups sifted flour
1	egg		

Cream butter; add sugar gradually. Beat in egg and vanilla. Blend in flour. Dough is soft. Remove 1/4 cup dough to add to walnut filling. Knead remaining dough in hands until pliable. Use star shaped cookie press plate. Press dough through cookie press onto ungreased cookie sheets to form 3-inch strips. Join ends to make wreaths. Make Walnut Filling.

Walnut Filling:

1/4	cup reserved cookie dough	1/4	cup light corn syrup candied cherries
1	cup finely chopped walnuts		citron
1	teaspoon vanilla		

Combine 1/4 cup reserved dough, walnuts, vanilla and syrup. Place a teaspoonful of filling in center of each wreath. Decorate with bits of candied cherries and citron. Bake at 350 degrees for about 15 minutes or until delicately browned. Makes about 4-1/2 dozen.

Vanilla Sour-Cream Rosettes

Tender, pretty cookies with a hint of cinnamon flavor.

1/4	cup butter	1-1/2	cups flour
1/4	cup shortening	1/2	teaspoon cinnamon
1/2	cup sugar	1/4	teaspoon salt
1	egg	1/8	teaspoon baking soda
1/4	cup sour cream	1/2	teaspoon baking powder
1/2	teaspoon vanilla		

Cream butter and sugar. Add egg and beat well. Stir in sour cream and vanilla. Blend in sifted dry ingredients and mix thoroughly. Force through cookie press into rosette shape onto ungreased cookie sheet. Bake in a 375 degree oven about 10 to 12 minutes. Makes about 48 rosettes.

Vanilla Daisies

Nothing prettier on a tray of cookies than a delicate buttery cookie with a cherry in the center.

1	cup butter	1	teaspoon grated lemon rind
1/4	teaspoon salt		
2/3	cup sugar	2-1/4	cups flour
1	egg, beaten	1/2	teaspoon baking powder
1	teaspoon vanilla		

Cream butter and salt. Add sugar slowly and beat well. Add egg, vanilla and lemon rind and mix. Blend in dry ingredients, mix thoroughly, but do not over-mix. Press dough through a cookie press using a star shape form. Place a candied cherry half in center of each cookie. Bake in a 375 degree oven about 8 to 10 minutes. Makes about 40 cookies.

Fancy Meringue Figures

Add these to your gift cookie tray for that special look.

1/2	cup egg whites	3/4	cup sugar
	pinch of salt	1/2	cup sugar
1/4	teaspoon cream of tartar	1	teaspoon vanilla

Mix egg whites and salt, beat until frothy. Beat in cream of tartar. Add 3/4 cup sugar by tablespoon, beating constantly. Fold in gently the remaining sugar and vanilla. Squeeze meringue with pastry bag and number 3 star tube into fancy designs onto a cookie sheet covered with parchment paper. Sprinkle the figures with colored sugar. Bake at 225 degrees for 30 to 40 minutes, or until they are dry and crisp. Let cool slightly. Remove from the paper to a cake rack to dry. Makes about 10 meringues.

Chocolate Strasburgers

Use your cookie press on these excellent tasting treats.

1/2	cup shortening	1-1/2	cups flour
1/2	cup sugar	1/4	teaspoon salt
1	egg	2	squares unsweetened chocolate
1	teaspoon vanilla		

Cream shortening and add sugar gradually. Cream well. Beat in egg, and vanilla. Blend in dry ingredients. Melt chocolate and blend into mixture. Press dough through cookie press. Use saw-toothed (spritz) plate, and make strips across ungreased cookie sheet. Bake in a 400 degree oven 6 to 8 minutes. While still warm cut into pieces about 2-inches wide and 2-1/2-inches long. Remove from pan. Makes about 24 cookies.

Chocolate Meringue Puffs

A melt in your mouth treat.

2	ounces unsweetened baking chocolate	3	large egg whites
3/4	cup confectioners' sugar, sifted	1/2	teaspoon cream of tartar
3	tablespoons unsweetened cocoa powder, sifted	1/2	cup sugar

Line baking sheets with foil. Finely chop chocolate in a blender, and set aside. In a small bowl combine confectioners' sugar and cocoa. In a medium bowl beat egg whites and cream of tartar with an electric mixer at medium speed until mixture thickens. Increase speed to high, and add sugar slowly. Beat until mixture forms stiff peaks and turns glossy. Gently fold in cocoa mixture and chopped chocolate with a rubber spatula. Fold ingredients into egg whites until mixture is uniformly brown with no streaks. Fill a pastry bag fitted with a large star tip with the meringue. Pipe meringue in decorative shapes onto foil lined baking sheets. Allow meringue to dry at room temperature for about 45 minutes. Bake for 1 hour in a preheated 200 degree oven. When cool, remove from foil with a metal spatula.

Note:
Don't try making these on humid or rainy days.

Chocolate Pillows

Sandwich cookies get a new look in these melt-away favorites.

2-1/4	cups flour	2	teaspoons vanilla
1/2	teaspoon salt		milk chocolate candy bars
1	cup butter		(about forty-eight, 1-inch
3/4	cup sugar		squares)
1	unbeaten egg		

Cream butter and sugar well. Add egg and vanilla. Stir in dry ingredients. Press dough through a cookie press, using saw-tooth plate (spritz) onto ungreased cookie sheet. Place chocolate pieces 1/4-inch apart on strips of dough. Press another strip of dough over candy covering pieces completely. Mark bars between chocolate pieces. Bake at 375 degrees for 12 to 13 minutes. Cut into pieces immediately. For a fancy touch, sprinkle with colored sugar, nuts or coconut.

Spritz

Buttery, almond-flavored Swedish spritz, probably the best known pressed cookies.

1	cup butter, softened	1/2	teaspoon almond extract
3/4	cup sugar	2-1/2	cups flour
2	egg yolks	1/8	teaspoon salt
1	teaspoon vanilla		

Beat butter and sugar, until fluffy. Add egg yolks, one at a time, and beat until smooth. Beat in flavoring; add sifted dry ingredients blending thoroughly. Place dough in a cookie press fitted with a design plate, packing it in firmly and evenly. Force out onto ungreased baking sheets, spacing cookies about 1-inch apart. If kitchen is very warm and dough is soft and sticky, refrigerate until firm enough to press easily. Decorate as desired. Bake in a 350 degree oven for about 12 to 15 minutes or until edges are lightly browned. Transfer to racks and let cool. Makes about 4 dozen cookies.

Decorations:

Before baking, top cookies with halved cherries; or sprinkle with finely chopped nuts, colored sugar, nonpareils, silver dragees, or chocolate sprinkles, or brush baked cookies with chocolate glaze; in top of a double boiler over simmering water, melt together 4 ounces semisweet chocolate and 1/2 teaspoon shortening. Apply with a pastry brush. Refrigerate glazed cookies for 10 minutes to harden glaze.

Chocolate Spritz Cookies

A tray of various spritz cookies is always a winner, especially with chocolate on them.

1/2	cup butter or margarine	2	cups cake flour
1	cup sugar	1/4	teaspoon salt
1	teaspoon vanilla	2	ounces (squares) unsweetened chocolate, melted and cooled
1	egg		
2	tablespoons milk		

Cream butter well; add sugar and vanilla and cream together; add egg and beat 1 minute. Add milk and blend. Sift together and add dry ingredients, mixing until blended. Add chocolate and blend well. Form cookies with a cookie press onto ungreased cookie sheets. Bake at 375 degrees for 8 to 10 minutes. Makes about 50 cookies.

Note:
Spritz cookies can be shaped into any desired designs, such as daisies, scrolls, rosettes, or fingers. Use chocolate or vanilla icing to fill out the center of daisies.

Spritzies

These are made with the same dough as Chocolate Spritz Cookies. Use large star tube of pastry bag and form into bars on ungreased cookie sheets. Bake at 400 degrees for 8 to 10 minutes. Makes about 3 dozen spritzies.

Chocolate Log Cookies

Add these to your cookie collection - you won't be sorry.

1	cup butter	2	teaspoons vanilla
1/2	cup powdered sugar	3	tablespoons cocoa
1/2	cup granulated sugar	1/2	teaspoon salt
2	egg yolks	2-1/2	cups sifted flour

Cream butter and sugars gradually. Blend in egg yolks, vanilla, cocoa, salt and flour; work dough lightly in hands. Use star-shaped cookie press plate; press dough through cookie press onto ungreased cookie sheets; make cookies about 2-inches long. Bake at 350 degrees for about 12 minutes. Frost with mocha icing.

Macadamia Macaroons

A little taste of Hawaii in these dainty cookies.

1	cup toasted macadamia nuts	1	teaspoon grated lemon peel
1-1/4	cups sugar	3	ounces semisweet chocolate, melted
1	can (8-ounces) almond paste	3	ounces white chocolate, melted
2	large egg whites		

Preheat oven to 425 degrees. Line 2 baking sheets with foil. In food processor, grind nuts with 1/4 cup sugar. In bowl, mix almond paste, egg whites and remaining sugar; beat in nut mixture. Place dough in pastry bag fitted with 1/2-inch star tip. Pipe 1-1/2-inch rosettes onto prepared baking sheets. Bake 8 minutes or until golden. Cool on wire racks. Dip half of each macaroon into 1 of the melted chocolates. Makes 4 dozen.

Fancy Chocolate Cookies

Pretty these up any way you choose.

1/2	cup butter	2	squares of unsweetened chocolate, melted
1	cup fine granulated sugar	2	cups flour
2	egg yolks	1/4	teaspoon salt
2	tablespoons milk		
1	teaspoon vanilla		

Cream together the butter and sugar until light. Beat egg yolks, add and mix well. Mix in vanilla and milk. Mix in the cooled melted chocolate. Sift dry ingredients and blend into chocolate mixture until smooth. Force through a cookie press in fancy shapes onto ungreased cookie sheets. Bake in a 350 degree oven 8 to 10 minutes. When baked and cooled, dip end, top or sides of each cookie into melted bittersweet chocolate frosting, place on waxed paper to dry. Or decorate the tops with fine lines or fancy designs. Use a small tube with melted bittersweet chocolate. Makes 3-1/2 to 4 dozen cookies.

Bittersweet Frosting:

Use any amount of bittersweet chocolate and melt slowly in a double boiler over hot water, while stirring occasionally. After it is melted, let it cool slightly. This coating will set immediately in a cool place.

Orange Spritz Cookies

A citrusy version of the traditional buttery spritz cookie.

2-1/2	cups flour	2	teaspoons grated orange peel
1	teaspoon baking powder		
1/4	teaspoon salt	1/2	teaspoon almond extract
3/4	cup butter		colored sugars for decorating
1/2	cup sugar		
1	egg		

Beat butter and sugar together until fluffy. Add egg, orange peel and almond extract and mix well. Add sifted dry ingredients. Do not chill dough. Pack into a cookie press. Force dough through press onto an ungreased cookie sheet. Decorate with colored sugars or candies, if desired. Bake in a 400 degree oven for 6 to 8 minutes. Cool on wired racks. Makes about 48 cookies.

Triple Chocolate Kisses

Love chocolate? Here are the best cookies made.

2	egg whites	1	ounce semisweet chocolate, grated
1/4	teaspoon cream of tartar		
1/4	teaspoon almond extract	24	milk chocolate kisses
1/2	cup sugar		unsweetened cocoa powder

In a small mixer bowl beat egg whites, cream of tartar, and extract on medium speed until soft peaks form. Gradually add sugar, beating on high speed until stiff peaks form. Fold in grated semisweet chocolate. Spoon meringue into a decorating bag fitted with a star tip. On a lightly greased cookie sheet pipe some of the meringue into 24 rounds, each about 1-1/4-inches in diameter. Lightly press a chocolate kiss into each meringue round. Pipe meringue around each kiss in concentric circles, starting at base and working toward top, until kiss is completely covered. Dust with cocoa powder. Bake in a 325 degree oven for 20 to 25 minutes or until light brown on the edges. Immediately remove from cookie sheet; cool on a wire rack. Makes 24 kisses.

Lorna Dunes

Tastes like the old-fashioned butter cookie did.

1-1/2	cups shortening	4	cups cake flour
1	cup sugar	1/2	teaspoon salt
5	eggs	1	teaspoon baking powder

Cream shortening and sugar. Beat eggs until light and fluffy and add to shortening and sugar. Sift and mix in dry ingredients. Color and flavor as desired. Press through cookie press. Bake on greased cookie sheets allowing room between cookies. A small gumdrop or nut may be placed on top of each cookie before baking. Bake at 350 degrees for about 15 to 20 minutes.

Norwegian Butter Cookies

A good way to use those leftover egg yolks.

1/2	cup butter	1/4	cup sugar
1	cup flour	1/2	teaspoon vanilla or lemon extract
2	hard-boiled egg yolks		

Cream butter, add egg yolks and beat well. Beat in sugar. Add flour and flavoring. Put through a cookie press or drop by teaspoon on ungreased cookie sheet. Bake at 375 degrees for about 10 to 12 minutes.

Coconut Macaroon Nests

A pretty new way to show off macaroons.

3	egg whites	1	teaspoon vanilla
3/4	cup sugar	2	cups finely chopped coconut
1/8	teaspoon salt		

Combine all ingredients in double boiler and mix until quite warm and pliable. Do not boil. Remove from heat. Squeeze onto well-greased cookie sheets with pastry bag and large star tube. To make ridges around the dropped cookies, use a fork. Add a maraschino or candied cherry to the top of each. Bake at 325 degrees for 15 to 20 minutes. Makes about 30 nests.

Peanut Butter Spritz Fingers

Everyone loves peanut butter especially when it's shaped into a finger with your faithful cookie press, then dipped into chocolate.

1	cup margarine or butter	3	cups flour
1/2	cup creamy peanut butter	1/2	cup semisweet chocolate pieces
1/2	cup sugar		
1/2	cup packed brown sugar	1	teaspoon shortening
1	teaspoon baking powder	1/4	cup finely chopped unsalted peanuts
1	egg		
1	teaspoon vanilla		

In a mixing bowl beat the margarine or butter and peanut butter with an electric mixer on medium to high speed for 30 seconds. Add the sugar, brown sugar, and baking powder; beat until combined. Beat in egg and vanilla until combined. Beat in as much of the flour as you can with the mixer. Stir in any remaining flour with a wooden spoon. Force un-chilled dough through a cookie press fitted with star plate or 1/2-inch tip into 2-inch long fingers onto an ungreased cookie sheet. Bake in a 375 degree oven for 8 to 10 minutes or until edges are firm but not brown. Cool cookies on a wire rack. In a small saucepan heat chocolate pieces and shortening over low heat, stirring until smooth. Dip ends of cooled cookies, on a diagonal, halfway into melted chocolate. Sprinkle nuts over chocolate. Let stand on waxed paper until set. Store cookie in an airtight container. Makes about 80 fingers.

Mexican Strips (CHURROS)

A light and crispy cookie that is sold by vendors in Mexico. Delicious served with a mug of hot Mexican chocolate.

1-1/2	cups water	1/4	teaspoon salt
1/2	cup butter	1-1/2	cups unbleached flour
2	teaspoons grated lemon peel	3	eggs, room temperature
			vegetable oil for frying
2	teaspoons sugar	1/2	lime
1/4	teaspoon ground cardamom	1	slice day-old bread
			sugar

In medium saucepan, combine water, butter, lemon peel, sugar, cardamom and salt. Heat to boiling. Remove from heat and add flour immediately. Beat with electric mixer until batter is fluffy. Cool slightly. Add eggs, one at a time, beating well after each. Spoon warm batter into pastry bag fitted with 1/2-inch star tip. In large, heavy saucepan, heat 2-inches of oil to 370 degrees. Squeeze juice from lime and reserve for another use. Add lime shell and bread to oil and fry until bread is dark brown. Remove bread and lime with slotted spoon. Pipe batter onto oil in 2-inch lengths. Fry several at a time, but do not crowd. Cook 1-1/2 to 2 minutes or until golden brown, turning occasionally. Drain on paper towels. Roll CHURROS in sugar and serve warm. May be reheated at 250 degrees for 5 minutes before sugaring.

Unbaked Cookies and Icings

*Festive trees and childs delight,
carols ringing through the night;
frosted panels aglow with light,
this is Christmas.*

Bourbon Pecan Truffles

Just a slight bourbon taste, give these cookies the kick they need.

2-1/2	cups sifted confectioners' sugar	2	tablespoons bourbon
1/2	cup plus 3 tablespoons unsweetened cocoa powder	2	tablespoons heavy cream
		1/2	teaspoon vanilla
			dash salt
		3/4	cup chopped pecans
1/3	cup butter, melted		

In bowl, mix sugar and 1/2 cup cocoa powder. Stir in melted butter, bourbon, heavy cream, vanilla and salt until blended. Stir in pecans. Cover with plastic wrap; refrigerate 4 hours. Form mixture into 1-inch ball. On sheet of waxed paper, roll balls in remaining cocoa powder. Place in airtight container; refrigerate until serving. Makes about 3 dozen.

Italian Cocoa Balls

"Mama Mia" these are loaded with almonds and rum.

2	cups crushed chocolate wafers	1	cup chopped, blanched, almond nutmeats
1/4	cup sifted cocoa	1/2	cup rum
2	cups sifted confectioners' sugar	3	tablespoons corn syrup
1	cup ground, unblanched almond nutmeats		

Mix crushed wafers, cocoa, sugar and nutmeats; add rum and syrup and mix well. Using about 1 tablespoon for each, shape into balls. If desired, roll balls in additional confectioners' sugar. Store in airtight container in refrigerator. Makes about 4 dozen.

Peanut Butter Squares

An easy-do cereal cookie.

1	cup light corn syrup	1	cup butterscotch bits
1	cup sugar	1	cup semi-sweet chocolate bits
1-1/2	cups cream style peanut butter		
6	cups ready to eat high protein cereal		

Combine syrup and sugar; bring to a boil. Remove from heat; add peanut butter; mix until smooth. Pour over cereal; mix lightly. Press into a buttered 13 by 9 by 2-inch pan. Melt butterscotch and chocolate bits; stir to blend. Spread evenly over cereal mixture. Allow to stand at room temperature until set; cut into squares. Makes about 48 squares.

Fruit And Rum Balls

Like rum balls? Try these with candied fruits and nuts.

1-1/2	cups crushed vanilla wafers	2/3	cup sliced pitted dates
1/16	teaspoon salt	1/3	cup chopped candied cherries
2	tablespoons white corn syrup	1/2	cup chopped candied pineapple
5	tablespoons rum		
1	cup chopped pecan nutmeats		

Mix ingredients well. Using about 1 tablespoon for each, shape into balls. If desired, roll in confectioners' sugar just before serving. Store in airtight container in refrigerator.

Peanut Butter Snow Balls

An unbaked cookie that children love to make.

1	tablespoon butter	3/4	cup powdered sugar
1	cup chunky style peanut butter	1-1/2	cups crisp rice cereal, slightly crushed

Mix butter, peanut butter, and powdered sugar. Fold in cereal. Shape level teaspoons of dough into balls. Refrigerate. Make glaze. Makes about 4-1/2 dozen cookies.

Glaze:

1	cup powdered sugar	3/4	cup canned flaked coconut or chopped salted peanuts
3	tablespoons hot milk		
1/4	teaspoon vanilla		

Blend sugar, milk, and vanilla until smooth. Drop 1 ball at a time into glaze. Coat well. Place on a rack for a few seconds to drain but not dry. Roll in coconut or peanuts. Refrigerate.

Toasted Almond Balls

These tasty balls are studded with toasted nuts.

1	cup semisweet chocolate bits	1/4	teaspoon salt
1	cup butterscotch bits	2	cups vanilla wafer crumbs
3/4	cup confectioners' sugar	3/4	cup finely chopped toasted almonds
1/2	cup sour cream		
1-1/2	teaspoons grated orange rind		

Melt chocolate and butterscotch bits at a low heat. Mix in sugar, sour cream, orange rind, salt and crumbs; chill. Shape into 3/4-inch balls; roll in almonds. Makes about 6-1/2 dozen.

Peanut-Mallow Clusters

These are so good they could be classified candy as well as cookies.

1	package (6-ounce) semi-sweet chocolate pieces	2	eggs
		1-1/4	cups confectioners' sugar
		1/2	teaspoon salt
1	square unsweetened chocolate (1 ounce)	1	teaspoon vanilla
		2	cups salted peanuts
1	tablespoon butter or margarine	2	cups miniature marshmallows

Melt chocolate pieces, chocolate square, and butter in top of double boiler over hot water. Beat eggs until foamy; stir in sugar, salt, and vanilla. Blend egg mixture with chocolate mixture. Stir in peanuts and marshmallows. Drop by rounded teaspoonfuls on waxed paper. Refrigerate 1 hour to set. Makes 4 dozen clusters.

Three-Layered Cookies

Everything you ever wanted in a rich candy-like cookie.

Bottom Layer:

5	tablespoons margarine	1	cup graham cracker crumbs
3-1/2	ounces semisweet chocolate, coarsely chopped	1	cup finely chopped walnuts
1	cup shredded coconut		

Melt margarine; stir in chocolate, stirring until melted. Remove from heat; stir in remaining ingredients. Put mixture into a greased 8-inch square pan. Press evenly in pan. Refrigerate 20 minutes.

Butter Cream Layer:

1	large egg yolk	3/4	teaspoon vanilla
1	tablespoon milk or orange liqueur	1-1/2	cups powdered sugar
1/2	cup butter		zest of 1 orange, optional

Beat egg yolk and milk; add butter, vanilla and orange zest. Beat until light and fluffy. Add powdered sugar and beat until creamy. Spread mixture over bottom layer. Refrigerate until cool and slightly firm.

Top Layer:

2	ounces unsweetened chocolate, coarsely chopped	1	tablespoon vegetable shortening
2	ounces semisweet chocolate, coarsely chopped		

Melt chocolate together, cool until barely warm to touch. Pour over butter cream layer; cover and refrigerate until chocolate is set, but not yet hard. Cut into bars; cover and refrigerate several hours. May be kept in refrigerator for a week. Freeze for longer storage. Makes 24 or 32 small bars.

Chinese Cookie Balls

Coffee powder gives these cookies a satisfying taste.

1	cup semi-sweet chocolate bits	2	teaspoons instant coffee powder
3	tablespoons corn syrup	1/2	cup hot milk
2	cups confectioners' sugar	1-3/4	cups graham cracker crumbs
1	cup finely chopped walnuts	1	teaspoon vanilla

Melt chocolate chips over hot water. Remove from heat. Add corn syrup and sugar and mix. Combine coffee powder and milk and stir in; add nuts, crumbs and flavoring. Mix well. Shape into balls about the size of a walnut. Roll balls in confectioners' sugar. Chill. Makes about 70 balls.

Note:
Fruit juice, brandy, rum or a liqueur may be used for half the milk, but then the cookies will taste of the new ingredient and less of the mocha or coffee.

A wicker covered basket makes a beautiful gift, loaded with decorated cookies.

Simple Decoration Icing

Use this easy to decorate icing in a pastry bag or just to paint on cookies.

3	egg whites	16	ounces confectioners' sugar
1/2	teaspoon cream of tartar		assorted food colors

Beat egg whites and cream of tartar until frothy. Add sugar and continue beating 5 to 7 minutes until smooth and thick, using high speed of mixer. Place in container with tightly fitting lid until ready to use. Can be kept up to 2 weeks in refrigerator. Once you begin working with icing, be sure to keep covered with damp cloth to keep from crusting on top. Using small bowls, mix small portions of icing with assorted food colors; mix until desired color is reached. (See color chart below.) To Pipe: Use pastry bag with small writing tip or use wax paper cone.

Color Chart:

NUMBER OF DROPS PER 1 TABLESPOON ICING:

COLOR	RED	YELLOW	GREEN	BLUE
Orange	1	3	–	–
Lavender	1	–	–	2
Purple	3	–	–	1
Olive Green	–	–	3	2
Chartreuse	–	12	1	–
Lime Green	–	6	1	–
Turquoise	–	–	1	3
Bright Red	7	1	–	–

Little Cookie Tips:

Practice makes perfect. Learning pressure control of your pastry bag can be fun. Start with simple dots; hold bag straight up and squeeze with steady pressure. Stop by breaking away to the right. Go in a circular sweep for rosettes. For lettering, hold bag nearly parallel to cookie, glide with even pressure.

Decorating Frosting

2	egg whites	assortment of food
2-1/2	cups powdered sugar	colorings
1/4	cup light corn syrup	

Beat egg whites until they hold a soft peak. Add sugar gradually and beat until sugar is dissolved and frosting stands in peaks. Add syrup and beat 1 minute. Use food coloring to get desired color. Add a few drops of water if a thinner frosting is desired. Keep well covered when not in use.

Fancy Orange Icing

1-1/2	cups sifted confectioners' sugar	2-1/2	tablespoons orange juice
1	teaspoon butter, at room temperature	1	teaspoon orange rind

Combine all ingredients. Beat until smooth. Mix until well blended. The grated rind may be omitted for plain orange icing. For another delicious orange frosting use 1/4 cup orange juice and enough confectioners' sugar to make a smooth thick icing. Beat in 1 teaspoon melted butter. Use at once. Makes about 1-1/4 cups icing.

Pecan Frosting

1/4	cup butter	1/4	cup chopped pecans
2	cups confectioners' sugar	2	tablespoons light cream
1	tablespoon light molasses		

Cream together butter, sugar and molasses until well blended and smooth. Stir in pecans; add cream gradually until frosting is of spreading consistency. Makes about 2-/34 cups frosting.

Cocoa Icing

1/2 cup unsweetened cocoa pinch of salt 1-1/2 cups confectioners' sugar, sifted	5-1/3 tablespoons butter about 3 tablespoons boiling water

Place the cocoa, salt, and sugar in the bowl of an electric mixer. Melt the butter and pour the hot butter and 3 tablespoons of boiling water into the bowl. Beat until completely smooth. If the icing thickens too much while you are icing the cookies, thin it carefully with a few drops of water. Lift a cookie and hold it while you partially frost it with a generous teaspoonful of the icing. Allow some of the marshmallow to show through, preferably 1 side of the marshmallow. The contrast of black and white is what you want. Also, don't try to cover the entire top of the cookie itself or you will not have enough for all the cookies. Place cookie on rack. Ice all the cookies and then let them stand for a few hours to set. Icing for Fudge Mellows on page 205.

Chocolate Creme Frosting

2 ounces (squares) unsweetened chocolate 15 ounce can sweetened condensed milk	1 teaspoon vanilla pinch of salt

Melt chocolate over hot water; add condensed milk. Stir and beat as mixture begins to thicken. Continue beating until of spreading consistency. Remove from heat and from the hot water. Stir in vanilla and salt. Use immediately, while still warm. Best for cooled brownies while they are still in pan and uncut. Makes about 1-1/2 cups.

Chocolate Butter Cream Icing

4 large egg whites	1-1/2 cups butter, softened
1 cup plus 2 tablespoons sugar	1/2 teaspoon vanilla
3 tablespoons shortening	3 to 4 tablespoons bottled fudge topping
6 tablespoons sifted powdered sugar	

In top of double boiler over simmering water, combine egg whites and sugar. Cook, stirring with whisk, until sugar is melted. Transfer egg-white mixture to large mixing bowl and beat with wire whisk until soft peaks form. Stir in shortening, powdered sugar, butter, vanilla and fudge topping. Mix until well blended and creamy. Makes about 4 cups icing.

Bittersweet Frosting

2 squares unsweetened chocolate	1 cup powdered sugar
2 tablespoons butter	1 teaspoon vanilla
2 tablespoons milk	1 or 2 teaspoons cream if necessary

Warm chocolate with butter and milk until chocolate and butter are melted; stir to blend. Mix in sugar and vanilla; mixture is crumbly; keep saucepan over low heat; stir until sugar melts and frosting is of spreading consistency. Thin with cream if necessary.

Perfect Cookie Frosting

Most cookies don't need a frosting; some taste and look better if left unfrosted, but for special occasions you might want a little color or different appearance.

1	cup powdered sugar	3	drops food coloring
1/4	teaspoon salt		grated rind or orange or lemon, optional
1/2	teaspoon vanilla		
1-1/2	tablespoons cream		

Blend all ingredients until smooth; add just enough cream to spread easily. Spread on cookies with a spatula. Decorate with chocolate sprinkles, colored sugar or whatever you desire.

Note:
Good for cut-out cookies, sugar cookies, even hermits.

Pastel Butter Frosting

1/3	cup soft butter	1	teaspoon vanilla
1/8	teaspoon salt		red and green food coloring
2	cups powdered sugar		
2	tablespoons cream		

Cream butter; add salt, sugar, cream and vanilla. Beat until smooth. Tint half of frosting a delicate pink, other half green. Frost cookies. Makes about 6 dozen.

Mocha Frosting

3	tablespoons soft butter		green food coloring
1	cup powdered sugar	1-1/2	tablespoons water
2	tablespoons cocoa	1-1/2	cups finely chopped walnuts
1-1/2	tablespoons cold coffee		
1/2	teaspoon vanilla		

Combine butter, sugar, cocoa, coffee and vanilla; mix until smooth. Add a few drops green coloring to water; stir into walnuts; mix until evenly coated. Spread in shallow pan. Place in a 350 degree oven about 8 minutes to dry. Dip ends of cookies in frosting, then in green walnuts. Makes about 10 dozen.

Browned Butter Icing

1/4	cup soft butter	1	teaspoon vanilla
2	tablespoons cream (approximately)	1-1/2	cups confectioners' sugar

Brown butter in heavy skillet; blend in vanilla, sugar and cream. Stir until smooth.

Colored Walnuts

	green food coloring	1-1/2	cups finely chopped walnuts
1-1/2	tablespoons water		

Dilute green coloring in water. Blend into walnuts. Spread into shallow pan. Place in a 350 degree oven about 8 minutes to dry.

Colored Sugar

1   cup sugar
      red, green or yellow
      food coloring

Mix together, add 1 or 2 drops of 1 color until sugar has taken the color evenly. Spread colored sugar on pan covered with waxed paper. Allow to dry for a few minutes. Put through coarse sieve or rub between your fingers and the sugar is ready to use. Lemon sugar, mix 1 teaspoon finely grated lemon peel with 1/4 cup sugar.

Simple Syrup

4	tablespoons sugar	2	tablespoons white corn syrup
4	tablespoons water		

Bring all ingredients to a boil. Follow directions and apply with pastry brush to cookies while they are still hot. Makes about 1/2 cup.

Glaze Icing

1/2	cup sugar	1/4	cup confectioners' sugar
1/4	cup water		(approximately)

Boil together sugar and water until it threads from the spoon, 230 degrees. Remove from heat. Stir in confectioners' sugar to make right consistency. Brush hot icing lightly over cookies. Also called white icing glaze when 1 teaspoon cornstarch is sifted with the confectioners' sugar. Brush while hot over Lebkuchen. Makes about 1 cup icing.

Notes

Index

INDEX

ROLLED COOKIES

Almond Butter Sticks 36
Almond Cookies 14
Austrian Butter Cookies 3
Best of All Sugar Cookies 1
Biscochitos 37
Brazil Nut Diamonds 44
Bread Crumb Cookies 23
Brown-Eyed Daisies 16
Butter Horn Cookies 28
Candy Bar In-Betweens 6
Caramel Sugar Cookies 4
Chocolate Filled Dreams 11
Chocolate Shortbread Hearts 12
Chocolate Sugar Cookies 1
Christmas Miniatures 34
Cinnamon Jelly Gems 10
Cinnamon Maple Rings 39
Cinnamon Stars 33
Coffee Crisps 35
Cream Cheese Sugar Cookies 37
Date Crescents 29
Dutch Sugar Cookies 2
Finska Kakor 3
Gateau Bonbons 8
German Anise Cookies 2
German Spice Cakes 22
Gingerbread Cut-Outs 23
Hazelnut Crescents 41
Hazelnut Shorts 34
Honey Graham Crackers 31
Hoot Owl Cookies 40
Ice Cream Cookies 7
Ischler Hearts 43
Lecheri 19
Merry Christmas Molasses Cookies ... 17
Merry Mints 13
Mibs Molasses Cookies 22
Mickie's Date-Filled Oatmeal Cookies 25
Mississippi Cookies 15
Molasses Wafers 16
Mondchens 26
Nut Rolls 7
Oatmeal Christmas Bells 29
Oatmeal Cookie Crackers 30
Paintbrush Cookies 4
Parlies 14
Peanut Cutouts 45
Pecan Praline Rounds 27
Pepparkakor 20
Peppermint Pinwheels 38
Ragalach 36
Ramunes (Daisies) 15
Rolled Sour Cream Cookies 35
Rum Mocha Treasures 44
Snowflakes 13
Speculass 24
Spicy Crisps 21
Spicy Molasses Crisps 21
Stone Jar Molasses Cookies 18
Sugar-Nut Sticks 30
Swedish Wafer Cookies 32
Sweet Pastry Pockets 46
Swiss Almond Bites 32
Swiss Chocolate Cookies 12
Trilby's 26
Triple Treats 42
Viennese Almond Wafers 33
Viennese Jam Rounds 10
Viennese Specials 5
Walnut Filled Treats 5
Walnut Walkaways 45
Zucker Hutchen 9

DROP COOKIES

Almond - Oatmeal Cookies 75
Almond Cookies 61
Anise Drops 110
Apple Butter Cookies 82

i

Applesauce Cookies 73	Coconut Gingers 58
Applesauce Oatmeal Cookies 77	Coconut Maples 59
Bachelor Buttons 111	Coconut Mounds 59
Banana Oatmeal Cookies 78	Coconut Sponge Drops 60
Bear Track Cookies 89	Cowboy Cookies 65
Bittersweet Chocolate-Chip Rounds .. 98	Creamy Chocolate Cookies 97
Black Walnut Cookies 80	Crispies 86
Brown Almond Drop Cookies 62	Date Lemon Sugar Cookies 48
Brown Sugar Kisses 52	Double Chocolate Potato Drop
Brownie Drops 93	Cookies 92
Cake Mix Chewies 55	Eggnog Cookies 48
Candy Cookies 108	Florentines 96
Cape Cod Oatmeal Cookies 77	Frosted Holiday Cookies 71
Caramel Oatmeal Cookies 75	Frosted Pecan Drops 112
Carrot Oatmeal Cookies 82	Fruited-Orange Cookies 67
Cashews and Coconut Cookies 90	Ginger Creams 85
Cherry Chocolate Chip Cookies 94	Ginger Drops 84
Chewy Christmas Macaroons 51	Ginger Jumbos 84
Chewy Orange Drops 68	Glazed Apple-Spice Drops 69
Chewy Peanut Butter Cookie 88	Golden Nut Drops 62
Chocolate Almond Bites 100	Golden Yam Drop Cookies 70
Chocolate Bonnets 101	Hawaiian Cookies 83
Chocolate Chip Cookies 91	Holiday Fruit Drops 76
Chocolate Coffee Drops 96	Honey Crunch Cookies 86
Chocolate Cracklers 109	Lemon Drops 60
Chocolate Cream Cushions 102	Light-Brown Oatmeal Cookies 81
Chocolate Dipped Kisses 54	Little Chocolate Drops 54
Chocolate Drop Cookies 99	Macaroon Top Hats 55
Chocolate Lumps 107	Macaroonies 50
Chocolate Marshmallow Cookies 103	Mammy's Plantation Drops 57
Chocolate Orange Puffs 100	Maple Pecan Cookies 49
Chocolate Sundae Cookies 95	Marbles 106
Chocolate Surprise Cookies 108	Marmalade Drops 111
Chocolate Walnut Clusters 106	Meringue Fudge Drops 57
Chocolate Walnut Kraut Stacks 107	Mint Chocolate Meringues 52
Chocolate-Chocolate Cookies 104	Mocha Cookies 109
Chocolate-Coconut Mounds 104	Molasses Prune Drops 85
Chocolate-Malted Cookies 93	Mom's Favorite Christmas Cookies ... 66
Chocolate-Pecan Meringues 53	Mother's Milk Chocolate Pecan
Chocolate-Pistachio Macaroons 53	Drops 91
Christmas Lizzies 72	Nuggets 72
Cocoa Oatmeal Drop Cookies 80	Oatmeal Cherry Cookies 81
Coconut Almond Haystacks 58	Oatmeal Lace Cookies 76

Odds and Ends Cookies 66
Old-Fashioned Cookies 47
Old-Fashioned Soft Sugar Cookies 47
Orange-Glazed Banana Cookies 79
Oriental Tea Treats 70
Peanut Butter Carrot Cookies 78
Peanut Jumbles 87
Pistachio Angels 51
Pistachio Orange Drops 67
Potato Chip Cookies 49
Powder-Puff Tidbits 73
Pumpkin Spice Cookies 71
Pumpkin Whoopie Pies 63
Ranch Cookies 87
Reese's Chewy Chocolate Cookies ... 90
Salted Peanut Crisps 88
Scottish Reels 74
Self Frosting Anise Drops 110
Sour Cream Cashew Drops 89
Spell-Binders 64
Stachelschweinchen 56
Sweet Treats 61
Tea Time Macaroons 50
The Best Chocolate Chip Cookies 94
Triplets 65
Val's Oatmeal Cookies 83
Wheatie Coconut Macaroons 56
White Chocolate Cookies 99
Wicked Chocolate Drops 105

REFRIGERATED COOKIES

Almond Icebox Cookies 139
Aristocrats 137
Banana Whirls 152
Black and White Slices 145
Black Walnut Charms 148
Butter Crunch Confection-Cookies ... 133
Butter Nut Cookies 142
Cherry-Cream-Cheese Slices 153
Chewy Cranberry Gingers 114
Chocolate Nut Refrigerator
  Cookies 148
Chocolate Shot Cookies 151
Chocolate Tweed Cookies 151
Cinnamon Icebox Cookies 136
Coconut Shortbread Cookies 134
Cookie Jar Cookies 113
Danish Sugar Cookies 144
Frosted Anise Drops 127
German Christmas Cookies 122
Ginger Pinks 118
Gingersnaps 117
Holiday Cookies 128
Holland Dutch Cookies 126
Kipfel 130
Lemon-Pecan Wafers 146
Malted Milk Rounds 150
Marble Refrigerator Cookies 135
Mary Ann Cookies 121
Meringue-Filled Cookie Pastries 129
Molasses Cookies 118
Molasses Crisps 115
Mother's Special Cookies 131
Oatmeal Refrigerator Cookies 149
Orange-Flavored Snails 140
Peanut Butter Pillows 138
Peanut Butter Swirls 114
Pecan Delights 134
Pecan Turtles 147
Petticoat Tails 133
Pfeffernuesse Fruit Cakes 124
Pfeffernusse 125
Polish Pastries 132
Ribbon Cookies 141
Rum-Pecan Meltaways 132
Scotch Scones 149
Simple Sesame Slices 142
Slice O'Spice 113
Soft Ginger Cookies 117
Spiced Almond Thins 146
Spiced Nut Cookies 116
Spicy Refrigerator Cookies 119
Striped Cookies 144

Sugar Crisps	143
Sugared Sherry Fingers	141
Swedish Chocolate Pinwheels	135
Swedish Ginger Cookies	119
Wagon Wheels	123
Windmill Cookies	120

MOLDED COOKIES

Accordion Treats	215
Almond Crescents	166
Almond Fingers	183
Anise Butter Cookies	180
Apple Cobbler Cookies	230
Berliner Kranze	162
Brazil Nut Shortbread	213
Brittle Filbert Cookies	192
Brown Eyed Susans	179
Butter Nut Drops	171
Butterscotch Melt-A-Ways	193
Candied Apple Cookies	231
Cardamom Butter Cookies	158
Cashew Triangles	191
Cherry Nut Bells	188
Chinese Almond Cookie	182
Choco-Peanut Butter Cookies	195
Chocolate Aggies	199
Chocolate Chiffon Cookies	196
Chocolate Cookies	202
Chocolate Crackle Tops	198
Chocolate Curls	208
Chocolate Dipped Creams	203
Chocolate Macaroons	212
Chocolate Pretzels	207
Chocolate Sandies	198
Chocolate Shadows	206
Chocolate-Coconut Candies	200
Chocolate-Print Cookies	204
Cinnamon Almond Cookies	164
Cinnamon Sugar Butter Cookies	157
Coconut Grove Cookies	229
Coconut Jam Fills	208
Coconut Pennies	172
Coconut Pompons	182
Coconut Surprises	169
Coconut Washboards	175
Cocoroons	209
Crunchy Coconut Cookies	174
Danish Dandies	180
Date - Nut Jumbos	190
Date-Coconut Confections	186
Double Chocolate Chews	203
Easy Peanut Butter Cookies	194
Fortune Cookies	231
Frosted Cookie Canes	161
Frosted Crisp Molassies	218
Frosted Eggnog Logs	211
Frosted Melting Moments	155
Frosted Pecan Cuplets	210
Frosty Date Balls	173
Fruitcake Cookies	217
Fudge Cups	197
Fudge Mallows	205
Ginger Spice Cookies	217
Glazed Almond Cookies	183
Gold Cookies	175
Graham Cracker Marguerites	227
Greek Cookies	222
Grossmutter's Pfeffernuesse	213
Grybai	233
Gumdrop Macaroons	212
Hazelnut Puff Balls	166
Hazelnut Sugar Dusties	167
Hermits	220
Hidden Chocolate Cookies	201
Holiday Bon Bons	176
Holiday Hats	168
Honeyed Apricot Biscotti	221
Java Sticks	184
Jumbo Peanut Butter Apple Cookies	216
Kringla	161
Kris Kringles	160
Ladyfingers	224
Lauren's Sugar Cookies	156

Lemon Angel Halos 170
Lemon Peel Sugar Cookie 163
Little Gems 181
Maple Rice Crisp Cookies 177
Marshmallow Clouds 206
Meltaway Maple Crisps 177
Mexican Wedding Cakes 184
Mix and Match Cookie Tarts 159
Molasses Cookies 218
Molasses Rum Balls 220
Molded Brown Sugar Cookies 165
Norwegian Christmas Wreaths 162
Nut Cluster Cookies 214
Nut Strudel 164
Nut Toasties 228
Nutmeg Butter Balls 168
Oh' So Good Cookies 190
Orange Coconut Crisps 173
Orange Madeleines 225
Orange Sun Bursts 163
Orange Tuiles 223
Parisian Orange Cookies 178
Peanut Blossoms 215
Peanut Butter Cookies 194
Peanut Butter Crisscrosses 195
Peanut Butter Kisses 179
Peanutios 193
Peanutty Chocolate Crinkles 192
Pecan Balls 186
Pecan Delights 201
Pecan Fingers 186
Pecan Nut Puffs 226
Popcorn Macaroons 226
Powdered Sugar Cookies 155
Princess Delights 176
Rosettes 232
Rum Apple-Raisin Cookies 216
Rum Bubbles 167
Russian Teacakes 185
Salt Dough Decorations 234
Sandies 178
Scandinavian Drops 171
Senoritas 174

Sesame Cookies 181
Short 'nin' Bread 157
Slice and Serve Cookies 187
Snickerdoodles 207
Spiced Cherry Balls 189
Spicy Gingersnaps 219
Springerle 225
Sugar Cookies 156
Sugar-and-Spice Madeleines 224
Surprise Teacakes 227
Swedish Gingersnaps 219
Tea Time Tassies 165
Tiny Fudge Tarts 196
Totcicles 228
Vanilla Krumkake 232
VI's Pecan Fingers 185
Wheaties Cherry Blinks 191

BAR COOKIES

Almond Fudge Topped Shortbread .. 268
Almond Toffee Bars 263
Apricot Shortbread 244
Banana Oat Bars 242
Baseler Leckerle 273
Blitz Kuchen 257
Brown Sugar Jan Hagel 261
Brownie Petit Fours 303
Butter Chews 289
Butter Pecan Turtle Bars 266
Buttermilk Cinnamon Bars 280
Butterscotch Chewy Logs 261
Calypso Bars 259
Candy Bar Brownies 301
Candy Bar Squares 238
Caramel Brownies 298
Caramel Candy-Bar Cookies 237
Caramelitas 237
Checker Bars 291
Cheesecake Cookies 299
Cherry-Coconut Bars 289
Chewy Chocolate Brownies 296

Choco Peanut Pan Cookie 252	Kentucky Cheese Cake 255
Chocodiles 255	Lemon Creme Bars 245
Chocolate Buttermilk Squares 309	Lemon Filbert Tea Bars 246
Chocolate Cake Brownies 311	Luscious Apricot Bars 245
Chocolate Coconut Slices 305	Macaroon Polka Dots 235
Chocolate Covered Cherry Squares 294	Maple Date Bars 282
	Maple Walnut Bars 269
Chocolate Meltaways 307	Marbled Cookie Squares 308
Chocolate Nut Squares 306	Marzipan Bars 258
Chocolate Oatmeal Peanut Bars 251	Merry Christmas Bars 284
Chocolate Peanut Bars 254	Merry Mincemeaters 273
Chocolate-Almond Cookie Bark 267	Milk Chocolate Caramel Bars 236
Chocolate-Cherry Cookie Pizza 294	Mississippi Mud 312
Chocolate-Cherry Squares 295	Mother's Chinese Chews 280
Chocolate-Chip Cheesecake Fantasies 293	Norwegian Almond Bars 262
	Oatmeal-Fudge Bars 313
Chow Mein Date Bars 282	Old-Fashioned Raisin Bars 275
Coconut Crunch Bar 271	Orange Gumdrop Slice Bar 239
Colonial Pumpkin Bars 278	Oriental Crunch 247
Congo Squares 253	Peanut Brittle Bars 249
Cranberry Crunch Bars 243	Peanut Brittle Cookies 248
Cream Cheese Brownies 300	Peanut Butter Crunchies 251
Crispy Date Bars 281	Peanut Streusel Banana Bars 250
Crisscross Jelly Squares 257	Peanut Strips 252
Date Brownies 311	Peanut Toffee Diamonds 250
Delta Bars 262	Pecan Pie Surprise Bars 266
Double-Frosted Brownies 297	Plantation Fruit Bars 274
Dutch Chocolate Bars 314	Rickety Uncle 247
Fig Bars 285	Rocky Road Fudge Bars 310
Frango Mint Bars 288	Rocky-Road Oaties 236
Fresh Lemon Bars 246	Scottish Yule Bannock 258
Frosted Fig Bars 286	Sesame Seed Bars 260
Frosted Fudge Bars 304	Sherry Date Strips 283
Fudge Four O'Clocks 305	Snowcap Brownies 298
Glazed Lebkuchen 272	Spice Bars 274
Graham Pecan Treats 267	Spiced Prune Bars 277
Heavenly Hash 287	Strawberry-Filled Butter Slices 241
Heavenly Honey Bars 256	Sugar Plum Squares 240
Iced-Spiced Ginger Bars 275	Sunshine Dream Bars 292
Jan Hagel 260	Swedish Almond Brownies 299
Jeweled Bars 239	Swedish Butter Slices 241
Jiffy Jimmy Bars 276	Tangy Banana Bars 242
Kahlua Chocolate Squares 306	Toffee Filled Brownies 302

Toffee Squares 256
Toffee-Nut Bars 265
Two-Way Almond Bars 264
V.J.'s Cookie Surprise 290
Walnut Bars 270
White Fruit Bars 272
Winter Squash Squares 279
Zucchini Bars 278

PRESS COOKIES

Butter Gems 316
Chocolate Log Cookies 323
Chocolate Meringue Puffs 321
Chocolate Pillows 322
Chocolate Spritz Cookies 323
Chocolate Strasburgers 321
Coconut Macaroon Nests 326
Coconut Wreaths 318
Fancy Chocolate Cookies 324
Fancy Meringue Figures 320
Fruit Filled Spritz 317
Lemon-Cheese Dips 315
Lorna Dunes 326
Macadamia Macaroons 324
Mexican Strips 328
Noel Wreaths 319
Norwegian Butter Cookies 326
Orange Spritz Cookies 325
Peanut Butter Spritz Fingers 327
Spritz 322
Spritzies 323
Triple Chocolate Kisses 325
Vanilla Daisies 320
Vanilla Sour-Cream Rosettes 319
Wreaths 318

UNBAKED COOKIES

Bourbon Pecan Truffles 329
Chinese Cookie Balls 334

Fruit and Rum Balls 330
Italian Cocoa Balls 329
Peanut Butter Snow Balls 331
Peanut Butter Squares 330
Peanut-Mallow Clusters 332
Three-Layered Cookies 333
Toasted Almond Balls 331

ICINGS

Bittersweet Frosting 338
Browned Butter Icing 340
Chocolate Butter Cream Icing 338
Chocolate Creme Frosting 337
Cocoa Icing 337
Colored Sugar 340
Colored Walnuts 340
Decorating Frosting 336
Fancy Orange Icing 336
Glaze Icing 341
Mocha Frosting 339
Pastel Butter Frosting 339
Pecan Frosting 336
Perfect Cookie Frosting 339
Simple Decoration Icing 335
Simple Syrup 340

*When Christmas Eve has come at last
And Santa's on his way,
My prayers for you and everyone
"A Blessed Christmas Day"*